Praise for
I Remain Yours

"With its innovative epistolary structure, Katherine Cottle's
I Remain Yours provides a fascinating window into
Mormon culture—at a time when Americans have reason
to be more interested in that than usual."

-Madison Smartt Bell, novelist
Author of *All Souls' Rising* & *The Color of Night*

"An American story."
-Clay Goss, playwright, Author of *Homecookin'*

I Remain Yours.

I Remain Yours.

Secret Mission Love Letters
of my Mormon Great-Grandparents
1900-1903

Katherine Cottle

Apprentice House
Loyola University Maryland
Baltimore, Maryland

First Edition

Printed in the United States of America

ISBN: 978-1-62720-006-6
Ebook ISBN: 978-1-62720-007-3

Cover design and photo by Kate Tafelski
Internal design by Kate Tafelski
Pre-press design by Alexander Namin

Published by Apprentice House

Apprentice House
Loyola University Maryland
4501 N. Charles Street
Baltimore, MD 21210
410.617.5265 • 410.617.2198 (fax)
www.ApprenticeHouse.com
info@ApprenticeHouse.com

Also by
Katherine Cottle.

Poetry

My Father's Speech (2008)

Memoir

Halfway: A Journal through Pregnancy (2010)

Acknowledgments.

I would like to credit the following people and sources with helping to provide me with information about my great-grandparents, the Mormon religion, history, and the stories that make lineage so much more than pictures and names on a page.

Joyce Palmer Cottle, my mother, was instrumental in providing feedback, editing, and answers. Clay Goss, professor at Morgan State University, saw the stories and my role in this project even before I did. My husband and children continued to survive on frozen pizza and fish sticks while I spent many hours during the last three years either distracted at the computer or in my head.

Yes or No? Letters of Nellie Brady and Peter Sundwall, Jr., 1900-1903, contained the typed, compiled, and edited letters that inspired this project. Mary Fairbanks deserves enormous credit and gratitude for providing this service and for distributing copies of the letters to the descendants of Nellie Brady and Peter Sundwall, Jr.

Other important family history books utilized for this project included *Lindsay Anderson Brady*, compiled by Ressman Christopherson, Peter Sundwall/Johan Nyvall and Their Descendants by Kenneth W. Sundwall, as well as *Forty Years Among the Indians* by Daniel Webster Jones, and *On the Other*

Hand: A Life Story by Fay Wray.

I consulted various church records and resources including *The Book of Mormon, The Doctrine and Covenants, Mormon Doctrine,* and *Markers and Monuments Database of Utah State History.*

Various newspapers and magazines were also vital for researching topics relevant to the turn of the 20th century, as well as the turn of the 21st century, including *The Chicago Tribune, The Smart Set, Ladies' Home Journal* and *The Star Tribune.*

There are, inevitably, spelling and type errors that have occurred, both naturally in the original love letters, as well as in the two transcription processes of the letters (first into type copy and then into electronic copy). I edited a few errors that seemed logically unintentional and that, in my opinion, would potentially distract the reader from following the narratives of the letters. However, I have left the majority of the letters in their original format, including the content and structural mistakes that, in my opinion, provide the voices that make them original, and human, letters. The letters are also presented in the order that they were received, as opposed to chronological date, allowing the reader to understand the exchange of content and conversation that did not always follow linear time or instant messaging and/or response patterns.

Some of the included poems were previously published in the following magazines:

Free State Review: "Actress"; *Grub Street:* "My Grandmother Lives in the Laundry Chute"; *Welter:* "5:45 A.M."

For Ellie.

Contents

I revealed myself to those who did not ask for me;
I was found by those who did not seek me.
To a nation that did not call on my name,
I said, "Here am I, here am I."
-Isaiah 65:1

Introduction.

I have to admit. It took me awhile to get to the letters.
Properly that is. In fact, it took me 36 years, two degrees, two
miscarriages, two children, a few anxiety attacks, numerous
deaths in my extended family, and hundreds of rejection letters
to be exact, before I was willing to begin tackling the pages.
I knew the letters were buried in my mother's cedar chest,
resting comfortably between a shoebox of black and white
pictures and a tattered 1968 copy of *A New Pictorial History of
the Talkies*. I wanted to keep the letters there, within the warm
safety of others' lives, and I realize now it was because I had
to come to terms with myself before I could turn their pages
and begin to understand my role as a great-grandchild, an
inactive Mormon, a wife, a mother, and a writer.

Reading the letters any earlier in my life would have been
premature, like eloping to Vegas or winning a small lottery,
or getting a book published before I was thirty. It would
have been initially pleasant, but fleeting. I would have smiled
and turned the pages of the letters, but I wouldn't have truly
connected to them. I wouldn't have been mature enough
to feel the pull of love across an ocean and two different

continents, and I wouldn't have had the distance and life experience to appreciate the faith and belief in the Mormon religion that carried my great-grandfather through the two and a half years he spent in Sweden doing missionary work and that also kept my great-grandmother waiting patiently for his return.

My life has been pretty typical for the late 20th and early 21st centuries. My rebellion from the Mormon religion and more conservative paths is probably more expected than unexpected. My marriage juggles the fine line between business partners, household mates, and childcare guardians, as so many marriages do these days. When I began to read the letters it was this contrast that struck me the most, the differences in our lifestyles and the religious beliefs. I wondered what my great-grandparents would have thought of this young woman, trickled down from their genes as she read their secret letters and then passed them along to the world. But then, as I progressed through the exchanges, I began to see two completely vulnerable people, struggling with their own flaws, talents, and emotions in a world that was just as contemporary when they experienced it. I found both favorable and unfavorable traits also noticeable in my grandparents, my parents, me, and my children. The surface of the letters reflected another time and place, but the people in the text were hauntingly familiar, even though I had never met them. For these reasons, I wanted to tell all of our stories, not to spill secrets or to be disrespectful in any way, but to find the place where we met, not in real time, but in connection. I wanted to explore our links, to capture the physical and literary passion they and I found on the written page, and to provide an open route that my own great-grandchildren might find one day in which to place their own words. My descendants' entries might be dated 2100 or 2109, written in some future writing tool that has yet to be invented, but I am betting their letters will also contain love, desire, insecurity, and the hardships of their lives. Their entries will also weep, celebrate, long, and mourn. I begin my journey, neither backwards nor forwards in time, but within, and welcome those after me to begin theirs when their time is right.

*

My great-grandmother, Harriet Eleanor (Nellie) Brady was born in Lehi, Arizona on March 29, 1882, the second of three children born to John David Ward Brady and Eleanor Ann Jones. Their first child, a son named John Franklin Brady, died at 6 months of age and their third child was a daughter named Vina Brady, who is mentioned throughout the letters. Nellie's father was the son of Lindsay Anderson Brady, a polygamist, and his second wife, Susannah Ward Allen. Nellie's mother was the daughter of Daniel Webster Jones, the author of the autobiography, *Forty Years Among the Indians*, published in 1890. The book chronicles Jones's life as an orphaned child, a Spanish/English translator and mediator during the Mexican war, in which he states he, "indulged in many wicked and reckless ways," followed by his conversion to Mormonism and his eventual leadership of the Mexican Mission. One of Daniel Webster Jones's other daughters gave birth to a girl who would one day grow up to scream in the palm of a terrifying beast named King Kong. Fay Wray's own autobiography quotes from her grandfather's book:

> After the war, enroute to California with a large trading company, the hammer of his pistol caught on the edge of his holster, causing the gun to go off: "The ball ranged downward, entering the groin and thigh, passing through some fourteen inches of flesh." The company expected that the youth would die and must therefore be abandoned. But the company guide thought that if the youth was to be left behind, he should at least be abandoned to the

possible care of nearby Indians. He planned to fetch
them. My grandfather wrote: "I can never forget their
looks of kindness. They offered to take me and try
to cure me." The company, thus challenged, made
a frame to carry the wounded boy on the back of
a mule for the remaining fifteen day's journey into
Salt Lake Valley. "I felt almost disappointed not to
go with the Indians for my heart was melted toward
them and I felt as though I could always be their
friend and trust them." In Salt Lake City, Mormons
nurtured him to recovery and inspired him to join
the church and forego continuing to California.

I used to thumb through the pages of my mother's *Talkies*
book for hours as a young girl, in awe of Fay Wray's beauty
and her ability to capture the love of beast that could have
killed her with one squeeze. I secretly wished to be as
beautiful as Fay and to be carried away to an island without
the annoying and catty girls that surrounded me every day
at school. I imagined there was a place where love could
transcend physical forms, as well as a boat that could make it
to this undiscovered land. I chose not to think about the end
of the movie and Kong's horrible demise. I chose to pretend
that Kong was never captured, and that he and Fay lived
happily ever after, though the flashes of firing planes and the
heartbreaking growls from the confused beast repeatedly cut
through my adolescent dreams. I cried when Jessica Lange
took over Fay's role in the 1976 version, because my relative
was now replaced by a woman in color, delivered with fancy
camera angles that made Fay look like an amateur. To me, Fay
was the real Ann Darrow, not Jessica Lange, and certainly not
Naomi Watts, who took on the role in 2005. Like everything
in the past, nostalgia painted its thick layer of validity. In
my mind, no one could have lived up to Fay's portrayal
of life in black and white, both stolen and protected by a

misunderstood animal, her screams for help and love echoing
from a skyscraper that rose higher than any possible sky. I
clung to my vision of Fay for years, until one day I saw an
interview with her on the television in which she was at least
ninety years old, looking out the protective glass windows of
the Empire State Building while she answered the usual array
of questions. Her face was wrinkled beyond recognition, and
her white hair was thin and dry, yet she still carried an air
of longevity and confidence that broke through the camera's
capture and refused to look down, or away. In elementary and
middle school, when I needed her the most, she was there:

Actress

She was my grandmother's cousin,
my mother told me when I was twelve,
pointing to page 86 of the *Talkies* book,
Fay Wray captured in still motion,
caught between frames of a smoking Bette Davis
and blonder than blonde Jean Harlow.

I spent the rest of my summer thumbing
through the book, earmarking the page
where Fay is mid-scream, her eyes frozen
in the clutches of the desperate Kong.
In my mind, I transformed
my own thick thighs into petite curves,
my wiry horse hair into greased Hollywood curls.

I explained to the other junior high girls
that there was a girl before Jessica Lange,
in a black and white film, miles away
from the prickly and impossible rope of gym class
and the Jordache jeans with the gold seams
that Mom said we couldn't afford.

Fay lived high above,
in a city that looked too dark and hard
for the mean girls in my grade to ever survive--
the Empire State Building sharp enough
to cut through the clouds,
while Fay's legs dangled out of reach
of any passed note or caddy insult.

She was my possible futures:
that I might get asked to board
a foggy ship in the middle of the night,
that the natives might capture me
because my face was that beautiful,

that a large beast would one day
hold me in his palm,
and I would be the only one to understand
he was a harmless creature,
just lonely, and looking for something
other than his ordinary world

Fay's first cousin, my great-grandmother Nellie, was four years
old when her mother moved them to Utah after Nellie's father
was accidentally killed after his gun discharged on a mining
prospecting trip to Mexico with Daniel Webster Jones. After
their return to Utah, Nellie's mother married a man named
Wasatch Pritchett (after the Wasatch Mountain Range). The
family then moved between Arizona and Utah during the next
few years, doing ranch and field work. While in Mammoth,
Utah, Nellie saw an advertisement in the paper by a young
male artist from Fairview, Utah who was looking for display
work. That young male artist was her future husband, the
young man who would become my great-grandfather, Peter
Olofsson Sundwall, Jr.

*

My great-grandfather, Peter Olofsson Sundwall Jr., was born on
January 26, 1876 in Fairview, Utah. His parents, Peter Olofsson
and Anna Cajsa Johannesson, were from Stockholm, Sweden.
Peter Sr. left Sweden for America in 1872, in large part to join
the Mormon exodus to Zion (which Mormons refer to as the
physical and symbolic state of Utah). Upon his immigration
he changed his name to Peter Sundwall, after the largest
city in Northern Sweden and the capital city of Noorland,
veering away from the Swedish practice of patronymics, the
practice of a son taking a father's first name as his last name,
and potential confusion he thought might be caused by the
popular name in his new country. Anna Cajsa Johannesson,
an apprentice seamstress in one of the clothing stores that
catered to the Swedish royalty, soon followed, and the two
were married in Salt Lake City in 1875. Peter Sundwall, Sr. was
a very ambitious and successful business man and civic leader.
Some of his various positions in Fairview, Utah included that
of school trustee, city councilman, mayor, postmaster, and
county commissioner. He was the President of a Cooperative
Sheep Company (which he modeled after the cooperative
system he had seen in Sweden), manager of a Cooperative
store, and the founder of a State Bank. Peter Sundwall, Sr. and
Anna Cajsa (changed to Catharina) Sundwall had five children,
the first being Peter Sundwall, Jr., and also raised the son of
Anna's sister after her early death. Peter, Jr. showed early talent
as an artist and a musician. He was an excellent student and
was self-taught in telegraphy, photography, calligraphy, pen-
sketching and music. His first job was as a telegraph operator,
60 miles east of Fairview. He was then transferred to Provo,
where he worked until he was called to go on a mission by
the Church of Jesus Christ of Latter Day Saints, otherwise
known as the LDS or Mormon Church.

*

The love letters were kept secretly, and separately, by both my great-grandmother and my great-grandfather. My great-grandmother's letters were found in a brown paper sack above the kitchen rafters in their home in Fairview, Utah after my great-grandfather's death in 1961, 60 years after their creation. My great-grandfather's letters and many of his sketches were found in my great-grandmother's trunk after her death in 1970. Peter Sundwall, Jr. and Eleanor Brady Sundwall were married for fifty-seven years. This is their early story, as well as mine.

Departure.

The letters begin on the night Peter is packing to leave, having been called to serve a two-year mission in Sweden, the birthplace of his parents. He has recently visited Calder's Park in Salt Lake City, one of the first amusement parks built in the early 1860's. The park had a dance pavilion, a racetrack, ballpark, merry-go-round, and a natural spring that was converted into a lake for boating.

July 21, 1900
Salt Lake City, Utah

Dear Nell:

I started to write with ink on advice of my friend Miss Britt
who said it would be almost vulgar or anyway inappropriate
to write with pencil. However, I am much in a hurry and have
but a few hours in which to pack up for my long voyage so
discard the pen—I have to leave at 8:05 pm via Rio Grande
Western to go to New York—thence to Philadelphia. Ten or a
dozen of the company left this morning via United Pacific and
three of us go tonight. I think I get benefit of better scenery via
R. G. W.

Last night in company with friend, Brother Nielson. I saw the
"Battle of Manila" reproduced at Calder's Park. While the battle
was not a successful imitation of the real battle, however, the
spectacle of cannon shots, rifle shots, fire works, ships, water,
and foot militia was a lurid, interesting scene.

I was in a shop-music store and tried some of the sheet music
there, and among some of the pretty selections I saw was one,
"Will She Always Be True?" Of course, I can't invest in such
songs for a while and shall have to turn my mind in another
direction. The song was suggestive and set me to pondering. . .

Miss Larsen (Bertha) is in the room and talks to me between
lines—My letter as a result is rambling. Miss Larsen is a
University girl. Miss Britt is an artist and lives here also. I just
called to see her before I leave and asked for privilege of
writing. Miss Britt sends with me to her esteemed friend Evan
Stevens, across the water, a "note"? --evidently a love letter.
Miss Britt is talented. Four of her pretty paintings hang about
in the room. She is also a musician. Can you read music?

I shall not hear from you, perhaps, until I get across to

my destination—will write you again from Philadelphia or maybe before. My parting with Mother was not altogether the pleasantest—But you will vindicate—myself and you. I hope it will come out alright. It would be my desire that no one know of the situation which it is my fortune to be in.

> I remain yours,
> *Peter*

N.S. Excuse pencil this time, please. If you can't read this send it to the following address for interpretation. Bertie M. Larsen/ Hooper Eldridge/ Salt Lake City/ Room 19.

January 12, 2009
Baltimore, Maryland

Dear Peter,

I remember the poster I made in the summer of 1985 was almost as big as I was, and it rubbed my shins as we made our way down the blocked off streets of Towson, Maryland for the annual Fourth of July parade. The theme of that year's parade was "Ancestors," and the entire youth of the Towson Ward Mormon church penned their relatives' names and country origins onto the bright white rectangles before marching down toward the old court house. Mine read "My great-great-grandfather, Peter S. Sundwall, was from Sweden." I was in the seventh grade. Needless to say, I cared more about attracting the attention of the boy behind the "My grandmother, Joan Flockton, was from England," poster than I did about understanding my lineage.

The following fall I would stop going to church, choosing instead to stay home with my dad watching Laurel and Hardy movies on late Sunday morning television, refusing to accompany my mother and my two siblings to the three-hour spiritual marathons, broken into a never-ending rotation of Sacrament Meeting, Sunday School, and Relief Society/ Priesthood Meetings.

That summer I had already discovered Madonna and hundreds of black gummy bracelets that crawled up my arms like baby garter snakes. It was the summer of Katrina and the Waves and 'Til Tuesday, long hot days full of potential and rushing hormones. I hid behind my diamond studded sunglasses and marched on while the unforgiving July sun burned its mark into the back side of my legs.

Your great-granddaughter, *Katherine Elizabeth Cottle*

July 26, 1900
Philadelphia

Dear Nellie:

We have now been in town some 3 or 4 hours, coming from New York. We arrived in New York yesterday at 4 pm. And from what little I have seen of the town, I do not like the place much. We may not have been in the pleasantest part of town and so this may account for my opinion of the town.

The streets are so narrow, and paved with hard, brick-shaped rock. And the elevated cars and the ground track cars, together with the continual rattling of wagons and the tromp of horses hoofs, makes so much noise that it tires one. With all this noise you can scarcely speak audibly—Cars can scarcely make their way through the jam of vehicles, and drivers occasionally have a "Set to" as a result of a collision. I saw a case of this yesterday, wherein one driver was about to "scrap" another.

I like Philadelphia. It is more agreeable, cleaner, & quieter, than is New York. It is, as you know, a historic city.

My friend Mayley and myself have just been out on a jaunt through the city. We have just seen the famous Independence Hall and Benjamin Franklin's grave. I shall take a snap shot of these places tomorrow. We saw other places of interest and will see others tomorrow.

For miles before arriving at here (from the west) the railway is lined with pretty homes, having either neat or artistic lawns in front of them. Nature has provided shade for these homes with an abundant supply of pretty trees & shrubbery the most of which grow wild.

The scenery along the Susquehanna River is grand—sublime. I shall not attempt to describe it to you as I could in no way do justice to the scenery or picture.

We unfortunately did not get to see much in New York, as a heavy rain shower began just as we pulled into town, and continued all the time we were there. We intended taking in Coney Island, Brooklyn, and other places, but the storm would not permit. We could not help, of course, seeing the "sky scrapers," and I am wondering often as to where there is any value in those buildings outside of its being a novelty.

Well, I wonder how you are getting along. I should like to hear from you. Will not ask you to wait until I am located before you write. I should like for you to write me a good nice letter at once and address it to me c/o St. Paul's Gade #14, Copenhagen, Denmark, and by the time I will have spent 2 weeks in Paris and get to Denmark, I will have this letter in hand to interest and please me. About that time the blissful part of my trip will be at an end, and I will then if at any time, feel inclined towards homesickness. This mission president will be advised to locate me in Stockholm.

The hotel has just been treated to music by 2 Italians or Egyptians—I do not know which, one is a gent, the other—a girl who handled a tamboras—the gent handling a new style of music box—a large one of wheels, which has, when in operation, a piano effect. It is something I have never seen before and the music is attractive to me.

I send you today copies of McClure's and Ladies Home Journal. I thought I would enjoy Kipling's story in McClure's but can not say that it interested me much. You may find something of interest in the magazine.

Well, I close. The next time I write will likely be on the steamer, "Rynland," which letter, some incoming steamer will bring back. We leave Saturday next in the morning. Then goodbye to America, to my home, to you. I could continue to write on, but the landlord's stationary is going & it is late.

Tell me how the 24th went off. Representation of Utah by you was, no doubt, successful. You know the drawings that the sour orange joke inspired—I have unfortunately lost one of the parts of the drawings. I had it in two parts. It must have either been left or taken on the sly by one of the people at my boarding place in Salt Lake. I am sorry. It will do me no good now, and I will not have time to make another. Well, what young man has had the fortune to have your company lately? Brother John will soon be home from school and he will likely call occasionally and take you out, as will also Mr. Nielson of Salt Lake. How is Vina and Mr. Clements getting along?

> Write and tell me everything.
> I remain,
> *your Peter*

N.B. & P.S.

My friend Mayley is quite a bright young man who goes to England on a mission. However, he goes to Paris first. He served in Utah volunteers, and is the author of the book, The Utah Batteries. Unfortunately he is habituated to using cigars, which habit he contracted in the Philippines. He says he will quit when he gets to his field.—

Excuse haste and poor writing. I supposed you read my S.L. letter. Best wishes to you all. P.S.

January 16, 2009
Baltimore, Maryland

Dear Peter,

I was the only girl in my Sunday School class whose father smoked a pipe. I remember the awe on my church member friends' faces when they came over to play and saw the white billows rising up toward the ceiling of the living room. A few tried to catch the disappearing puffs, but most just stared at the smoke like it was the poison boiling over from a witch's caldron. Smoking was forbidden in all Mormon households, as well as alcohol, coffee and tea, and usually caffeine. It was, and continues to be, all a part of The Word of Wisdom, taken from the Mormon text, *The Doctrine and Covenants*, Section 89:

> *Revelation given through Joseph Smith the Prophet, at Kirtland, Ohio, 27 February 1833. As a consequence of the early brethren using tobacco in their meetings, the Prophet was led to ponder upon the matter; consequently, he inquired of the Lord concerning it. This revelation, known as the Word of Wisdom, was the result. The first three verses were originally written as an inspired introduction and description by the Prophet.*
>
> *Verses 1–9, The use of wine, strong drinks, tobacco, and hot drinks is proscribed; Verses 10–17, Herbs, fruits, flesh, and grain are ordained for the use of man and of animals; Verses 18–21, Obedience to gospel law, including the Word of Wisdom, brings temporal and spiritual blessings.*

My mother, baptized into the Mormon Church when she was sixteen, married my father, a non-Mormon and her high school sweetheart, when she was twenty one. Of course, because he was not a member, they could not marry in the temple (a temple marriage being a marriage in which an active male and female Mormon are spiritually sealed for all Eternity). So, they did the compromised version, marrying in her local Mormon church, with my mother's Bishop performing the ceremony. Her ward (a set of local parishioners meeting at a particular church branch) and their families were able to see the entire ceremony, like most weddings in the world. Temple marriages can only be viewed by people who hold a temple recommend, a bi-yearly recommendation from their local Bishop and Stake President. My parents' wedding album resembles any other early seventies portfolio: wide collars, empire waists, yellowing prints that still smell like dusty possibility.

I have often wondered if my mom ever had second thoughts about marrying a non-Mormon, having to attend church by herself, dragging her three young children there year after year. She has never mentioned any regret from being spouseless in the pews, or resentment that she must enter the Washington D.C. Temple with another widowed woman to do her temple work instead of her husband. However, she had a blueprint to follow, as her own mother, my grandmother Katherine Sundwall Palmer, your and Nellie's 4th child, also married a non-Mormon man, Cecil Ambrose Palmer. He was a man who also smoked a pipe and had trouble sitting still in your family's home while he courted your daughter in Fairview, Utah in 1935, his restless temperament too restless for anything that required much patience or compromise.

My mother has stuck to the Word of Wisdom for the most part, with the exception of caffeinated soda, which finds its way into the pantry closet, next to the dry dog food and the snacks for the grandkids. My father continues to live on nicotine and coffee; filter-less Camels and vast amounts of bitter brew that keep the local Dunkin' Donuts is business. The caffeine rule seems to shift, depending on the family and the decade in the Mormon Church (and how close you live to the Mecca centers of Mormon culture, like Provo or Salt Lake City, Utah). Coffee and tea are always big No-No's, but Mountain Dew and Coke are like the hidden stepchildren among some of the members. This strict diet is intended for both spiritual and physical health. Overall, I think Mormons do tend to live longer than the average Red Bull-guzzling-cigarette-smoking individual. But, in my own extended family at least, most of the people who have passed away prematurely have been the healthiest ones, and the smokers and drinkers have made it well into their senior years.

When I was a young teen, life expectancy statistics weren't an issue. I didn't want a few short lines in a book to dictate what I would or would not put into my body. I secretly puffed on my father's pipe when he wasn't around (though it tasted like old, dry shoes) and sipped the forgotten last drops of his black coffee (though it tasted like congealed dirt).

"Make more rings," I pleaded with my father, and stepped back to watch the circles dissipate into the air above my head.

> Wanting to see,
> *Your great-granddaughter*

July 27, 1900
Philadelphia

Nellie,

I take advantage of my last opportunity to write you again before I bid goodbye to America. We leave in the morning at 10 o'clock.

Have spent the day in sightseeing and have been much entertained. First went down to ship yards, where two large battle ships for our navy are in course of construction. Was in Independence Hall & saw the cracked liberty bell, as to the important incidents connected with that historic building you are aware of. The city building is a magnificent edifice and covers a show square. On the outside of the building, at different points on the broad side walks are statues, built to the honor of our leading generals. Spent some time looking in the art shops, and saw some beautiful drawings that fascinated me much. They are so full of inspiration, and they so infuse in me an interest to that extent that I would almost feel sorry that I cannot devote myself exclusively to the work.

At times, before leaving for my mission, I actually felt a little indifferent with regard to my calling, for I wanted to accomplish myself in the other direction, but since receiving my blessing in Salt Lake, at the hands of one of the apostles, I am quite content and satisfied. I am assured success in the pursuit of art, but am admonished to bear in mind that my mission work is primary. My blessing will be forwarded home from Salt Lake. You may get to see it.

I hope you will find some way in which to cultivate yourself in the direction you desire. One with your ambition and desire certainly is worthy of and merits every opportunity she can get. However, you already embrace the virtues and education that speaks much for you.

I saw Fairmont Park this evening. To think what Dame Nature, under the designing hand of man can accomplish, is wonderful to me. The arrangement of flower gardens, fountains, ponds, lilies, trees, lawns, and shrubbery go to make the park a veritable paradise. This park eclipses the central park of New York. In the park are located the celebrated memorial and horticultural buildings. The latter was a maze form, for I felt transplanted to the tropics. Among this elaborate display of trees, plants, flowers from many climates, especially the tropics were trees as follows:

Fan palm from Africa
Fan palm from Australia
Bamboo from China
Rubber tree from India
Aculeate from Mexico
Palm from Brazil
Palm Cabbage from West India
Rose apple from East India
Oil palm from Honduras

Some of the palms, I suppose, reached up 50 feet in height. I enclose you a leaf from the fern tree of Australia that I plucked without the guard's notice. I do not suppose though, it will retain its form till you get it.

I feel that before I leave this country of America, I should in some little way at least, give you something as a token of my esteem for you. Am sorry, Nell, that I can do so in no better way than by offering you a year's subscription to the Ladies Home Journal. I have heard you say that you liked it. I like the magazine very well, myself, and hope you will enjoy it. I was in the home of The Journal and can say that things are kept prime and nice.

Excuse me for coming so near to talking you to death. It will gratify me much if you will come so near doing me up in that

Copenhagen letter that I am looking for as I have "done you" in these two or three documents that I have written you.

Does any one imagine our relationship? Or do they ask you any questions much. In your letter tell me everything and "Tell Me That You Like Me"—a pretty new song—at Fairmont Park, I thought to myself, would be an ideal place, were you here, to get cider (side her)—and even drill you on the new military salutes—Hobson's, for instance—Ha!Ha! Should my folks guess the situation with you & myself, they would say something is radically wrong with my mission work and that I am not fully consecrated to the duties before me as I ought be. Please let no friends no that I send you the Ladies Home Journal.

All my friends are to bed. So I close and say Good bye.

N.S. Remember St. Paul's Gade #14 Copenhagen, Denmark. Am I not a "cracker Jack" of a writer? Here are six sheets filled up.

January 28, 2009
Baltimore, Maryland

Dear Peter,

Already, I am aware from your early letters that you have
the condition that is now coined the disability of ADHD. I'm
well versed in ADHD since my son was diagnosed two years
ago, after months of "distractive" and "impulsive behavior" in
his first grade classroom. Add in a desk that looked like the
remnants of the wars that your generation will live through
and coin with capital letters and Roman Numerals, and I was
handed a letter "strongly recommending that you discuss
the current behavior issues with your child's pediatrician."
But in your day, even in my own childhood days, there was
no such thing as ADHD. We didn't have initials, only words,
to categorize people who were scatter-brained, distractible,
temperamental, or just plain weird.

Your admission of your longing to continue your artistic
work is a glimpse into your internal struggle to find balance
between your creative impulses and your spiritual duties. I
have learned, both from my children and my own experience,
that you cannot have unexpected discovery without
impulsiveness, creation without distraction, or production
without being hyperactive, either in the mind, body or
both. However, these are the three elements that organized
institutions, in particularly rigid churches and schools, resist
the most.

Discovery, creativity, and curiosity tread the dangerous waters
of new findings, new directions, and the inevitable questioning
of hierarchies. Even if my son wants to accept his school
environment, he must fight to go against his natural instincts,
which automatically push the boundaries and rules away from
his growing skin. As his pediatrician explains to me in layman's

terms, "It is like telling him to write neatly when he has both of his hands tied behind his back."

Your internal struggle must have been just as physical and psychological, feeling pulled in both the direction of your art and your religion. The strict requirements of a mission are written for the masses, not for an individual artist. Even today, in 2009, missionaries must follow strict rules that specify every aspect of their waking lives. This attention to time, neatness, detail, and lack of personal privacy is particularly difficult for people with ADHD to follow. The amount of rules that missionaries must follow is daunting. The following missionary expectations list is taken from the February 9, 2007 issue of the *Star Tribune*:

1. Internet access is allowed only 1 day a week, and only permissible if companions can see each other's screens. Missionaries may only access Mldsmail.net, lds.org, mormon. org, and josephsmith.net.

2. Make sure carpet is covered where bikes are stored to prevent stains. Bike stains are the biggest reason why we lose our deposit money.

3. Please only wear nice business style ties. Flashy or bright ties that attract attention should not be worn. This includes, but is not limited to '70's style polyester, pink, and purple based ties.

4. The following music is approved: Especially for Youth, church-produced music, LDS hymns, Mormon Tabernacle Choir, appropriate Christmas music, and classical music.

5. Please strictly follow the Elbow Rule: Always be near enough to your companion to hear him at a whisper while outside of the apartment. Do not separate for long periods of time within the apartment.

6. 100% on the plan [7 days a week for two years, with only minor variations on preparation days and Sundays]. Out of bed by 6:30 a.m. (not 6:31). One full hour of personal and companionship studies (not 59 minutes). Out of the apartment by 10 a.m. (not 10:01). One hour for lunch at the most. One hour for dinner, the latest time being from 5 p.m. to 6 p.m. Be out of the members' houses by 6 p.m. (not 6:01 p.m.) Be in by 9 p.m. If you are teaching, you may be out until 9:30 p.m. at the latest. Plan the next day's activities starting right when you get in the apartment. Be either in your bed or praying by 10:00 (not 10:01).

7. Letter writing is allowed only on preparation day during preparation hours.

Will your letters become your creative outlet during the next two years, providing the descriptions and metaphors that are the urgent and necessary releases for your existence? Already, your letters' intensity, length, and digressions spell it out with their own words: creativity cannot be put on hold. Your rebellion is subtle, yet undeniable. And, as the pamphlet I shoved into the top drawer of my desk states: ADHD is usually genetic and passed down from generation to generation.

> One hundred and ten years later,
> *Your great-granddaughter*

S. S. Rhynland
August 8, 1900

Dear Nellie:--

Have just had dinner- at home we'd call it supper- and now that I'd make an attempt at writing you a letter, not-withstanding fact that I have written you some 3 times, and, as yet, have not heard a solitary word from you. However, I do not look for any word from you until I get that Copenhagen letter.

Am still on the sea though indications point to a probability of our journey coming to end, for all day we've been travelling along the coast of Irish land, the celebrated country of the shamrock. About an hour and a half ago, our ship "Rhynland" anchored in the bay fronting the Irish sea port of Queenstown, and the steam tug "America" sallied proudly up, and made connection with our S.S., and then we exchanged passengers, some getting off and some getting on. Among those to get off our "Rhynland" were two D.D.'s –reverends. These people don't particularly like the "Mormons" because some of them (Mormons) sometime come out a little too direct—with questions that embarrass the ministers a little to answer. There was a profusion of handshaking & "Good byes" just before our resp. D.D.'s left us, but they avoided the "Mormons." Some of our people overheard some one say to the distinguished men below, jokingly: "Have you said Goodbye to your Mormon friends?" The reply was not audible.

When the S. tug "America" steamed away with her Irish passengers, the "Rhynland" people sang a farewell song. The scene of kerchiefs waving looked to me a little interesting, and so I "snapshot" the outfit just as the tug pulled away. There will be I think a bit of Irish landscape in the background.

It seemed quite like a holiday day, for we've just been sailing along the land, interesting land of the Irish, and as I stood gazing on the fields that stretched up the hillsides, I fancied I saw those West hill farms at home. We have been sailing, you know, for 12 days without seeing anything but water and sky. So you see this long monotony was happily broken today. People all day have been viewing the green hilly landscape with the fields of grain and vegetables, partitioned off with what the fieldglass reveals to be hedges. Dwelling places & buildings dot the land here and there, and sometimes a group of houses nestle in some hollow or vale—these, you know are protected against the winter winds and once in a while, some big mansion or castle environed by smaller houses, and then the fields. This means that some landlord owns the premises—it may be a thousand acres of some less he owns—which is worked by a great number of poor tenants. I have enjoyed looking over the land so much sung of in song, poetry, and other wise.

We shall next land at Liverpool tomorrow at about noon. Then the "boy preachers" will scatter over Europe. Four will go to Scandinavia, four in England. Two to Holland & one will go to Berlin to accomplish himself in singing.

Unfortunately, I suppose, I shall have to go to France alone. Unless Bro. Mayley goes along. As yet he is not decided. Maybe he will go and maybe not.

Just now had some little crackers and cheese. The tables are usually set at 9 o'clock when the above named articles with coffee are served to those who care to eat. I usually do not eat at this evening repast, but the cheese & crackers being shoved in front of me, I mechanically set my paper aside & went to eating with my other friends. We eat at 7 am., 12 n., and 5 pm. and are served pretty good chuck. My health has been good,-- have eaten at every meal, and to my surprise was affected with sea sickness. Have enjoyed myself every day!

There are 15 in our company, (5 ladies and 10 Elders)—Two of the ladies go to Scandinavia to see relatives; one goes with her husband to do missionary work in England, one goes to meet her husband, and one goes to meet her sweetheart. See the 5 ladies have been more or less sea sick, while 3 of the brethren have also been likewise affected, one poor fellow being sick the entire voyage.

I had intended to devote myself to the study of the Gospel, my language & some other things while on this ship, but the surroundings and sea have so fascinated me that I have accomplished but little. But then I am no worse off than my brethren. It seems that one can be on deck & never tire of looking out on the sea. My time has been devoted to doing this together with game of playing, studying, writing and sketching some. I am regarded as quite a notorious artist here on board. My "Mormon" sisters are rather responsible for this reputation that I have. I have written and sketched for merchants, M.D.s, and other individuals, and I believe my efforts have made good impressions, as I have received plenty of compliments, free gratis from professional people of all kinds. Today, I made a pencil portrait of one English lady's boy. I think the attempt was first rate. Yes, I did better with this than I did with that girl that Sunday afternoon if you remember. I can't quite do justice to good looking people—Excuse me, I mean no flattery, I assure you. I can handle children and old people better. Some jobs that I have contracted, I guess, I cannot fill. Met a Mr. Mooney, editor of the Memphis Commercial Appeal and had a little pleasant conversation. He gets $300.00 per month as salary. Excuse my reference to my hobby. I'll shut up.

Mrs. Smith is just playing the piano. She is a clever player, also singer. Her husband sings cleverly and also plays fairly well. In the concert last night, he played while she sang a pretty song, then later in the program, she plays while he sings. They are apparently just married, as she looks quite young.

Miss Edge, evidently a high born lady, so conducts herself
that no one has much respect for her. She is accomplished as
a musician. She is either talking or laughing continually. With
the waiter especially is she making application of her wit--,
instead, renders herself impudent and disagreeable with her
passenger friends as well as with the ship's crew. She rather
tired me by describing how well packed her two chests were
with music, "just only music."

Our English people are quite nice, and I rather enjoy my
association with them. One of them, a saintly looking woman
of about 33 years of ago unfolded to me the other day, a
chapter from her life's history. A pathetic tale it was, and its
recital aroused in me a deep sympathy for this lady with the
Christian bearing. For the other character, in the story, her
husband, who cruelly and shamefully deserted her 12 years
ago, I would have but little mercy for. Three years after they
were married, he left wife and child, sailing for America,
beguiling her with the tale that he would send for wife & child,
to come to a new home. She did not hear from him, and for
12 long years she has hoped and waited with a fortitude and
patience that is admirable. This summer she was bound she
should meet her husband and have an understanding that
should be fine. She heard of her truant husband, left the home
at her parents and sailed for America and found him dissipate
& wrecked. Now she returns to her English home fully
resigned to the "blighted" life that she feels she is consigned
to. She says she will bear up under the situation as well as she
can, "though I once thought to make away with myself," she
said in her broad English,--"but I've changed my mind. Yes,
my life is blighted." I feel sorry for her, she is, indeed a good
woman. I respect her. It is my opinion that the fault is all with
the man whose inhuman traits, at the time of her marriage,
were too well concealed for her to see. No one would guess
that any sorrow had crossed her way, for she conceals her
unfortunate position gallantly. Yet down in her heart, there is a

wound, a laceration which cannot heal and for her, the life, no matter how short, will be long, comfortless, and unpleasant.

I asked her for her name and address. She hesitated, saying, "I have to think about that first." She likely fears that I make misuse of the story and her name. She asked me to say nothing of this or to give her away. I assured her I should make no gossip, and that she could regard me as a friend. I feel, though, it will not hurt to tell it in the brief way that I have done.

I could say more, but I tire you. Have written quite a long letter. Perhaps, too long to read all at once. I should have divided it off in chapters or something that way. So that you could read a division or two, then lay the letter aside for a while, but then by the time you have read this far, my suggestion will do little good, for then you will have read most of the letter.

How is Vina and who is her refuted caller? How are your Sundays? For 3 Sundays, I have now spent without your company in your shady rendezvous and I guess quite a number more will pass before I can look for that pleasure again.

Supposed you write every two weeks, if you feel patriotic enough, and I shall in return, of course do the same. Fire them to St. Paul's Gade #14. Copenhagen, Den. When I get located in Stockholm, I will let you know my address. I think I can conduct a correspondence with you without it interfering with me fully consecrated to my work.

Au revoir, my Bonne et Bell, Bonne foi, Le bon temps viendra.

> Affectionately,
> *P. Sundwall, Jr.*

N.B.—If I go to France land I must know a little French, hence I practice a little French. P.S.

February 1, 2009
Baltimore, Maryland

Dear Peter,

The "boy preachers," as you call your group of traveling missionaries, truly are boys by today's standards, averaging 19-24 years old. You would have been 24 years old when this letter was written, at the older end of "boy" in my book. There was a time, back when I was a little girl in the church, when male missionaries did look like older men, with clean shaven cheeks and newly broadened shoulders. I saw no difference in their authority and the power of the other married men holding the Melchizedek Priesthood, sitting up straight in the raised upholstered chairs facing the pews in our weekly Sacrament meetings. The main difference was that they traveled in pairs, always two black suits, or two name tags, two spotless ties, or two sets of shined shoes. This duality seemed to increase their influence, and I remember avoiding them in the church halls because they made me nervous, not because they would do anything bad to me, but because they were so impenetrable. I always felt guilty around them, like I would be caught just for opening my mouth, my quivering lips never sure of the correct response to their overly friendly smiles. I calculated the quickest escape route past them and down the carpeted hallway to my Sunday school class.

While I was growing up, my mother invited the "traveling" missionaries over to dinner at least every other month, whipping up big pots of spaghetti with lots of garlic bread and carrot salad for their voracious appetites. I would quietly sit there and listen as conversation was exchanged and my father constantly quizzed the missionaries with his trivia tidbits about current topics they knew nothing about since missionaries are not allowed to watch television. It was a

revolving door of new missionaries every six months, some
pimply and tall, some with glasses and curly hair, some
fat, some pale with freckles: but always the name tags, the
politeness, and the referral to each other as "Elder." I was
particularly fascinated when we had female missionaries over
for dinner, as they were less common and tended to have
large breasts that could never be completely hidden under
their baggy suit jackets and long wavy black skirts that swam
as they walked. A lot of the missionaries were from the west,
from large families in which all boys was expected to attend
a mission and girls were expected to marry young or to go
on a mission if they were still single at age 21. But I only
learned about their origins from my father's blunt questions,
as the missionaries never talked about themselves unless you
asked them a question straight out, staying focused on their
plates and the required after-dinner scripture readings.

I was always curious about the missionaries' backgrounds
and the lives they had before the dark colors and uniform
hair styles. Did any of them flunk any classes in high school
or go just a little too far with the girls before receiving their
callings? How did they honestly feel when they received
their mission callings? Did they immediately fill with the
Holy Spirit, or did they gulp and feel butterflies and beetles
crawling all through their stomachs? Was it pleasurable, to
know you were going to give up two years of your life to
God, or did it feel like someone was about to saw away part
of your body, priming up another duplicate half to become
the weight that would keep you from getting into trouble? In
reality, the missionaries were a lot like conjoined twins, one
unable to move without the other one coming along for the
ride. How interesting, I thought, to have a semi-permanent
twin who didn't come from the same mother. They scraped
their forks along the bottom of their plates, just like I did.
They drank when they were thirsty, just like I did. Yet, I felt
a wall of difference between us. I kept quiet, without a twin,

and listened. They talked, when asked, already knowing what they were going to say.

Without a sound,
Kathy

Fairview, Sanpete Co., Utah
August 5, 1900

My dear boy:

Hope this reaches Copenhagen by the time you get there. Haven't had time to write sooner. Am staying at Clarence Pritchett's and we are so very busy, gathering and packing fruits, besides the housework. Am so tired when night comes that I cannot stay awake long enough to write. Have this afternoon off, and am spending it in the most pleasant way possible—writing to you.

How grand it must have been to see those old buildings and all those other beautiful things. Have often wished I could visit some of those eastern city's. Never imagined I should like to live in the east though. How one must miss the mountains going from here there . . . our mountain home. Would so much liked to have been with you while there, especially at the park. Think I should have submitted to have been drilled on the new military salutes—Hobson's especially—How grand it would have been. Haven't been to a party or social since you left. The young men do not call. They are afraid or do not care to call. Need never call for all I care. For some cause or other I do not care to go out as I used to.

Went with John and Carl down to the meadow for a load of Hay, had a jolly time. Reminded me of the day we were down by the old mill. Do you remember?

The fern leaf is just as pretty as can be. It retained its shape very well. Must have been most beautiful to see those palms and trees. Suppose one can't imagine how very beautiful they are, until you see them. Am so glad you were fortunate enough to secure the leaf. When I look at it, it brings so vividly to my mind the park and your thoughts while there. I imagine I have seen the park.

Wish you were here to go to meeting with me. Such lovely evenings we have—moonlight—I shall not spend these moon light evenings so pleasantly as I did the last, nor will I until you return.

It would have been very nice, could you have gone on with your work of art. But there will be time after you come back. You know you will be successful. As soon as I can I am going to call at your home, so I may see your blessings. Hope I am successful in gaining all I desire to. Think I shall. Ah! I will.

Dear boy you could not have given me token any better than you have. How I appreciate it. How I shall enjoy reading the magazine. Thank you very much. You are so good. Will keep them all, and when you return, we shall enjoy reading them together.

You said in your first letter that the song entitled, "Will She Always Be True?" set you to pondering—Well, you think I won't remain true to you, but I will. You know I will. If not, wait until you come home.

Am so glad you can locate at Stockholm. The sketch you sent me is fine, so natural. I can scarcely write there is such a confusion in the room. You asked me to write a good nice letter, but I have not because I am not capable. Wish I could write such good refreshing letters as you.

Must tell you how Vina treated Mr. Clement. On the twenty-fourth he came in the afternoon. Amanda, Vina, and I were sitting on the west side of the house. Some one came through the gate, Vina said, "There is someone with light clothes on, wonder who it is?" I said, "Maybe it is some one going to take me to the dance." I seen who it was then, told Vin. Well you should have seen her. Ha! Ha! She did not wait for anything. Jumped over the fence and ran up the road—It was about seven in the afternoon. I am sure he seen her. Well it fell to Amanda and I to entertain him. We were so full of laughter, we could scarcely talk. I was ashamed of myself. He did not stay long. And he "has'ent come back anymore." Poor boy!

I did very well on the 24th, so everyone said, was so frightened I did not know how I said my speech. Will send you a copy of my speech next time I write. I think it is very nice Amanda helped me get it up. Amanda is quite ill. Nothing serious though.

I may go to the city this fall. Aunt Vina has written for me to come.

How nice it would have been could I have gone with you as far as Phila. to see all the pretty scenery, and gone through the park not so much the pleasure of seeing as being with you. I think no one imagines our relationship but there are some very curious people here. Ask such bold questions. I have to turn it off in jest. How glad I shall be when I will not need to keep it a secret. When all may know.

You said for me to tell you that I like you. Ah! I love you, and my love grows stronger every day. Well, I have nearly "talked you to death," but it will not interest you. Hope I will do better next time.

> I remain true to you.
> *Nellie*

February 6, 2009
Baltimore, Maryland

Dear Nellie,

I had to do some research on Hobson's salute. I had never heard of this salute before, and at first I suspected it might be some type of fancy hand signal. Turns out, Lieutenant Hobson had quite a reputation of kissing the ladies after his lectures in late 1898, to the tune of hundreds of kisses at a time. Apparently, this was in all of the papers at the turn of the century, and Hobson reported that the number was greatly exaggerated, as it was only a few women, not hundreds. So, Hobson's salute becomes campy code within your letters: a kiss, rather than a hand to your forehead; a way to convey "I desire you" without ever having to write out the words.

Your letter also brings up Peter's mission blessing, a verbal ceremony or formal prayer called "setting apart," performed before church members embark on missions, which is both a literal prayer and an abstract blessing which will be materialized for the missionary and his family. Blessings are only presented by the priesthood, male members of the church in the highest level positions. The priesthood member performs the blessing by placing his hands directly on the recipient's head, after which he states a verbal prayer that can vary in content and length depending on the particular recipient's situation. Blessings can be performed for significant life events, such as baptisms, mission farewells, or marriages, as well as for private issues and challenges by individual member request. They contain a person's lineage, including which tribe of Israel the member belongs to, as well as blessing promises, warnings about temptations, and other life counsels and advice.

I can remember watching one blessing that occurred when I

was younger, when my little brother was very ill. He had been running a high temperature for days and was disoriented and still, as opposed to making his usual hyperactive destruction paths throughout the house. My mother carried him out into the living room in a white sheet, his face drenched with sweat. I sat on the couch and just watched as two men in black suits quietly arrived and surrounded him, placing their hands on his hot forehead. His tiny body disappeared behind the mass and material of their bodies, and I remember thinking that I couldn't even see my brother, hidden in the impenetrable huddle. I sensed that something was wrong because my mother's face was a map of tears, and my father was even silent, not cracking his usual inappropriate jokes or interrogating the men with the "What if?" questions he saved exclusively for Mormon visitors.

The blessing was probably only two or three minutes long, but it seemed endless to me at the time. I was worried my brother might stop breathing, and that he would be scared to death among the big hands and the thick adult bodies. I wanted him to break out of the closed circle, to jump back on his Big Wheel and peddle down into the TV room, but he didn't. He didn't even whimper. The blessing finally ended and the men stepped back. My mother's face lifted for a second-- the room now open, my brother unlatched from the spiritual and physical hold.

"Thank you," my mother cried, and I did, secretly, hope that some power had passed through their large white hands, an invisible lightening crack, and that healing would now begin, and we could go back to our regular lives. And, a couple of days later it did, as my brother's fever broke, and he returned to popping the heads up and off of my Barbie's, then kicking them down the hallway.

> "Prayers go up and blessings come down"
> -Yiddish Proverb
> *Katherine Elizabeth Cottle*

Orebro, Sweden
August 28, 1900

Dear Nellie,

Sunday morning just as we were up the postman called and
left us one solitary letter. It was mine, and the way it had
been scratched, readdressed, & patched up was a terror. The
missive had come a distance of about 6000 miles so it is not
to be wondered at that the envelope could not quite stand
the pressure. The envelope is patched up on end and side. I
suppose that friend Carlston of the Copenhagan office did it to
make sure I should not receive an empty envelope only.

Kind of him. I was glad to get the letter. It was forwarded from
Copen—to Stockholm and from latter place to here. There
is on the envelope some 6 or 8 awkward pen strokes run
through names of cities and places and as many other places
or names put on. You shall see it sometime.

You will be surprised when I tell you I did not go to the
fair. When I reached L. Pool I saw that I could not do so
without making too many implement sacrifices, so concluded
not to go. I shall not now take time to state them to you—
reasons why I did not go. I wrote to Bro. Nielson stating
the circumstances. I learned of afterwards that he went
down in company with other Elders, and so has plenty of
company, and, I suppose he will not miss me much. I shall,
for the present, have to forego pleasure of telling you some
particulars of our travels to England, North Sea, and Germany.
Day after our arrival in L. Pool our Scandinavian Co. left.
I stayed because I wanted to see some sights. I enjoyed
myself immensely at Walker's Art Gallery—was there two
times and saw upwards of two hundred or more original
paintings, statues, etc., the main attraction being a painting
entitled "Christ or Barabbas," size 12 ft. by 20 ft. long. It was a

masterpiece. I can tell you much about the painting, but will do it some other time. Elder Kirkham, (who goes to Germany to study singing) and I travelled as far as Hamburg together. I should like to tell you about our "compulsory" dinner while on the North Sea,--about our time in finding the customs office in Germany where none could understand us nor we understand the Germans,--about the pair of shoes that Kirkham was taking to a missionary friend, that the custom office inspected so closely because Kirk had the night before attempted to scratch the gloss off the soles with the pocket knife so that the shoes would go through without duty. Kirk. Got out of it by paying only duty. He felt as though he would be handled on charge of attempt to smuggle or defraud—quite comical it was. From Hamburg I had to make my way up to Copenhagan alone. At Kiel in northern Germany I went out into the suburbs of the city to get a shapshot of the old style gable straw roof houses. In my travels there I collected about 30 German boys & girls & children that followed me about in my hunt for scenery. Had quite a time—a pleasant time—Will tell of it some other time.

There are quite a number of fine saints there in Copenhagan— between 3 and 4 hundred of them, and the organization can boast of quite a number of pretty girls, too, and accomplished—about as nice a set of girls as I ever saw, excepting one—you know who. We've visited one lady that is without question the prettiest girl I saw in my travels from Utah and barring neighbor Jew, Jentile, or any other Christian. I took her photograph. If it is good, I will send you a copy. The lady is an expert at sewing. Enjoyed myself in trading with the Danish girl clerks. They enjoyed my attempt at talking Danish. I generally had an interpreter along to help me express myself and help me out of a predicament.

The Copenhagan choir gave a party last night I was there. I was invited and of course attended. We had a good time, were treated to chocolate, cake, dancing, etc. One girl who sang in the choir was very much like you, about your height and complexion and wore a sailor hat, very much like the sailor hat you used to wear. Of course, she made me think of you, Miss Jewson her name it, and she works at the Copenhagan office.

Took look at Copenhagan and went to Malmo, a city of about 65,000 population on almost the southern extremity of Sweden, a pretty city Malmo is, modern and up to date. Some good saints there too. One good Mormon girl I must admire for her courage. She has a rich aunt who tries to induce her to forsake Mormonism and come and enjoy the luxury of the aunt's home. She prefers to stand by the gospel and so chooses to live with some friends in a tenement house that is not inviting. She makes her living by doing odd work. She is an excellent singer, and used to sing in one of the popular churches to appreciative audiences. She doesn't go to the big church anymore, and there is now none else to admire her singing but the few saints that she sings with on the Sunday afternoon. She with some other ladies treated us to chocolate in the evening and we spent the evening in the park. Sunday evening it was. It would have been more pleasant could I have talked Swedish a little better. Next day I went to Stockholm. I was there but a few days until the Pres. got word to the affect that an Elder was wanted at Orebro as the one was ill. I, a green, row American was the only available man and so I went down to Orebro. I have been here since last Thursday and now I realize I have a colossal job to do. Can I do it? To preach the gospel is hard enough, but when you have to learn the language, too, the job is about twice as hard. I hope to succeed. Elder Pearson is a young man of 28 years of age, a university graduate, and like myself, could speak no Swedish when he first came. He does first rate now. Has served about 16 months of his mission. He is bro. to the Leut. Pearson who was in the Manila battle. Elder Pearson has now had some 3 attacks of appendicitis and is advised by M.D.'s not to do much walking. At close of the month I will go back to Stockholm where I will be installed in my field there and pursue my

studies. I have a very strong notion to ask them (the mission
& branch pres.) to let this action be deferred until the Spring
Conference and instead let me go out into the field or some of
the other branches to get good practical missionary training for
some 6 months. It will be for my good and besides my friends
at home, and friends here will have not occasion to think that
to fill a mission was not my main object.

I could tell you much about Stockholm, the "northern Venice",-
-its beauties and attractions, but shall do it some other time.
Do you know that the Swedes are the most polite people
I have seen? And according to one author, the most polite
people in the world. I could write you a half doz. sheets of this
paper just on the subject of the Swedish manners, sheets on
the subject of Swedish landscapes, scenery between Malmo,
Stockholm and here. Inland water, or lakes & ponds can be
seen from any point on the land. There are very, very many of
them, and these lakes, channels, rivers together with the thick
woodlands—verdure that abound in profusion make Sweden
and its scenery romantic and lovely. I don't want to tell you all
these things now. Will do it some other time.

You say you have not been out to a party since the 4th and
further more that you do not care. Am glad you feel that way
about it. Am glad that you recognize the sort of mission that
you have imposed on yourself which will take some time
and effort to accomplish. It will be a pleasant one for you I
believe, for I believe your tastes and inclinations run in that
direction. You will certainly be successful. The time and efforts
you expend in the avenue that we before have discussed you
can never regret. What interest you take in religious duties
and matter of self accomplishment will bring you respect and
praises from the community and put you on a level with the
other popular and respected girls of your town. Two years will
flit away and an individual who centers attention on parties,
amusement, etc. more than on anything else will not after the
elapse of that time be much better off for it. You may not be

situated financially that you can go to school. I do not look for that, but you can acquire something in the time you like through self effort & study that will be quite an attainment for you. I can commend Miss Lundquist's company. There is a refining, educational atmosphere about her. I also wish you could associate with my sister, but I do not suppose she goes out much. She is likely engaged in the more serious affairs of life. She is a sister that I can well be proud of as she pursues a character that is spotless. You will find other girls in the community whose company you will like and appreciate also.

You speak of going to Salt Lake. I hope you will enjoy yourself in your work and at the same time find some opportunity to accomplish yourself in the line you wish to. Before you go down I hope you will be in full fellowship with our ward and while in the ward you will succeed in so gaining the respect from the entire community and especially the one or two individuals so that none will need wonder at my becoming attached to the "stranger girl."

> Your
> *Peter-*

N.B. The girls are planning about ride tonight into the channel. The channel is a slow moving river, and commerce is carried by boat between here and Stockholm. The water is very still, at night the electric lights of the city are reflected in the water, and the scene is very pretty. I shall tonight have my first row-boat ride in Sweden. While in the boat I will think of another and wish she were here. However, perhaps that other and myself can enjoy a similar amusement after a lapse of two years. P.S.

If this letter is hard to read because poor, I must attribute it to Swedish ink & pen—they are poor. Don't like Swedish bread either.

Address me at #80 Hornsgatan, Stockholm, Sweden.

February 15, 2009
Baltimore, Maryland

Dear Peter,

I cannot help but smile at the thought of your companion
trying to deface the soles of his shoes in hopes of alleviating
a German duty tax. One wonders what the two of you would
have thought if I whispered in your ears that missionaries
would be taking their shoes off for every airplane flight, a little
over a hundred years later, not for the sake of a glossy new
shoe tax, but for the inspection of explosives. It is ironic to
picture you and your companion, holding your breaths while
the German officials searched you, to know that neither of the
World Wars have erupted, and that the shoes of the Jews are
still on the feet of their owners. It is hard to imagine that the
world has changed so much in a century, and that so many
lives have been lost for the sake of dominance and religion. A
century is the life span we all desire: one circular bracket in
history; two bookends around a full anthology set, including
the birth of flight, the beginning of space travel, the world
leading—then, being led by technology.

Am I stretching it to compare one person's life span next to
the weight of the world's century? Is it ever possible to truly
know the value a century holds for one human life? You two
missionaries, Elder Sundwall and Elder Kirkham, carefully
eye each other while the customs officials are looking away,
talking in a language you do not understand. The lack of your
linguistic connection with the German officials is tangible. If
you were not so afraid, could you trace the empty space with
your hands? Could poke holes through the language shade
that has been lowered in front of you? No, you hold your
hands at your sides. Today, in my year, over a century later,
the missionaries continue to keep their hands to themselves,
walking forward through metal detectors and sniffing dogs,

x-ray machines and body searches, continuing to move on into different countries, a small tax on their new shoes the least of their worries.

> You cannot know my address
> or my name,
> *a great-granddaughter*

Orebro
September 10, 1900

I go out just as soon as I get ready for a tract distribution
trip—my first experience, so will drop you a line or two
before I venture out on a 50 or 60 mile trip into rural
Sweden. I think I shall enjoy the trip although I shall have
to walk, and probably have to eat some horsemeat besides,
and to top the situation off, can talk but little Swedish. The
trip will do me good though. Two weeks now since I heard
from you, but 'er I get back from the country trip there will
likely be a letter waiting for me. How are you now days? Still
putting up fruit? How did my sister's wedding come off? The
affair comes very near making me a little homesick. I feel
that I am now minus a sister—her leaving home to embark
on a new journey—thus severing me to some extent the
close affectionate ties of brotherhood and sisterhood. But
this cannot well be helped. All our days cannot be spent in
our early, blissful homes. Sorry that I could not be at the
reception or at the dance in the evening—with you. Did you
attend the reception & the dance?

Just heard from my friend Sw. Wm. Nielson, while he
expressed disappointment at not meeting me at Paris, he
feels that he cannot blame me in doing as I did. I suppose
I missed something big in not taking the fair in, but then if
I arrange to go home when I am ready to return home, via
Hamburg, Cologne, Rotterdam, Brussels, and perhaps Berlin,
and London, and see the acts, libraries, museums, parks, and
the magnificent gothic cathedrals of these respective places. I
will see more and learn more than I would at the fair—After
devoting two years to work and study after having spent
some two or 3 short weeks at the fair, one could scarcely
(have) anything more than a faint recollection of what
happened at the exposition. So I am not so very sorry that I

missed the Paris Exposition.

Yesterday, I photographed our Sunday School class—about the nicest branch in the mission. The Saints treat us nicely, as we are invited out to some 6 or 7 meals per week. Orebro is a pretty place of some 22,000 inhabitants. The channel running through the city with theatres, amusement halls, parks etc. bordering on it adds attractiveness and beauty to the city. Should like to tell you about the market day affair, which occurred on the 4th but must forbear this time and tell you some other time.

Am occasionally taking a "snapshot" picture. Have as yet none finished, however they are at the photographers.

Tell me of what is transpiring among the young people of the town. Annie says that a number of couples will get married this fall. Tell me who they are. Does Emma C., Nellie Nielson still have their entertainers Frank and ? How about D.K. and Helena, Minnie, and Will?

I saw just the other night and for the first time since I crossed the Atlantic, a nice bright moon light—My thoughts reverted to home a little. We had such a lovely moonlight there just before I left.

How about Sadie—She is my relative now you know—a sister. I shall have to write her one of these days. She kindly invited me to. I supposed she is teaching now. How is Amanda L. thriving?—teaching also I suppose. And lastly, but certainly not last tell me of yourself. I could express my adoration & all that for you. I sometimes feel much inclined to do so, but it is rather my duty to consecrate myself to my mission and forget things pertaining to home as much as I can. There will likely be plenty of opportunity for that after 2 years—when yours and my mission is through with and I can return home and feel that I merit the particular girl of my choice.

Address me at No. 8 Hornsgatan, Stockholm, Sweden.

Yours in haste,
P. Sundwall Jr.

Baltimore, Maryland
March 2, 2009

Dear Peter,

The World's Fair that you missed in Paris, "The Exposition Universelle of 1900," debuted inventions such as talking films, the telegraphone, Ferris wheels, and the Eiffel Tower, as well as an appalling human zoo diorama titled, "Living in Madagascar." The World's Fair that I attended in 1982, "Energy Turns the World," in Knoxville, Tennessee, included a large, automated Rubik's cube, an unwrapped Egyptian mummy, Pac-man and Astroid video game arcade tokens specially minted for the event, Cherry Coke, and my own personal picture taken next to a walking human zoo from the Korean exhibit: two young women in Hanbok and full make-up, half-smiles that held the requested pose on either side of me, an artificial "Cheese," hissing through their bright red lips. They didn't look as beautiful in the developed picture, printed two weeks later, as I remember they seemed in person, their brilliant green and blue skirts bigger than my whole life, their faces challenging the light not in language, but in mime, while my own chubby cheeks stood out awkwardly and uncomfortable above faded denim overalls.

Your great-great-grandson, my son, continues the need to capture proof of life of "the other" in the frame, taking at least 300 pictures of graffiti by the time the Light Rail, Baltimore's above ground subway, reaches Mount Royal, the stop where we get off and walk a block to the Art College for his weekly drawing class. Each week he pesters me non-stop until the pictures are loaded into a virtual folder on the computer, safer within the cyber-heart of our computer than in any physical box or file in our messy house. Each week, he snaps the same shots through the dirty windows of the train, yet each week they are different squares of the time and place, different because of the changing light, the season, and who he has aged into within the span of seven long days.

There is no delay in today's photography—between shot and processing, start and finish. Within less than a second my son declares, "Got it!" then nods at his successful frame of sprayed letters and tags. I picture the professional photographers of the 1900's like magicians, hidden under darks cloaks, the camera pops accompanied by smoke and illusionary possibilities. Today's photographers carry purple Dora the Explorer cameras and download pictures before they are even able to read.

And, once upon a time, somewhere in-between your world and my mine, little gold Fotomat huts bloomed across America, tiny cubes with enough room for one thin person and a few rows of film. It remains, in my mind, the transition of the first eliminations of the distance between film and processing—a fast food style photo service that attempted to claim its credibility next to the multiplying yellow arches of McDonald's. My mother used the Fotomat in our local shopping center a few times in the 1970's, until it magically disappeared one day in the 1980's, as magically as it had appeared on the shopping strip center's parking lot, with just a slighter lighter shade of concrete left as its footprint.

"What an amazing job," I remember thinking, to work in an office where no one else could literally fit, where it was just you and thousands of pictures: birthdays, weddings, baptisms, lost teeth, and first pony rides. However, I wondered if one worked there was there the chance one might grow glossy and rectangular, like the handled pictures? Most of the young men working there looked that way, stuck between a 2-dimensional and 3-dimensional world. Would it be too much to be the only breathing thing in that gold hut, so far from the sea and Caribbean waters of the customers' proud prints? Or, would it make one feel like God, in control of so many others' lives, free to destroy or lose others' memories at will? I didn't realize it at the time, sweating in the backseat of my mother's gold station wagon, but I was just beginning to grapple with the role of the artist—the exploration of the line that straddles ego and motivation, risk and inappropriate action. I saw the pimply teenage boy in the Fotomat as something special, something different in both his isolation and control. We pulled up next to his window, and I peeked into his confined world, and what was there was exhilarating and frightening, the thin walls of his tiny building both caging and protecting him from the outside winds.

Without his image,
Kathy

Fairview, Utah
September 2, 1900

Dear Peter,

This is the first opertunity I have had to write. Have been
staying at Grandpa Pritchett's. They have had so much honey
to attend to, besides the other work, that I haven't had a
moments spare time. Came home last night, most to confining
to stay there.

Vina and I are alone this afternoon. Vin is reading and I—
well you know what I am doing. Conference at Mt. Pleasant
yesterday and today. Would like so much to have gone, but
no one was kind enough to condesend to take me. Can't get
a fellow. Vina takes them all. It is "all off" with Vina and Oren
since the twenty forth.

You must have enjoyed your journey to the fullest extent.
How grand it must have been to view the coast of Irishland.
What a pretty picture it will be and what a pretty sight it must
have been to see the people, the "Rhynland" and "America"
bidding farewell to each other. Am so glad you got the
picture.

You surely must have appreciated the sight of land. Seemed
very strange did it not to see nothing but water and sky?
Suppose one can hardly imagine how it would be.

Those D.D.s with all their knowledge cannot answer some of
the most simple questions the "Mormons" ask of them. Wish
you could have heard their reply to the question, "Have you
said Good bye to your Mormon friends?"

I can imagine I see those mansions. I have read of them so
much. How grand it all must have been.

Indeed you "boy preachers" will be scattered over Europe.

I did not think there were so many. Read a sermon of Bro. Q. Cannon's, and he said "There are many people yet to be warned." Therefore it will take many missionarys to warn them. Ah! What sacrifices they all make. But what do they care for that, go in a cause. You all know you will get your rewards.

Hope Br. Maybery desired to go to France. I hear there are so many people there that they cannot supply them with food. If so, I should think one would not enjoy themselves.

"Chuck" is that what you call your food on board ship? You say to your surprise you were affected with seasickness—Then you enjoyed your food every day. I should think it would be anything but enjoyable to be seasick. Maybe you meant to say, you were not affected. Did you? Am so glad you enjoyed yourself, seasick or not. Rather sad the one fellow should be sick the whole time. Very nice to be entertained, as you were, concerts, game playing, etc. There will be plenty of time to devote to the studying of the Gospel and those other things. It is well you enjoyed the voyage.

You may someday gain the world wide reputation, as the "notorious artist." That will be fine wont it?

You must have meant that you can do better with good looking people. Am sure you did alright with that girl that Saturday afternoon. She wished you were here to make a sketch of her this afternoon.

Was so nice you had such pleasant company.

Wish I may go to meet my sweetheart when he returns as did the lady on board the "Rhynland." I have heard of this Mr. Mooney. It is well he gets such a large salary. It would be very nice if some people could get half the amount.

It is very sad indeed that the English lady should have her life blighted. What a wicked man her husband is or was. I suppose there are many who hear her sad story. T'is well that she can conceal trouble so gallantly. I suppose there are many lives that are blighted if we could but tell. Did you learn her name before you parted?

Well today is Wednesday. Went to church Sunday evening. Had such a nice meeting. Went to Mt. Pleasant Monday and did not get back until today, was visiting with a lady friend; just could not get away to come home.

Peter Anderson died this morning. Isn't it sad such a young man should have to go?

I enjoyed reading the Journal very much. Am looking forward to getting the next number. So much nice reading in there. I usually go to meeting Sundays. John was at the house last Sunday evening a week ago. Had a nice time. Was with him at the circus, Mt. Pleasant Aug. 13th, Enjoyed it very much. Ringling Bros. show it was.

You may divide your letter off in chapters if you wish, I shall read them all before I lay it aside. Yes many more Sundays will pass before we can see and be with each other, but we will have to wait. I wish the time of waiting was over with. I think we can carry on a correspondence with each other without it interfering with your work. I hope so anyway. I haven't divided this letter off in chapters, but if you get tired of reading, lay it aside until you can read some more. Cannot send a copy of my speech this time, will try to next.

I do not know the France language, hence you will have to translate this little French you speak to me.

Anna and Oscar went to Manti yesterday. Am going to the reception tomorrow. Hope it will be as John said, "It will be you and Peter to go next," but I told him it would be he next. Don't you think I ought to stop? I do.

I am every yours
Nellie

N.B. "Write to me often letters are links that bind loving hearts to each other."

Baltimore, Maryland
March 8, 2009

Dear Nellie,

I suspect the Ringling Bros. & Barnum and Bailey Circus
performance that I saw as a child in the late 1970's was
brighter than the one you attended in September 1900. There
were so many lights and so much electronic movement, that
I remember feeling completely overwhelmed and needed
to constantly look down in my lap to center myself, my
eyes choosing the slick pages of the circus program as their
anchors. Everyone around me seemed to be yelling and
applauding, while simultaneously chomping on popcorn and
peanuts. I was just a small pin among the thousands of people
around me: two eyes on the top of a girl's body clenched into
a metal chair, two feet, jeans and her favorite black sweater, a
mouth that stayed closed amidst the noise around her.

One person stands out in my memory from that night at
the circus. She was the performer on the highest swing, the
seductive acrobat with full breasts and smooth hips, dazzling
underneath a diamond encrusted light blue leotard that
somehow stayed in place, though it looked like it would
fall off at any moment. She was the only artist who kept my
attention for more than a few seconds, and it was not because
of her legwork, or her fancy twists across the bar. It was not
even due to the death defying swing from her harnessed hair
braid, her body swinging underneath like a tightly wound
metronome. It was her ease with her body and her comfort
with the thousands of eyes watching her that baffled me.
I couldn't even make it to the front of my second grade
classroom, fully dressed, without wincing. She moved like a
natural wave, like the easy flow of an evening tide. Even the
winks of her sexy costume spelled fluidity, movement without
breaks or brakes. It was her silence within this confidence that

kept my attention, and the rest of the loud and glaring circus dulled in comparison, the lights and sirens fading into the background like my little sister's annoying crayon scribbles on the frame of my bed. I could have cared less about the clowns, the elephants, and the cannons. I realized then, I wasn't a child born to laugh. I was a child born to look. I watched the woman dangling by her hair, and tried to find the actual point where pleasure met pain.

Nellie, your letter does not mention a sexy woman swinging by her hair from a bar, and it is my bet that she is only a glimmer in her performing grandparents' eyes at that point in time, maybe the wink between the equestrian pair you saw clutching hands while they rode into the recent addition of three rings to their practiced act. What was it that caught your own attention? Was it the danger of the lion's open mouth and how close his tamer came to being eaten? Did you close your eyes when his greased, bald head finally disappeared between the lion's razor teeth—or did you watch?

"Don't you think I ought to stop? I do," you write to Peter. I know, as well as you know, that Peter's answer is "No, don't stop."

> Last row, the last seat to the right,
> *Your great-granddaughter*

Fairview, Utah
September 17, 1900

Dear Peter:

Monday evening. Haven't had time to write before. Was at
Clarence Pritchett's when I received your letter. Came home
Sat. evening. Planned to write last night, but John Alred and
Will Taylor came in. I was quite prevoked. I have "snubbed"
John so much, did not think he would call. He won't come
again. Will is a "stayer" too. Vina said "He is a chump if he
comes here any more." Suppose the boys are nice, do not
know much about them. But we do not care to go with them. I
do not care to go with any boy here. You know why.

This place is so still, nothing going on. It will probably liven
up after a while. There has been two weddings in town since
Anna's. Peter Christenson and Teresa, Moroni Tucker and Miss
Bills. There will be more next month. Won't be many young
folks left in town. Most of the boys excepting those that are
to be married have left—or going to leave town. Johnnie and
Cris—have gone.

The Lawsen girls, the Christenson girls, Nell Miner and I have
decided to be "old maids." Isn't that interesting? Can't tell much
about Nell Neilson. She and Andres are still very dear friends.
See Miss Larson occasionally. The night after Anna's wedding
dance, we—John S. and I—went into your fathers. Miss
Larsen was there, waiting for Andrew. She played for us. That
night when I hoped I might be able to play for you—as she
played—when you return. Do you remember?

The wedding was a success. Everything was grand. All passed
off so peaceful. Anna looked so sweet. I told her I hoped I
might look half as sweet as she when I am—Ah!—when I am
a bride—

They left next day after wedding. I would liked to have been with Anna more than I was. But I know she is as you say pure and good. I have learned to love her very sincerely. Seen your Mother quite a good deal the day of the wedding, as I helped some in the kitchen and dining room. She is a lovely lady. I am sure I could love her very dearly.

That letter was torn up pretty badly sure. Very kind of that friend to patch the envelope.

So tell me about everything you did and seen "some other time." I enjoy reading about it so much.

It would have been very nice had you gone to Paris. Maybe it is just as well you did not go. It was very nice that you were able to visit Walkers Art Gallery. What a beautiful painting the "Christ or Barabbas" must have been. Was well Bro. Kirkham got off as lucky as he did on the shoe question.

Had no idea there were so many Saints in Copenhagan. Will be more than pleased to get that beautiful lady's photograph.

You must have enjoyed yourself at Copenhagan. Talking with the Danish girls and sight seeing. I would like to see that girl that looks like me. I too admire that girl for staying with her religion instead of going to her Aunt's home. Sad Bro. Pearson is ill. Hope he will soon get well. Indeed you will succeed in your work. It would be much better had you known the language. But you will learn it soon and the preaching of the gospel won't be so hard.

Hope you succeed in getting your six months training in your missionary work. It will help you, but as to your friends thinking you have any other object than your mission work don't think they would.

I have decided to stay in Fairview this winter. Mr. Pritchett being away and Vina is going to Milburn to stay with Amanda and go to school. So if I left it would leave Mama alone. I can take music lessons and will have plenty of time for study of other things and as you say gain the respect of the community. I hope to, and think I can. Mr. Pritchett has bought a home here. I am glad of that. Hope my folks won't roam around anymore.

You will appreciate bread made at home all the more, if you don't like Swedish bread. Would it have been grand had "that other" been there to row boat ride with you, and the girls. Hope that you and she will enjoy a boat ride some day.

    Your Nellie

P.S. or N.B. Johnie and I had a good long talk before he left. Said you told him all about our relationship while you were at Salt Lake City.

    Nellie.

Baltimore, Maryland
March 19, 2009

Dear Nellie,

The "secret" of your and Peter's relationship is that of young
lovers, meaning not so secret since it is fact that very few
people, especially young people, can keep secrets, no matter
what century it is. Your "secret" is more an unspoken truth,
expressed through your letters and delivered across the
ocean, than an outright lie or deception. Your families likely
suspect your relationship, but stay silent, due to the church's
preference for missionaries to stay focused on their mission
work.

I consider the age old question: If something is not heard,
does that mean it does not exist? The poet in me thinks both
sides are possible, and your and Peter's letters juggle the dance
between public "no" and private "yes". The division between
public and private realms is blurry when it comes to any
religion. There is an unspoken open space of uncertainty—
especially, when you are handed a thick pile of scriptures as a
child and are expected to understand a language of old men
with beards as long as anchors and speech that seems to be
directed more to cliffs and alters than places that I could ever
see. I would have preferred a Religion for Dummies collection,
as opposed to the unbendable spines of the leather bound
scriptures. And even then, I would have wanted to make edits,
and add my own chapters and illustrations.

I always viewed religion as a big piano on my right shoulder.
Growing up, all of the neighbors to our left were Lutheran and
all of the neighbors to our right were Catholic. Our house,
with its Mormon Matriarch and Primitive Baptist Patriarch, was
at the top of the hill, like a lighthouse, standing and shining for
all to see. I knew the Mormon Church, especially, was a little

different from the religions of my neighbors and friends, but I didn't quite know how it was different. What I did know was that I was jealous that both of my neighborhood girl friends got to drink sips of wine at their weekly communion while I was left to sip cool water-fountain water from a clear plastic cup during the Sunday Sacrament meetings. Even our bread tasted second rate compared to the other religions who has bread with special names and textures. Our bread was plain old Wonderbread crumbled across the bottom of a silver tray. While my friends cracked crisp hard wafers with their braces, I was left to dissolve soggy crusts in the middle of my tongue.

"I got a piece without crust," my brother would brag before I elbowed him in the ribs.

"Are you a Christian?" one boy asked me in my public school third grade class, when I was still following obediently along on Sundays.

"What?" I replied, unsure about what he was asking.

"My mom says your family is weird. You aren't Christian," he mocked, then turned back to picking his nose.

I tried my best to keep my tears from releasing until I got home from school.

"Mom, a boy in my class told me we're not Christian. Is that true?"

"We believe in Christ," she said, like it was the silliest question in the world, and then changed the topic. I realized then, even she wasn't quite sure of the answer.

Mormonism is among the contemporary millennial religions, like Seventh-day Adventists or Jehovah's Witnesses, religions that are still trying to find firm grounding in a world where other religions have roots and claw marks dating back for centuries. Mormons are sort of like Twitter or Facebook—

everywhere and nowhere all at once, still somewhat fresh in their new rings within the global religion tree. Loyal Mormons feel the pull way down into the core of their homes and their beings. But the rest of us, some inactive, some excommunicated, and many, many non-Mormons, stand outside of this religion's huge eggshell and can't find an opening, or just don't know quite what to make of it. People naturally say what it isn't, what it couldn't be, what their friends tell them it is. Like children, some people knock it, some shake it, and some kick it. And some, if it doesn't quite fit their fancy, just leave it for the next child who will come along, simply wanting some answers.

Looking for cracks,
your great-granddaughter

The following is Nellie's 24th of July, Pioneer Day speech. It accompanies her letter of September 17, 1900.

Greetings to you, my noble sons and daughters on this my happy birthday, and along with my greetings I bring a deep and sincere feeling of gratitude to you who have helped to make me what I am. While looking with pride upon you and noting your prosperous condition, my heart goes back tenderly to the noble pioneers, as you call them, but I call them my foster parents, because when I was alone unknown among my sister states, they adopted me never looking at my barriers nor reproaching me for my want of beauty for they saw that like the diamond I would shine forth by being polished, and how earnestly they set to work. Some even at the cost of their lives in order to make me a kings daughter, for you must remember that those who adopted me belonged to a higher kingdom then any earthly king possess, and what a great cause they had to put forth. How glad I saw to shelter them among my stately mountains giving forth the cool silvery stream reminding them of the River of Life.

It was not long before I began to blossom and grow beautiful under their untiring efforts of making me to sparkle like a gem. Was I not grateful for having been freed from obscurity and being the abiding place of a people chosen by God? To be an instrument in His land to further his work?

Such an hour was not bestowed upon my sister states, and is it any wonder that I should feel somewhat elated and proud of my sons and daughters who have passed through many trails in order to bring me forth? Although persecutions have followed my noble sons and daughters yet the time will come when they shall rise in glory and I shall be glad to do honor with them. Since my first birthday I with the help of my foster parents and sons and daughters, increased rapidly and if you will bear with me, shall briefly speak of something of which I am proud. Look at My Colleges and Academes that raise their stately walls towards the sky in token of a desire for improvement, also my public schools which mark second in none I may say in this whole Union. Then there are my mines which give employment to thousands, putting forth great wealth.

You will pardon me if I speak boastingly of my agricultural products in that I have excelled myself, for you must remember that at the day of my birth I was nothing but a dreary desert over which the wild beast roamed, and now I am a garden of Eden in some places. My cereals are fine, my wheat is one of the best the market affords, and my fruit is simply delicious.

I am proudest of my children, who have been so abundantly blest by Providence in being placed in such a choice portion of the earth, where the sunshine days pass into cool evenings, leaving a pleasant influence on the mind and body. My children betray this in their pleasant manner and bright faces. And now I call upon you too faithful and patriotic liberty loving children, striking down oppression wherever it appears, always rallying to the rescue of truth when it is crushed down, remembering at what price I was bought. Live my children so that you will be sustained by an unfaltering trust in the Supreme Power that allowed the pioneers to find me and give you a place of shelter for a time.

May his richest blessing fall upon you, is my sincere desire, as year by year you celebrate my day of birth.

My speech, composed by Amanda. What do you think of it?

Nellie

Baltimore, Maryland
March 26, 2009

Dear Nellie,

Pioneer Day will always be synonymous with the middle of
the sweaty Maryland summer in my memories of my first years
in Mormon Sunday School, where I watched biblical characters
peel on and off of the felt easel, passed around packets of
lessons about "Choosing the Right", and glued scriptures onto
the sides of popsicle sticks or uncooked ziti.

Some of the Mormon traditions, such as celebrating Pioneer
Day, felt like a foreign holiday to me, like reading another
country's birthday card, with different customs, food, and
sayings than my own. Maybe some of this was due to our
location on the East Coast, far from any oxen or deserts or
rising mountains of Zion. Maybe some of the distance was due
to our present time and the lack of connection to the Pioneer's
early frontier days next to the easy crunch of my father's hand
on the alarm clock in 1979, before he went out to the driveway
to warm up the car each morning and then commute thirty
miles down the highway.

Unlike you, Nellie, who had a personal connection and
closeness to Pioneer Day and its relationship to your home, I
thought more about the outfits and the cute bonnets that we
got to wear for that special Sunday lesson in July (and the
extra large pot-luck lunch), than I did about the reality of early
Mormon life in Utah.

I never felt celebratory about my home state of Maryland. The
state just seemed like a random point in which I emerged one
day, another black dot amidst the millions of black dots that I
saw on our population graphs at school. My parents did not
move to Maryland for protection from religious persecution,

or for a chance to find Eden and the Promised Land. It was their fathers' jobs that landed them in the same neighborhood, just outside of Washington, D.C. My mother's father, your son-in-law, will become an architect in his late thirties, and will be quite successful with designing schools and buildings in Maryland and the District of Columbia. My father's father, a coal miner, will move to D.C. out of necessity, after his coal mine closes in West Virginia in the early 1960's. He will follow a cousin up into the most Northern state of the South, finding a job as a produce manager for a grocery store in Georgetown. Both families will discover that Washington, D.C. is far from Eden or Zion, so they will move to the suburbs of Montgomery County. My parents, your granddaughter and her husband, will be happy to settle down an hour north to start their family in Baltimore County.

My neighborhood was still quite rural in the 1970's and 1980's, the years of my childhood. There were horse and cattle farms and enough untamed landscapes to keep us busy for hours. My biggest mountain, though, was the sled riding slope of the next door neighbor' horse farm and the closest desert existed in the sandpit behind our barn.

I pictured the land of the Mormon Pioneers like the settings in my fairy tale book: ephemeral, fleeting, distant, being able to be opened and closed like our thick and dusty Yellow Pages. It was a pretend time, a pretend day, when photographs couldn't even reach far back enough to capture a mother's anxious brow, as she wiped the sweat from her forehead and ran her finger across the lips of her hungry child, born too soon and too early in our world to be documented, or missed, or even really there,

Kathy

Orebro, Sverig
September 24, 1900

Dear Nellie,

Just had dinner—a very nice dinner for people of humble circumstances to fix up, but the Saints here seem to think that nothing can be done too well for the Elders. There are 3 of us here in Orebro and we get from 5 to 7 meals per week with the Saints, the balance of the meals we eat we prepare ourselves at our hall. Most of the Saints here are poor,--have to rent and live in tenement houses. The city is made up of business and tenement houses, scarcely no private residences whatever. Yet quite a few of these saints manage to move out and get to Zion. Quite a number have done so, a number will leave in about 2 or 3 weeks and more go in the coming Spring.

Since last I wrote you I have been on a tracting tour, in company with Elder Farby, out in the country, covering a distance of between 50 or 60 miles. Notwishstanding my inability to handle Swedish, I got along quite well and enjoyed my trip first rate, and contrived to sell as many or more tracts than my more experienced friend. Had none of the "Bonders" (farmers) kick me out of their houses or even say anything seriously bad. We travelled the "Stor lands Vagen" (big country road). These roads are fine and excellent to travel, having been graded up and graveled for years. The varagated scenery and new phases of country and farm life that I saw on this trip I much enjoyed. Could tell you of what I saw, but will have to forbear this time. Have distributed and sold quite a number of tracts here in the city and I have had what I considered fair success in selling them.

Don't know if you arranged it purposely or not but your letter came to hand on a Sunday morning again, just 4 weeks later from date of first letter arrival. Postman brought 2 letters

around—1. for Elder Pearson, from his wife. One for me
from my "alskad" Nell. Unnecessary to say that I was glad
to hear from you. Too bad about Vina's monopolizing all
the young men in town. Don't know what'll become of you.
Grow to be an old maid, likely. Vina should be a little more
considerate with her older and more unfortunate sister. I have
no particular liking for an individual or combine that combines
to make a monopoly of a thing. Neither do I like entangling
alliances and who knows but what such an alliance might
be affected between you and some of those young men in
Vina's monopoly should you succeed in infringing on Vina's
monopoly of young men. Should such a thing as an entangling
alliance or any other sort of alliance be probable, of course I
would then prefer that Vin monopolize them all. But I believe
Nell to have good diplomatic judgment so that such anything
as an entangling alliance is hardly probable.

Yes, I should have said that I did not suffer any sea sickness
what ever. A most pleasant trip it was. No, the lady on board
the ship did not give me the name. She was rather afraid
that I would misuse the story she told me and her name, so
I decided it best not to do so. She was a very good Christian
lady and I shall remember the incident of her telling the
story for a long time. I saw her last in the customs house at
Liverpool. It was there she said that while she enjoyed my brief
acquaintance on the ship, and also had every confidence in my
integrity she hardly felt as though she ought to leave me her
address. I would much liked to have sent her tracts, etc.

Shall have to adopt a rigid rule of excluding English from
my reading, though I much hate to do it. Besides, English
magazines cost a good deal here. I bought some 3 or 4 of
them when down at Kopenhagan. Though a Swede I am not
at all sorry for what English I know, rather glad of what I
know. The Swedes you must remember are not so slow. Their
literary standing ranks pretty high. A Mr. Tegner is a much
admired Swedish poet. Even Longfellow admired his Swedish

productions and translated some of them. I shall send you a specimen of a Swedish magazine so that you can form an idea of it.

Apparently you are quite busy these days putting up fruit, etc.—Fruit at Pritchetts no. 1, the honey at Pritchetts no. 2. I wish there was an easy way of transporting some of that stuff over here. It would improve our 6 months winter's "chuck" (Yes, "chuck" stands for grub.) There is not much fruit here. Scarcely nothing outside of apples, gooseberries, and a few plums and pears can be cultivated, and people somehow don't go much on fruits as part of the menu. "Blo" and "ligen" berries grow abundantly in the forests. A number of times we sat in the pretty Swedish forests and ate these berries, when out on our tracting trip. A great many country girls and women go out into the forests and gather berries on market days (Tues. Wed. & Sat.) bring them into Orebro to sell, usually getting 9 or 10 "ore" per leiter (about 3 cents per quart.) These berries are the favorite fruit for preserving. As for honey, I have seen no honey since I came to this "land of the midnight Sun." Bees I suppose don't thrive so well here. Honey, I used to eat and enjoy it, but now need not look for any such article as a part of my food diet now. I guess I do no better than use it (honey) synonomously with some other word—a proper name. Then you see, honey will not fade out of my vocabulary by its occasional use. What do you say? Will have to close my letter now I guess. It is getting rather late (about 7:30 pm). We're to have a social tonight. The Saints are arranging for it in honor of the Elders here. The 3 of us leave Wed. for Stockholm, so the Saints decided to give a farewell party first. We shall likely have a good pleasant time with chocolate cakes and apples for refreshment.

Do not think I shall stay in Stockholm when I now get there. I shall prefer to spend the next 6 months in some of the other branches when I can get a good practical training in missionary work. What if you should get called on a European

Mission? I met some lady missionaries down at Liverpool. Two of them, a Miss Booth and Miss Chipman labor in Glascow. I met a Miss Mortenson down at Copenhagan. There are also some girl missionaries in Germany. The effectiveness of girls for missionaries is now past experiment, and I do not doubt but that they will call more of them into the mission field.

Is it asking altogether too much if I ask you for a new photo of you. If I could conveniently do so I should be glad to stand the expense of such a photo or photos, but as matters stand I shall have to be gone for the present & square the bill when I come home. Should much like a bust photo in the platinum finish—one that will do justice in any position you like. The one you so thoughtfully let me take with me is not quite complete enough. The boys, however, can see from it that she's good looking, but still doesn't show her features & countenance in detail quite enough. If it isn't asking too much send me a picture in the near future. I'll settle for it some time or other.

Now Nell, what disposition do you make of these letters of mine, rambling and spontaneously written letters. An individual of no particular concern would say that the letters exhibited a fickleness in me, and should some "gossip starter" get a hold of a letter, she would find some subject matter that, in her estimation would be worth talking about. I treasure your letters, of course, so take care of them.

You say you will be glad when you will not have to keep the matter of our relationship no longer a secret. So shall I, but for the present let it be strictly secret. My folks would think of the matter of my disposing of such a question of such magnitude not right of me, and at such a time, out of order. Yet I am not sorry myself & glad you are not. May be your mama would not think it right of her girl, for she to do as she did either. Have you told her yet? Let me say again, if you like the young man to that extent and you think him worthy of you, and you are willing to take upon yourself the mission of establishing in the minds of the folks whom this matter will sometime concern, your true worth, highminded-ness and other excellent womanly qualities you possess, why I say, wait for him, and he will return for all your trouble—if trouble it is—try and aim to render himself worthy or partially so of his Nell. For the present, though let no one guess our connection.

> I close, and remain,
> Yours affectionately,
> *P. Sundwall Jr.*

N.B. Excuse any bad spelling, I realize my English is getting defective through being in Swedenland. My penship is also bad. This letter is written with 3 pens—first with an ordinary pen, then for a while I used a stub, then finished with a fountain pen. Address me at Hornsgatan, N. 80, Stockholm.

Baltimore, Maryland
April 10, 2009

Dear Peter,

I thumb through the daunting family history book, as thick as an unabridged dictionary, and find a picture of Vina, Nellie's younger sister, the one who seems to be stealing all the attention of the local guys, "monopolizing" Nellie's chances of any male suitors while you are away.

She is an old woman in the first picture I see, with horn-rimmed glasses and a tangle of white sitting on the top of her head like an old Q-tip. She is saggy within her polyester dress, her belt just tight enough to suggest waist where there is actually no longer one. The caption states she is Vina Brady Steele, a great-grandmother at this point, an older-than-old woman, with no hint of youth, beauty, or the scent of suitors on her personage.

Then, I turn the page and see the young Vina, unable to be distinguished from her older self—pale and sure, a thick bun holding down a dark hat, a mesh of undefined fabric that nests and tilts just about her right eye. She looks confident, healthy: young. Part of me is afraid to flip back to the index, to then find my own portrait, drawn into this book of lineage, my brother and sister boxed to my right like building blocks, my own face the first slab of our triangular foundation. I like to think I will find a young girl there, too, healthy and confident, intent on gathering and directing the neighborhood boys together for an afternoon play in her parents' living room, learning quickly how to talk them into dressing up into her favorite dance costumes to re-create *The Muppet Movie* with the record player scratching out "The Rainbow Connection" from behind the corduroy couch.

But I know full well that girl no longer exists. The real girl has more wrinkles than freckles; more gray hairs than ponytails. The girl waiting under my name is just another aging woman, someone no one can quite put their finger on, partly because she blinks so much, with the sun always hurting her eyes.

I stay on the page with the old Vina and notice a woman almost cropped out of the same photo. She is old, too, smiling, and looking at Vina with understanding. Her mouth droops down, vertically, while Vina's pulls to the left and the right. The other woman's eyes are tired, in a more open way, like life is still clinging inside her pupils, still willing to try movement, even with the risk of injury.

It takes me a moment to realize the other woman in the picture is your Nellie, and that it is a shot of two sisters, probably one of the last pictures taken in their final months, a long decade after you have passed. It is hard to believe it is the same woman as the one in the picture frame on my mother's dresser, the one I grew up seeing every day, a twin frame with pictures of you and Nellie, taken separately, not long after you were married. The sepia prints always seemed so mysterious and haunting, your beauty coming from another dimension, not just another time.

The young Nellie on my mother's dresser is still quiet, her dark hair pulled back in a loose bun in the same way you will draw her portrait, the sketch that will somehow survive through more than a century. She looks like she already understands all there is to know about the world and doesn't need to offer more information. I wonder if you were standing there when the picture was taken, or if Nellie was thinking of you. Your picture is more stoic, a handsome blond, blue-eyed man with a serious countenance. You could be an actor with your steady demeanor. You could be anything, and you will be.

I decide to close the book before looking up "Cottle,

Katherine" in the index. I know there is a picture in there, but it is of a child, and I do not feel like seeing her today. The difference will do more harm than good when I glance in the mirror and find five new grey hairs. Today, I will not look, though I am glad someone else noticed her, and took the initiative to pause time, for just a moment, to capture the girl, and to label her with a name and a family, right before she disappeared.

Aging, as I write this,
your great-granddaughter.

Stockholm, Sverig
October 3, 1900

My Dear Nellie:

Received your letter, yesterday. Rather surprised me, as I hardly looked for a letter for a week yet. However, I was glad and enjoyed the letter immensely well. You seem to be feeling O.K. Glad you exercise prudence as to whom you will allow, of all your callers, to entertain or take you out. Only the best young men who are also respectable, are worthy of Nell's association, and I am glad that she recognizes this. You expect to stay at Fairview the coming winter. Glad you will find opportunity for study, music, and otherwise. Your efforts will be rewarded with success, I am sure.

Glad your mother and family will have a permanent home in Fairview. I wish I could locate in some little town of Fairview's size here. Am rather tired of the cities. Shall now spend next 6 mos. in Vesteras, a place of about 10,000 inhabitants. I asked to be sent out in the field. I have never been so impressed with the importance of our Gospel as I now am, and I want the credit of fulfilling a good mission. So for a time I shall try to dispel everything from my mind that is foreign to the Gospel. There is a salary attached to this mission work, that I have not quite comprehended before, almost have been ignorant of it, and I don't think that, I yet, comprehend its full significance. That part of the Great Master's pay roll that applies to gospel ambassadors is contained in Matthew 19 chapter and last two verses, I believe. Look it up and see what you think of it.

Have spent a week in Stockholm. All the Elders of this section have been here for conference. A fine, splendid time we've had, too. Hall was richly decorated with flags, verdure, flowers, etc. All with its two side rooms was filled with Saints and spectators during conference sessions, and the preaching was interesting.

The choir is excellent—in fact, better, I believe, than our Fairview choir home in Zion. An excellent little children's Sunday School choir they have also. The children are devoted to their Sunday School work. They even sing our English Sunday School hymns and while the dialect is not yet proper, they certainly do well. I admire the little boys and girls. They compare fully as well as the boys and girls at home. They are bright, intelligent, and happy. The other night the Sunday School gave a recitation or rendered a program. These little folks, or tots, carried the burden of the program and did excellent.

Last night the ladies fixed up a banquet for the Elders—a nice supper it was, and the whole affair was successful. The young ladies are certainly hustlers and, I might say, good cooks. A half dozen of them managed the affair. A pretty picture these girls presented, dressed in the national costumes, costumes pretty and girls pretty—A nice group for a "snap shot," would but the night have permitted such. We see many of these costumes. They seem to be popular. In some parts of the country people wear their particular costumes and nothing else,--the men wearing knee trousers with tassels attached, and the Fraken (Miss) a striped apron in different striking colors, red caps, etc., while "Fru" (Mrs.) wears ditto, excepting cap which is white.

Have visited a number of places in Stockholm—have been up to the King's palace, gardens, etc, the national museum and other museums. The art department in the National Museum is a big affair with hundreds of original paintings that are sublime. I intend to go there again or a number of times before I am through with Sweden. Stockholm is a pretty place, built upon rocks, hills and islands—even from where I am not I can look out of the window and see over the tops of the neighboring houses, and into the city. The house is built upon a granite rock. We have to climb a flight of stairs that reach from the end of the street up about 25 or 30 feet, to top of a granite hill on which the house rests.

Skansen and the Tivoli are popular resort or amusement places. Was out the other day and saw the places. Saw a typical Laplander's home and family—quite a novelty it was. Saw a great many other things which I shall tell you about "some other time."

What do you think of girl hod-carriers? I could scarcely believe myself, when the other day, in my ramblings, I saw an apparently happy, smiling girl waiting on the mason, supplying mud. What do you think of girl barbers? Lots of them here. One manipulated razor for me the other day. Perhaps I should not say what I thought when held captive in the chair—Suffice to say though, that if t'were another one there—a certain one, the captive would have instituted a little something as an intermission. It might be cheeky, but should this individual have ventured to come up in such close proximity to examine the captive's cheek, he'd been justified. Don't you?

No. I said nothing to John regarding you or I. He must have been joking. He was with me when I hurriedly wrote the S.L. letter, and in answer to a question I said only that we should correspond, and nothing more, do I think, was said. Did you say or confess to anything? Pardon me for sending the letter you doubtless have now received, without the usual introduction or "Dear Nell" and blank instead. I thought of it after posting. Wishing you success and happiness to be succeeded by a still better time in which another will be equally concerned.

> I remain
> P. Sundwall Jr.

N.B. Your speech is certainly nice.

N.B. Excuse pencil in this postscript. Just rec'd copy of

Pyramid. In column for Fairview I see my sister's name appear as Miss Anna Christiansen and that Moroni Tucker is given credit for wedding Trissa Terry. I presume these to be errors. I am surprised at Miss Johnson's engagement to that Mr. Vance. I do not know much about him, but I am inclined to think that George is a little hasty, and that she merits one with some better qualifications, than I believe he possesses. I think about the same of Miss Terry. A day of her attainments isn't making so much of an acquisition in getting the groom she gets.

Now this is just my personal opinion. What do you think of the matter? What have you to say of the Tucker-Bills nuptials? Glad to learn that you call occasionally at our home. Hope you will find more occasions or opportunities to call and extend your acquaintanceship with the folks.

Do not fear about writing too long or too much.
P. Sundwall Jr.

We leave in the morning by boat at 9 in the morning—a 6 hours ride it will be.

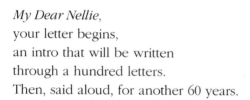

Baltimore, Maryland
March 19, 2009

Dear Peter—a poem for you:

A Shave
   Stockholm, Sverig, October 3, 1900

My Dear Nellie,
your letter begins,
an intro that will be written
through a hundred letters.
Then, said aloud, for another 60 years.

What do you think of girl barbers?
you ask, from across the Atlantic,
mid-way through your Swedish mission,
mailed in secret to your girlfriend,
the woman who will one day wear
your ring in the rising Rocky Mountains.

One manipulated razor for me the other day.
It is before your marriage,
before your six children.
You are still young,
and the world has just shifted
into the first year of the century.

Perhaps I should not say what I thought
when held captive in the chair—
You are the handsome man
from the early pictures of our family history book,
the one with the eyes so piercing
they look blue even in black and white,
not the old man in the back pages,

who looks like anyone's great-grandfather,
besides my own

Suffice to say though, that if t'were another one there-
a certain one, the captive would have instituted
a little something as an intermission.
and Nellie is the beautiful woman next to you
in those few aged shots,
long black hair swept up above dark eyes,
a soft confidence that shows
you are not afraid of strong women,
that you want someone other than the ordinary.

It might be cheeky, but should this individual
have ventured to come up in such close proximity
to examine the captive's cheek, he'd be justified.
You are clean faced in all of your photographs.
Very put together. You understand form.
Even in your 55th wedding anniversary picture
one can see control,
how your thick hands are folded,
how you sit upright through old age,
a straight tie and glasses that say
there is nothing that has bent me,

Don't you think?
except, that is, for love.

       Love,
       Katherine, your great-granddaughter

Fairview, Utah
October 1, 1900

Dear Peter:

I am sitting by the window where I can see the moon. And am thinking of the moonlight nights that you and I spent together. I often think of them, and of how many more just such nights will pass away before you and I can again enjoy them together. It is a most perfect night. Just such a night as that one was when we went driving. Carl and Mary you and I. Do you remember? Carl has gone with Mary longer than any other girl, since we came here and is still going with her.

School began at Milburn to day. I told you did I not? That Vina was going to stay with Amanda and go to school? I took them up to Milburn yesterday. Amanda has a house near the school house. They have everything comfortable. Two old maids living alone. Wonder what they would say if they knew I called them old maids? Amanda is going to try to get along without an assistant this winter. If she has very busy days, she will let the largest girls teach the smaller children. It will give them practice. Vina has been in the eighth grade for several years; but has never yet been able to go the whole year out, as hasn't gotten a diploma. Hope nothing happens to prevent her from going through the year.

Silma Lawsen and Sadie do not like teaching very well. They have over seventy pupils that is too many for one teacher. Had they less children they would like teaching better.

Yes, Sadie is your relative now. You must write to her by all means. Haven't seen Nellie Neilson for such a long time that I do not know whether Andrew calls now or not. She is in the City also. Think Nellie went in to be with her mother.

Frank Hails has not been at Fairview for such a long time. Think he is away from home. He and Emma had a little quarrel, so I heard. Do not know whether they made up or not. Emma has not gone with any one of late. We five girls do our best but we can't get a fellow. O.k. isn't in town. Winnie and Will, Ellen Peterson and Andre, George Terry and Agnes Anderson. James Henry Sanderson and a girl from one of the lower towns are to be married. Just think of it. There won't be any boys in town. We girls will have to send for some and have them come C.O.D. O yes! Petie Neilson and Philinda Terry are to be married this fall. Suppose you have heard from Johnnie since he began to teach. Prof. Sundwall. That sounds well doesn't it?

It would have been very nice indeed had you been here for Anna's wedding. The only thing that marred it, was that Johnnie had the toothache.

While at the dance in the evening I thought of you and wondered if you knew about the affair. And wondered if you were thinking of us. Did you know of it before it came off?

It will be very nice if you can arrange to go through all those large cities. Won't we be delighted at hearing you tell of the beautiful things you have seen and will see when you return? And to see all the pictures you will have taken.

The King's Palace is grand. I would like to see it very much. Thank you Peter for sending me the picture. What a grand affair the parade must have been.

I am still at home. Am going to take lessons in music very soon. We are rather undecided as to what we will do this winter. Mama thinks of leaving Fairview. Hope they do not. If they go, I think I shall stay here.

The mountains are most beautiful dressed in their autumn cloths. Two more autumns to come before you return. I almost wish the time had passed and your and my mission was through.

You won't be able to read this. I am sleepy, can scarcely write. Haven't time to write in the day time, am busy but not putting up fruit.

Am every yours,
Nellie

Baltimore, Maryland
March 23, 2009

Dear Nellie,

Over 70 students with one teacher? It is no wonder the woman
you mention does not like teaching. How could one woman
have been expected to supervise, let along teach 70 young
children? The answer is in your line: "If she has very busy
days, she will let the largest girls teach the smaller children."
The largest girls. I was one.

I was the oldest of three children, second in command: the
chaperone, the chauffeur, the babysitter. It was a particularly
challenging role to fill, as my mother was born a true teacher,
an elementary education major, and someone who took pure
joy out of making flashcards and color coded chore charts. I
was better at bossing my younger siblings around than I was
at "teaching" them. I excelled at slamming doors and yelling
insults.

Maybe, some of that guilt still lingers, that I wasn't keeping
a closer eye on my younger sister, that I never saw the early
signs which might have saved her years of grief from addiction.
Maybe, I could have been a more caring example. Maybe, I
could have been more patient and nice, like my mother, who
never yelled or snapped back. Maybe that would have made a
difference. I doubt it.

Maybe, like the girls your friend, Amanda, will commission
to help her run the school house, I was just a kid myself, just
born first and female, which placed me into that heavy role
called "Example."

As I write this, my sister now clean for over 8 years, I wonder
if you and Peter could have even imagined the drug issues that
will haunt the next century. At this point, you surely cannot

see anything but a field of unborn and happy offspring, ready to sprout in the sun. In the early years of my marriage, I thought just being a good wife and mother would guarantee a happy family. I didn't understand genetics, or the pressure of the world outside of the body.

You and Peter surely cannot picture your second daughter, my great Aunt Ann, breaking away from the church, choosing a Master's Degree, cigarettes, and an international social work career over a life without a husband and children. You probably can't even begin to imagine the schizophrenic pain of the son your daughter Katherine will adopt. You would probably hold your hands over your ears if you could hear his screams at the state hospital for 25 years, the way skin cancer devoured his body piece by piece, until he was unrecognizable, without face or race.

Another great-granddaughter's struggle with drugs is probably unimaginable in your thoughts, as is her interracial marriage. How could you know another one of your great-granddaughters would find her addiction in writing? You cannot. You live in the year 1900, without drug dealers waiting for the high school dismissal bell, with communities still defined by settlement dates and immigrant origins

I look at my children, now 8 and 4 years old, and cannot picture them as adults, or grandparents, or great-grandparents. Will my son's graffiti drawings still exist? Will graffiti still exist? If so, what will it spell? Will my daughter bare her own children? Will physical childbirth still happen?

On this day, October 1, 1900, not yet a wife nor a mother-- you are just tired. You are ready for bed, to put down your pen for the night. On this day, March 23, 2009, a wife and a mother-- I am tired, Nellie.

> I put down my pen for the night,
> *Kathy*

Vesteras, Sv.
October 22, 1900

My Dear Fastma, Nellie:

After an elapse of over two weeks of walking, walking, walking, in which I have covered a distance, I suppose, of over 200 miles, I am back to Vesteras, our headquarters, and, as I hoped and expected, the letter box contained a letter from you, also others from home, Mrs. Anna Christensen of Salem, Utah and a "Prof. John Sundwall" as you style him.

It may not be so pleasant to have to go out in the country for 2 or 3 weeks, and in all that time forgo pleasure of reading letters from home, girl and friends, and instead have to submit to allowing them to pile up in the letter box, but when one does get back there is a serene satisfaction, a complete contentment when one finds 3 or 4 letters awaiting him, and the reading of the letters—the pleasure attendant will almost repay one his loss for being out in the country. Now, in answer to your letter—rather short it was—I hardly know whether to write regarding what I have seen and done in the last 3 weeks or just to extol, upon, say, Nell?—her virtues, suppose. You speak of moonlight nights. Pretty, you say they are. No, I shall not forget them because the big, bright moon and Nell are perpetually linked in my memory now. Whenever I see a bright moon, or any kind of moon at all, (as yet have only seen one or two in Sweden) I am forcibly reminded of Nell, and my brief very brief escapade with her, which seems much like a romance, I enjoyed her company so much. Sometimes feel a little sorry that our association was so short as it was or that it did not cover a longer period than it did. Yes, I remember some of those bright moonlight nights. It was on one of those nights that we discussed on the propriety of "stealing" a little thing, or something or other when doing same would not materially injure anyone. What transpired as the result of this little affair, you perhaps remember. Perhaps, a little thing it was, but yet it was a big thing, too. As to the other nights when the bright moon smiled down on Nell, etc., they of course were sublime, immensely so.

Now I don't quite remember whether or not that moon was shining that one particular time when Nell's friend narrated something like it, in response. Do you? I perhaps, exhibited a little audacity that night in making the proposition I did or he did, but he's not sorry, far from it, and if she in her moments of sober reflections, has not come to the conclusion that she made a mistake,--why, then who can or will blame?

Quite a number of young people are to get married, sure, I hardly would have believed that Geo. T. and Agnes would embark off together. The last two or three years of Agnes' life has not been one of much pleasure or enjoyment. Nor that Will and Minnie would join hands. Now, Nell I hope you don't sacrifice too much of the good times or amusements in town. You likely have callers. Don't be too particular and reject them all, and thus be compelled to stay at home all the time. Bro. John, it appears, has taken you out some, as I hoped he would. I hope I did not emphasize this matter too much in my former letters, so that you would come to the conclusion that it would be best to not go out at all. I would suggest that you go out a few times with any nice young man. It appears though that there will not be many left, when one considers all the marriages that are to take place, and the other young men that have left town, so it is not all improbable that Nell will have to suffer mortification of being an old maid—

Anna and Osk have written me from Salem. Anna does not much like the town, and brother John says he is busy, very busy. He has, I believe he said, 11 teachers to manage. He also tells me some other things. I shall have to forgo pleasure of commenting upon them now, and instead do it "some other time."

I have now, written you a letter and have as yet said nothing pertaining to Sweden, or as to how I am getting along over here. My Senior companion, Elder Anderson is from Lewiston, Utah 32 years of age and has been in the field about 18 months. I don't go out to a nice meal every day as we did in Orebro, because there are but a few Saints here in the city. Our "skyson" (brethren and sisters) are scattered about in the country more. In my trip now, I saw nearly all of them. Some of them are genuine good saints, intelligent, etc. and I feel very much at home among them. My boat ride from Stockholm to Vesteras was most enjoyable. Such scenery of land, water and little island I have never, I think seen equalled before.

The weather is quite unpleasant these days. It has rained and snowed a good deal, and there has hardly been a sunshine day in the last month. All the time while in Stockholm it either rained or the weather was unpleasant. That accounts for my not, as yet, sending you "snapshots" views, as I have promised. Shall henceforth try not to make any promises unless I can at all fill them. You will get some views by and by, if not now immediately. Did I ask for too much when I asked for a photo of you? You perhaps are not situated so as to can afford to pay for a doz. of them, but you could, perhaps, get 6, 4, or 3. Now I expect to reciprocate your kindness by sending you one of your friend, likely in the Spring,--providing I can so pose that people will not say that I am looking at Nell. Well, I don't know if I care much if they do. I think now I have a right to do so—provided I could get a chance.

I am much advised to get a guitar. Music it appears is quite an important adjunct in missionary work and guitar accompaniment to singing is something that people appreciate very much. I have had hold of 2 or 3 guitars since I have been here, and have amused the people some in singing some of my English songs. There is one song that I have always admired and which now is of particular significance to me, more so than it ever was before. I once admired it because of its pretty tune, I now admire it especially because it completely mirrors my feelings & thoughts as well as can any piece of language. I have a notion to write a verse of it. Maybe, I sacrifice some of the preacher's dignity in so doing it. An ordinary individual would say it exhibited a spirit or disposition that would hardly become a fellow in my position. But as it fits the case I shall run the risk and so quote you a verse. No one but you and the writer will know of this affair, so no one but you can criticize my action, and if you criticize me too harshly, then I can offer some sort of apology later on:

Little darling dream of me while the stars are
softly gleaming
When I'm far away from thee. Keep me still within
thy dreaming.
Though I wander far from thee, still in spirit I
am near thee,
True to thee what e'r betide, waiting in my heart to meet
thee.

Chorus:
Smiling beaming brightly dreaming
Brightest visions come to thee
While the stars (and moon) are softly gleaming
Little darling dream of me.

Little darling dream of me, though in absence I am
from thee.
Love will bring me back to thee—For thy beauty I
live only
Slumber free from every care and at dawn awake light
hearted,
On thy lips this gentle prayer: "May we never more
be parted."

What have you to say by way of making a gentle comment on

the above? You speak of probability of your mother's going away this winter. Did or did you not make the transaction of buying your home?

Now, Nell, I do a lot of walking out in the country, and sometimes think that, in order to break the sometimes long spell of monotony, a chew of gum would be decidedly a nice thing to have. Now, I am no inveterate gum chewer, but still, sometimes, I long for a chew of gum, and as no gum is offered on the market in all of Sweden, I take this liberty of asking Nell to send. Enclose with her letter—a single stick—a chew— it won't add much to weight of letter. It would be a decided novelty. I can perhaps settle for it "some other time."

I may sometimes send you some telegraphic postal dispatches when in the country. So enclose you an alphabet so you can interpret same.

Yours,
P. Sundwall Jr.

Baltimore, Maryland
April 2, 2009

Dear Peter,

This month, my son received an electric guitar. My mother
was kind enough to buy it for him, or maybe just worn down
enough from his non-stop begging to give in to his request.
He has already learned how to play, "Smoke on the Water," by
Deep Purple and to turn the amplifier to ear-drum-breaking
level.

I took a few years of piano. My brother and sister were the
ones to take guitar lessons, encouraged by my father, who
kept a dusty acoustic behind the clothes in his closet. I
remember the guitar seemed awkward to me, the 6 strings too
close to the player, almost part of their hands, not protected
like the strings that were under the wood top of our upright
piano. Those strings were hidden away like my underwear in
my top dresser drawer, the drawer without a knob that had to
be pulled out with the tips of my fingers.

The guitar seemed more like a stubborn person to me, than an
instrument. The weight of the guitar, the height, even the open
hole where picks could fall into the hidden internal cavern,
seemed too much like a body, held tight against another body,
plucked and strummed like a comfortable lover. The guitar was
too external, too exposed. I liked my compositions hidden,
vibrating inside the closed case of the piano's coffin-like wood
planks, instead of right there, in my hands, in front of everyone
to see.

My son enjoys the exposure, his eyes wanting the stares,
his body constantly aching for more attention. He buys new
illustrated picks with his chore money: a skull, the Grim
Reaper, a bloody knife slicing down through the air.

"Aren't you supposed to practice some chords?" I ask him, recalling my long weeks of piano scales, up and down, up and down, up and down.

"I just want to play the songs," he replies. That is our difference. I really just wanted to play the songs, too, but I stomached the chords because it was homework requirement #1 that my piano teacher wrote down in my planner.

My son doesn't even remember where his head is, let alone a homework planner. He just wants to play songs.

I never realized the full connection between writing and the other arts until my thirties. They were different entities, and the lack of verbal language in my piano recitals never held the same intensity for me as my angst-driven poetry readings. Now, I understand that they are different waves within a larger ocean. My body just prefers the smooth lap of letters and words to the instruments of other currents, all tools in trying to create and understand a world that feels so unforgiving in its constant undertow.

My son packs up his guitar (or rather, leaves his guitar for me to pack up) and runs outside to spray more graffiti onto his tree house. My daughter slips into her dance costume for ballet class, and I close up your letters. I leave you for awhile, Peter, wishing for a guitar. Like all of us, you want more, the next thing, a new fin that might let you swim just a little further.

> Until "some other time,"
> *Kathy*

Milburn
October 15, 1900

Dear Peter:

Since writing to you last I have changed my place of abode.
Vina became so homesick that she could not endure to remain
at Milburn. She came home and I am staying with Amanda.
I assist with the teaching. After Christmas there will be more
pupils. Then I will get a salary. I am teaching now simply for
the practice. I am glad I was fortunate in getting the place as
assistant. I will be able to do other things that I wish to do.
Things that I could not unless I have the money. You know
what I want to acquire.

Amanda thought she would get along without an assistant. But
she has almost more work now then she can do. After Xmas
there will be so much more.

There is a large Democratic Rally here tonight and a dance
after. I would have gone had I not wanted to do something far
more pleasant then going to all the rallys and dances in the
land. Republican rally at Fairview. You can hear nothing else
but politics politics. You know how it is though just before
elections. Most people think "Bryan" will get elected. For my
part it matters very little as to which man is elected. Take no
stock in politics, as I can not vote.

Nothing special has happened at Fairview to my knowledge,
excepting the two weddings George Terry's and James Henry.
Their receptions and dance were given last Thursday and did
not attend either dance or receptions. Would liked very much
to have gone to them, but was at Milburn all day. Went home
in the evening, but was too tired to go out. Haven't as yet
to see James Henry's wife. Those who have say she is quite
pretty. We tease Nellie Lawsen and Adie now. James Henry
took Sadie a number of times. Poor girls! They are almost

walking skeletons. They have fretted so about the boys leaving them.

This paper is too thin to write on both sides so I will not do so more than this.

You surely did not think I would get into an alliance with any of Vin's young men? You know I was only joking. Indeed Vin may monopolize them all. I do not care to get into any entangled alliance with but more than one young man. You know who that young man is.

I shall be more then pleased to get a specimen of the Swedish magazine. I would like to surprise you by talking Swedish when you return home. Am very sorry you will have to exclude English from your reading. Isn't it harder to read the Swedish language then it is to talk it? I imagine it would be.

Am so glad you did not suffer from sea sickness. I imagine it would be delightful to travel by sea if you do not get sea sick. Wish you could have gotten the lady's address. Had she known you better she would have trusted you.

I know that isn't a good photo that I gave you. It will be hard of course to get a good one of me. But I will do my best to get as good one as I can. Will try and send you one for a Xmas present. If not by then, will as soon as possibly can.

As for "squaring the bill," you may do that before you come home by sending me a photo of yourself. When I get real lonesome to see you I look at the only photo I have of you. The one I had such a hard time keeping. That you know does not do you justice.

Oh! Wouldn't it be grand if I should get called on a mission right away so that you and I could return home together?

Yes, I wish we could transport some of our fruit over to you. As for honey you won't need any if you use it. Just say it as often as you please. Use it with a proper name if you like.

Yes, Mama knows of our relationship. She is overjoyed. I told her all and let her read your letters. She said she was anxious for me to get a letter from you as I am. Indeed she must be very anxious, because I am always anxious to hear from you. And then Mama can help me in many ways. Help me to be worthy of you and in other ways that I will so much need her help.

Indeed it is no trouble to do all I can to gain a good opinion of all the people, those whom will be concerned and those whom will not. Indeed I will wait for him, who is worthy of any girl. And shall be happy in doing so. Mama says it must be true affection because I seem so happy always. Before I was "blue" sometimes, but now I am always happy. Think of you and the future.

Do you think I would let anyone read my letters from you? I say my letters because they are mine now that I have them not but what I just as soon let the world read such pure letters, but as you say some "gossip starter" would have something to talk about. You can not treasure my letters more than I treasure yours.

I will not need to have my visiting cards printed when I am Mrs. Peter Sundwall, doesn't that sound well? My husband can make them for me. Those you sent me and the sketch will lead no one to think we are anymore than friends will it? Thank you very much for the sketch and the cards. I prize these above all. I mean all of them: the ones you gave me previous to you leaving, and those you sent me after you were gone.

You must be hinting at my bad penmanship and spelling. If I could but write and compose such as letter as you do, would give a great deal.

Maud Anderson is keeping her promise. Said she would

have gone to Kaysville with John, had she not made you that promise. It is all "cut and dried" between Maud and I that we will be sisters-in-law if the boy doesn't take someone else.

Mama sends her best regards. Am so glad you are doing so well in your mission work. May you do as well always. I remain as ever

> *Your Nell*

N.B. Continue to address me at Fairview as the letters come here from home.

Baltimore, Maryland
April 12, 2009

Dear Nellie,

I don't know what it feels like to be excluded from voting because of my gender, but I do know how it felt to look up at the rows of men on the priesthood shelf during Sacrament Meetings and realize I wasn't allowed among them. I really didn't want the power. In fact, I was glad there were other shoulders to hold God's decisions, as mine were weak and already starting to slump from so much reading. But, I didn't want to be told that I couldn't have the holy power, and by age 11 I had clumped every balding, suit-and-tie wearing man in the church into a category somewhere between parental enemy and substitute teacher.

The Sunday school classes started being divided by sex after elementary school, and I couldn't stomach knowing there were rooms full of boys in which I couldn't enter. I imagined the rooms to be much more exciting with their constant movement, pants, and lack of hand-raising. Now, I realize that there was probably just more snot and farting. But then, when we were told "no," I knew there had to be a reason. Were there secret pamphlets? Knighting? Or, was it the direct line of God that we couldn't witness, so strong it could only be harnessed by people with muscles and mustaches? The smell that was released when the boys' classrooms finally let out had to signify something, though I didn't know exactly what at the time—merely that it was a scent that was off limits, external in its origin, and full of something very potent and slightly dangerous.

> remembering
> *your great-granddaughter*

Vesteras Sv.
Nov. 10, 1900

Dear Nellie,

As expected, your much appreciated letter was on hand when I came in from my country trip. A pretty good letter it was too—I appreciated it. Things seem to be coming your way, considering your prospective position after Xmas, etc. Quite a manipulator of affairs you are. You've scored 2 or 3 points already in a brief time I've been away, and as for me, I don't know that I've accomplished anything. Of course, I wish you success,--all the success it is my place and duty to wish you. I believe you'd have a pretty good faculty for operating a stock or some other kind of exchange.

I was not serious when I offered that little suggestion with regard to avoiding a possible "entangling alliance" and when I spoke of "monopolies" etc. Like you I was jesting only. I don't think there is any occasion for my being sensitive or serious over Nell and callers.

No, it is harder to talk Swedish than to either write or read it. I have written 3 Swedish letters home, but to talk the language and do it correctly is a terror. Swedish grammar is hard to digest—gender of Swedish nouns hard to determine, and as the gender determines the form of the noun, also adjectives and articles it is important. A great many objects that naturally are neuter are by Swedish usage made either masculine or feminine and vice versa—for ex.—Fruntimmer, means woman, and one would naturally take it to be in the feminine gender, but it is in the neuter instead. A little fun isn't it?

Shall be glad to get a photo of you. Shall likely "square the bill" in the way you suggest. As to showing sketches— would prefer that you do not show them much, and only on occasion, as of course, your judgment may suggest—and not more than 2 or 3 of them. Hope that for a while yet no one of your neighbors or my neighbors or any one will have reason to suspect any "compact" or what you might call it—between you and myself. . .

No, I have not hinted at your "bad" spelling or writing. Now, I hope you haven't inferred that from my letters. You certainly write nice enough. When I talk about nice letters I don't refer to spelling, punctuation, etc., but rather something else. Spelling, etc., is not wanting in your case, and besides what ice should that cut with me. It isn't that that has anything to do with my attachment for Nell. "If I could but but write and compose like you" etc. you say. Now I hardly thought that my hurriedly written and rambling letter possessed any of the merits you speak of. I am hardly in a position to give the time and consideration to letters for Nell that they deserve, but on one of these long bleak wintery nights, when occasion will suggest, I may make attempt to write an "ode" or something else to Nell, and give her an opportunity to pass on its merits or demerits. Thanks for your Mama's regards. Best wishes in return. She can be congratulated in that one respect. She has a girl like Nell. What she thinks of Nell's "friend" though, I shall not pretend to know.

It is not yet 4 pm, and I can barely see to write. I shall have to light the lamp before I can finish.—This way every day. Sometimes dark at 2 pm. and after awhile, they tell me, we shall have to light our lamp at 3 pm. The sun has been hidden from view the last two months.

Lamplight—

Have had pleasure of seeing country auction since last I wrote, but cannot take space now to tell you of the affair. If my "snapshot" is any good it will give you a better idea than I can.

On night of your great election while out in the country I had my first experience at attending to the ordinance of baptism—An event I shall ever remember. We went down to the river "because there was much water there." Individuals were present to witness this act. The clouds cleared away from the moon for the first time during the evening and I believe, the last time for the night and the moon shown down on us during the few minutes we were engaged with this matter, and made the surrounding nature beautiful and sublime.

Will try to conduct myself in my next so that you need not hesitate to show letter to "friend" or sister, etc. should occasion warrant—or you feel that you would care to.

Yours
P. Sundwall Jr.

Baltimore, Maryland
April 28, 2009

Dear Peter,

The sound and the smell come back first in the memory, maybe
because it was crisp city water instead of the pungent well
water I was used to at home. The clear rush filled up the deep
baptism tub behind the accordion curtain, echoing against the
plastic basin pool as I folded my hands in my chair and looked
down at the flat chest of my smocked white dress. My mother
had picked it out for me the week before at Macy's, and then
stored it safely in her closet until the special day. I was sitting
next to another girl in white--I don't remember her name--but I
do remember her birthday was a few days before mine, which
made us both 8, the magic age of baptism in the Mormon
Church.

There was a few minutes of priesthood chatter, words about
washing your sins away and having the chance to start anew.
My sins had already filled up my whole body with their
weight: destroying my brother's new WWF cassette tape
by pulling out all of the ribbon, sneaking olives from the
refrigerator that were supposed to be for the Christmas party,
stealing pea pods from the next door neighbor's garden,
kicking the dog when he wouldn't get off of my canopy bed.
I was ready to have my slate erased, to start over with a clear
heart and a soul as transparent as water.

What I wasn't ready for was the strange priesthood man's left
hand on my back, raising his right hand into the air, repeating
the standard prayer for immersion, then pulling me down into
the water, covered completely in its liquid cocoon. I didn't
want to look at his hairy arms, descending out of his white
polyester uniform, his late 70's bar mustache prickly with a
few coarse grays. I wanted to immerse myself into the water,

at my own pace, down the three shallow steps, into the deep font, without a grown man next to me, guiding the way and determining the pacing of my re-rising. It would have been much better to have just floated on my back first, to let the little sins glide away from my spine, little flakes of corruption breaking off into the lukewarm water, before going completely under the surface and purging the rest of my transgressions.

I walked out drenched, the white polyester gown robe (worn just for the baptism) holding down my legs, while my long, wet braid pulled my neck and back with its enormous weight. The curtain closed, like the quick stop of a peep show finale, and my audience was immediately gone, and I was left to re-dress into my smocked, white dress in the changing room.

The other 8 year old girl was baptized after me and we sat quietly while the service was completed and our families took pictures and gave us special presents from the church gift shop, presents like scripture carriers and Book of Mormon name plates. I don't remember what I actually received, but I loved to read even then, so it might have been a book, published by the church press, every page guaranteed to be clean-cut and inspirational, the white paper advertising its purity like any eight-year-old virgin recently washed of her horrible sins.

Immersed,
Kathy

Fairview, Utah
Oct. 28, 1900

Dear Peter:

I came yesterday from Milburn. Was so busy last week that I could not write.

It seems very nice to be at home again. Milburn is such a lonesome place. Just came from meeting about two hours ago. First time Sadie has ever called at our house. We had a pleasant chat. I enjoy being with the girls again. I talk as if I have been away for a year. Gone two weeks only, but it seems so long. I like Fairview, even if it is rather dull. "There is no place like home."

Miss Lundquisst and I were at Mt. Pleasant yesterday. Seen Andrew and Miss Larsen. Had a nice talk with them. Andrew is getting along very nicely with this school. He hasn't been at Fairview for a long time.

We came home about dusk. As we drove along I thought of the evening another and myself were driving home from the Moroni conference. The evening the "Sour Orange" joke was invented.

The smallpox had such a hold on the town that they were about to stop all public meetings. There are only three cases now, so think they won't stop the meetings. Would not let Will and Minnie give a dance. They had a very quiet wedding. Did not go to the Temple.

A very sad thing occurred last Thursday. The death of Mrs. Swen Neilson. Sad that she should have to leave her family. But better she should go because she suffered very much. It will be hard for Willie, he being away.

They all seemed quite reconciled. Did not expect her to remain with them long.

We have been having fine weather up until today. It has been cloudy all day. Think it will be snowing tomorrow. How I dread the long cold winter. But time goes by very quickly. Winter will soon be gone, and then another and then you will soon come home. Time cannot go by and too quickly for me. That is if I accomplish what I want to before it is gone.

The Journals are just fine. I have four copies. There is so much good instruction in them, and so many pretty stories. On the front cover of the last copy there is a picture of a bride with her arms full of roses. It is such a pretty picture. I have subscribed for the "Young Woman's Journal," so you see I have quite a good deal of very nice reading matter.

Think I comprehend the meaning of the two last verses of the 19 chapter of Matthew. It says that "those who forsake Father, Mother, sister, brother, and friends to preach the Gospel in our Father's name, shall receive everlasting life, and many that are last shall be first and that many who are first shall be last." These are not the exact words.

It means that all those who go forth to preach the gospel are paid by receiving everlasting life. What a great salary it is. Who would want more?

Am so glad you had such a nice time while you were at Stockholm. T'is well the little children take such an interest in their Sunday School work. I imagine it would sound sweet to hear them sing.

Wish you could have gotten a picture of that group of pretty girls in their pretty costumes. I would so much like to see them.

I knew girls could do most anything but I never knew there were girl hod-carriers nor girl barbers before. How strange it would seem to see them.

What did you mean by "He'd be justified." You don't mean that he would be justified in practicing "Hobson's salute" do you? And who may the "certain one" be, one of those rosy cheeked Swedish maidens? Think I should like to be a barberess, and could manipulate the razor for a certain one.

Poor George. I feel sorry for her. I was well acquainted with John M. Vance, and I know what he is. She seemed so happy the day she left, hope she will always be so, but I too think she was rather hasty. Tis'nt as if she had to take such a fellow. I do not know much about Peter Christianson, but I rather think Miss Terry could have done better, even if she should have to wait a few years. Don't know much about Tucker or Miss Bills. Suppose they are well matched. They are in size. Don't you think so? What do you think about Will and "Swinnie"?

When John told me that you had told him of our relationship I told him he must have dreamed it and turned it off in a joking way. I tried to keep all from him, but he said he knew that you and I were engaged. I told him his knowing it must make it so. . .Just jokingly though. If he does think it true, he won't say anything to anyone. Do you think he will?

Peter Christenson and wife have had the smallpox, are much better now. Sam C. has had it too. His face is very badly pitted.

Anderson came home from school today very ill. Think she has pneumonia. Hope she gets well soon so that she will not lose much of her school work.

Cris is in town, has a few days vacation. Suppose Maud is delighted. Yes I received that letter without the usual introduction. I thought you had forgotten it or did not care to use an introduction at all. Mama sends her best regards. I wish you success and happiness. This you will have of course.

Sincerely yours,
Nellie.

P.S. N.B. Would like to see you tonight dear boy. Don't let me make you homesick.

Baltimore, Maryland
May 10, 2009

Dear Nell,

Today, my mother showed me an announcement she received
in the mail for a family reunion next summer. It is for all the
descendants of the brothers Olaf and Peter Sundwall, Sr., to be
held in Fairview, Utah at the dance hall you mention in your
letters.

The timing seems uncanny, since this is the first family reunion
of this sort, and I just started working on this book project
this past year. The last time I was out west was close to two
decades ago. We flew into San Francisco, and then drove
to Sonoma, California to stay with your daughter, Virginia,
for a few days. Afterwards, we headed to Salt Lake City to
visit your daughter, Ann. Ann will be your child who will
never marry, the woman who will keep a tight and practical
apartment, even when she becomes almost completely blind
in her older years. Her blindness won't stop her from guiding
us through the city, listening to the chirps of the WALK sign
at the intersections and pointing out the local spots of interest
and vagrant hangouts like any seeing expert. She will fill her
kitchen with Native American craft ware and tell us the history
of each pattern without ever looking away from her lap. She
will learn to move around her apartment with her hands
instead of her eyes. Until she passes away in her early nineties,
she will remain stubborn, louder and more opinionated than
the daughter who will become my grandmother, Katherine.
She will be, it sounds like, a lot more like Peter.

My family took a couple of day trips from Salt Lake City at the
end of that trip, a bit of a blur now that it has been so long,
but one clear memory that remains is the three houses of the
three wives of your grandfather, Lindsay Anderson Brady. The

idea of polygamy has always seemed abstract to me. I am not sure if it is due to being from the east coast, where cities climb on top of one another, and there is so little breathing room between people. I couldn't imagine a plural marriage, in the same way I could barely imagine room enough for a single marriage. When I saw the houses it suddenly did seem more real: the first wife's house standing strong, the largest of the three homes. The second wife's house was a little smaller and shabbier, and the poor third wife's house was like the typical third child: surviving, but without any real attention. It reminded me of my sister, tagging along, somehow making her way into the family picture though no one usually checked to see if she was looking at the camera.

The first: daughter and wife,
your great-granddaughter

Vesteras, Sv.
Nov. 25, 1900

Dear "Froken" Nellie Brady,

Received your letter some time ago for which accept my thanks. A newsy, breezy one it was.

You speak of your fine weather. Quite a contrast to that which we have. I think we have had but 2 or 3 days of sunshine weather in the last 60 days. It was quite a novelty to see the sun the other day. Away down south it was, quite a novelty to see it raise its animating disk but little above the horizon and then sink out of the heavens between 2 and 3 o'clock at times so that we have to light our lamp at 3 pm in order to write or read, and in some of the city's factories and stores the lights glimmer the day through. The weather is of a raining nature. This morning a coast of snow covered the ground but it did not remain long. It will not be long, now, I suppose, until it will be sunning in earnest, which will mean that we shall be held in the throldom of winter, but for a time. Cold they say it will be and much snow. But we are prepared for it, i.e. while we are located in our Vesteras home anyway. Double windows for our little bachelor house—something we don't have in America—and a "Kokeluyn" heater. Ask Sister Lundquist to describe it to you. As yet we make but one fire in the "Kokeluyn" (daily). That would be in the morning—After the fire burns down we turn the damper on and in 2 or 3 hours the "kokeluyn" begins to heat, and so the room begins to heat and continues for the rest of the day. We do not trouble ourselves to keep a fire up. If it is very cold we may make a fire in it at night and the room will be warm and comfortable the night through. Quite an idea the kokeluyn is.

Would like to experience a Swedish winter, so say let it come, even though it blows cold and penetrating and all nature appears dread, dressed in her white shroud. I shall enjoy seeing the lakes frozen, the trees bestrued with rime, and, lighted by the Northern sun, glisten as if they were covered with diamonds. The forests or woodlands will certainly look grand—immensely so, dressed in this shroud of immaculate snow. They say that in winter Sweden is the carnival of pleasure and society, and that this land is full of life and motion—

I said something about our "kokeluyn." I want to say that I can't recommend it for culinary or cooking purposes. If you saw my companion's or myself's "modi operandi" of making mush in the heater,--saw all the pains, trials, and sorrows incidental in our mixing and stirring, and cooking mush, you would sympathize with us or for us, and tears would likely trickle out as an expression of your pity for us. Now, this trouble is all because we have to cook in a "kokeluyn." You say that you and Amanda are "batching" it. Now I confess that girls know a thing or two that their masculine friends don't. Especially you who cooks or "batches." Now please give us an idea on mush cookin' some easy, automatic handy way you know. Some way that won't entail scorching of fingers, with subsequent swear words or almost equivalent.

Now Bro. Anderson thought out an idea, but I don't quite like it. He makes a complete mixture in cold water and sets same on to boil until done. The mush made this way doesn't taste quite right to me, but he thinks there is no difference. Now pardon me, I don't mean to tire you out with this narrative. It may be a little thing, this thing, but still it is often quite a bit item in our daily routine or work.

You speak of rosy cheeked girls. We have them, sure, some are strong and stout. Especially those out in the country, and some have cheeks as red and rosy as they are strong,--and some of them have such a profusion of natural red tint in their cheeks that I believe one could reproduce same with a Kamera. At any rate shall experiment and see—

You speak of L.H. Journals. Should like to know if Gibson's drawings appear in the journals. They were a feature of last fall and winter's Journals, but perhaps are not now.

Did Bro. Christiansen give up school for Mimie's sake and a matrimonial boat ride? Or is he attending the Stake Academy? I understood he intended to graduate in the Spring.

As to my missionary work, am perhaps getting along slow, but am, I believe, doing about as well as they expect young men in my situation. Do not like this preaching in the city. We have now held 3 Sunday meetings and I do worry over them. Wouldn't mind a preaching tour out in the country. Today, I had to speak and though defective as my Swedish may have been, I contrived to occupy 30 minutes. If I keep on this rate, according to ration and proportion by time the 2 years are up I had ought to be able to talk something like 4 hours—enough isn't it? But object is to talk well and with the spirit's dictation.

Had better stop my epistle. Would like to know from what locality Sister Lundquist comes. Some nice families of Lundquist in both Stockholm and Orebro. My best regards to her. Tell her I admire the forests, lakes, hills, and dales of Sweden, her "fosterland." Wishing you success in your enterprise, and with best regards to Vina.

> I remain yours,
> *P Sundwall*

Baltimore, Maryland
May 16, 2009

Dear Peter,

Missionaries and food go hand and hand. Perhaps this is
because most 18-22 year old males eat like horses, and a lot
of them are not too skilled on the kitchen front. You and your
companion's struggle to cook mush with the heater might not
be exactly comparable to today's missionaries burning rice,
and the pan, on the stove. But this is probably the rationale for
the missionary dinner sign up sheets: to decrease fire hazards,
cookware damage, and provide healthier dinners than Captain
Crunch with a side of Fritos.

The missionaries usually accept seconds and dessert, yet
you never see them eat. The food just seems to disappear
somewhere between the white plates and their clean mouths.
They speak when spoken to, yet don't start conversations. It is
almost like they are from another time period, with manners
that don't quite fit. If I am ever at my parents' house when
they are over, I usually ask them if they have any siblings and
the name of their home states. It is the standard missionary
questionnaire. The answer is usually Utah or California, and
the sibling number usually ranges from 5-8, which probably
explains another reason for their fast eating.

When dinner is over, they always politely ask if they can share
a lesson, after which my mother always replies, "Of, course."
My father follows this with 1 or 2 inappropriate jokes, to which
the missionaries don't know how to react, so they just smile,
nod, and clutch their *Book of Mormons.*

I am usually in the bathroom during their lessons, or on the
phone-- close enough to eavesdrop, but far enough away that
I do not have to be part of the conversation. I always feel
uncomfortable in pre-arranged church style lessons with texts,

like I am part of a book club for a book I did not read.

I felt the same way about my early school education. I hated the large textbooks, the regulated margins, the generic questions posed at the end of every chapter. None of it ever appealed to me. It all felt unnatural and institutionalized, with no regard to the individual, and certainly no respect for the girl who was drawing veins in the margins, even though she knew was supposed to return the book in the shape in which she initially received it at the beginning of the school year. I preferred the one-on-one discussions, or the independent assignments, where we could come up with our own original ideas, or essays where I could choose the topic without the help of an assigned partner or a teacher's recommendation. There isn't room for individuality in organized school or religion; the whole point is to stay with the text, whether it is *Literature for 6th Grade* or the *Bible*.

I think what I desire in religion is a temporary text, self-directed and fluid, without one-size-fits-all requirements and discussion questions printed neatly in its appendix. So far, I haven't discovered it—at least in a traditional "religious" sense. But I do think I use my own words to compose a surrogate religion, as happens when you cannot find what you need— you create your own spotty replacement.

That's what I do, privately and under my own terms: my pen creates its own texts, regardless of genre or topic-- doctrine that digresses and digs and isn't afraid of admitting human flaws and the need for revision. Maybe, at first glance, Peter, you would be shamed and embarrassed by my writing, and think me in the wrong. But I have the feeling, at second glance, you would understand and would see the spirit breathing and living just below the letters that we both share and cannot help but to use.

In digression, *your great-granddaughter*

Vesteras Sv.
Dec. 17, 1900

Dear Nellie,

What can be wrong Nellie with our correspondence? Should like to know what is the matter. You see its 5 weeks since I have heard from you. I aim to write you on the 10th and the 25th of each month and in comformity with this rule I wrote you on either the 25 or 26th of October, but as yet no reply has come to hand, and now that's 7 weeks ago.

I went on a country tour two weeks ago. For 2 or 3 days prior to my leaving I looked for a letter from you, but I had to go away disappointed. However, while I was out I looked forward with fond anticipation to day when I should return to town and find your letter awaiting me. I came back only to be again disappointed. It had also been my intention and desire to write you, in answer to this looked for letter, and expression of my well wishes and regards for the season as well as my love to Nell—to you, that would reach you Xmas time. But as your letter failed to come, I could not very well write. Now, I stayed in town a day, then had to go out on another country tour to see some saints. It wasn't much of a pleasure (in fact unpleasant it was) to leave town without getting the long due letter, or of writing one. I came back from the other trip only to meet with disappointment #3. Now I look for letter in reply to one written you the 10th or 11th of last month. Now, I hope this won't be very long in coming that it will throw a little light on this matter.

Now, Nellie my duty and pleasure is to wish you a Merry Christmas and a Happy New Year. Am sorry to say that no little present accompanies this letter as a token of my esteem and love for you. Couldn't decide on anything suitable that the mail would admit of, but Nell, I hope that for this time you will accept the will for the deed. I take it that Nell's love isn't of the kind that it requires to be fed by presents.

I want to express to you my hope that your life may be blessed and your path prosperous and happy and that you in all your undertakings in your school labors and in other pursuits may be blessed of Providence.

Again wishing you a good time during the coming holidays and a prosperous and happy year 1901. I remain

> Affectionately yours,
> *P. Sundwall Jr.*

N.B. Now this letter isn't very interesting perhaps, nor is it the style of a letter I had intended to write, but under the circumstances, you could hardly expect me to write in my best or happiest mood, when through some cause of other, I don't get to hear from you.

Baltimore, Maryland
June 3, 2009

Dear Peter:

I am learning that a lack of patience in creative people is inevitable. I see it in your letter, in your frustration at not being able to keep with your intended writing schedule because Nellie hasn't replied on time. I am learning the tendency for creative people to blame others when their plans do not work out: "If only she had written when she was supposed to, I wouldn't be mad. If only she. . ." I realize now, though it took many years, this opposition is the same fuel that drives us to continue to pick up the pen, or the paintbrush, or the ballet shoes, day after day: "If only . . ."

I remember my father blaming all kinds of things on my mother, snapping at her when she had nothing to do with the situations that were bothering him. There was always another force, another cause that was preventing his full happiness, never his own lack of patience or inflexibility. Like my father, your impulse is to blame Nellie for the late letters, not to take the time to imagine other scenarios that might have prevented the letters from arriving on time, like an illness or family tragedy. You do not want to wait, especially when you have an established plan that is working perfectly—for you.

My son lingers in punishment in his bedroom as I write this, yelling out into the living room, "How many more minutes?" His toes fasten at the line of his door frame, the closest proximity to freedom he can find.

"Still ten," I respond, and I hear him grumble.

"You said ten minutes a minute ago."

"And if you ask me again, it will be twenty," I snap back,

aggravated with the interruption of my writing. He is supposed to be thinking about his lack of listening and patience while in his room, but all he is doing is waiting for the ticks of the clock to advance, for this limbo to end so that he can get into something else.

All morning I repeated, "Give me a minute, give me a minute," to his demands, spurted out faster than I could process while I attempted to wipe my daughter's nose and pay the bills for the week.

"Can you turn on the lights downstairs? I need to play my video game," he requests for the third time from the top of the basement steps, "Give me TWO seconds, Addison," I huff, after which he replies, "One. Two. Okay. Can you turn on the light downstairs?"

I lose it, delivering out a twenty minute tirade about his lack of listening and patience before ordering him to his room.

"Think about patience and listening," I instruct, and then try to escape into the aggravated lines of your letters.

"I've thought about patience and listening," he announces from the door frame. "Can I come out now?"

"You've still got 9 minutes."

He doesn't see the room full of toys, books, and art supplies. He only sees what he can't do, what he must wait to do, which is simply leaving his room-- which is, right now, the only thing he truly wants to do.

> Am I so impatient and inflexible?
> *Your great –granddaughter, Kathy*

Fairview, Utah
December 2, 1900

My Dear Peter:

I do not know what you will think of me. Since writing you last I have been at Manti. Have been staying with Mrs. Madsen, Pre. Ethel Tucker. Have been kept so very busy. Mrs. Madsen has been quite ill. I had the managing of the house affairs, besides doing all the work. I was so tired when night came I just could not sit up to write or do any thing else.

I am sorry I have not written before. Will try never to wait so long again.

It seems so very nice to be at home again. I am going back to Manti. Madsens want me to stay with them until Xmas, or all winter. I will not stay longer than Xmas. Mama is going back to Mammoth for the winter. Vina and I will remain here until after Xmas. Then Vina will go over there. Do not know as yet whether I will go or not.

The trustees of Milburn say they won't have enough money to pay another teacher. If Miss Lundquist can possibly get along without help they much rather she would. It will be hard for her. There are several more pupils than there were when I was there and will be more after Xmas.

We had such a nice time at Sunday School this morning. It was such a pleasure to go to Sunday School again. Was so busy while at Manti that I could not go.

I have met the Miss Hougaards. They were here for the fourth you remember. Ida Hougaard goes with D.K. Hansen, and I never heard John speak of her. The Manti girls think the Fairview boys are alright. So they are. Lilma Neighburg is at Manti staying at Tuttle Hotel.

It was nice to have someone from Fairview to see occasionally. I get so homesick when away from home. Do not know what I would do if I should have to stay away very long.

The people of Manti are so classified. They are so hard to get acquainted with. I haven't been at but one party while there. Had quite a nice time. Boys are about as scarce at Manti as they are here.

Vina and I will go to meeting tonight. I go back to Manti Tues.

While on the train coming from Manti I met a gentleman from Arizona. One we were very well acquainted with. He was going home, after visiting relatives and friends in Southern Utah. It did me so much good to talk with him. Told me all about my friends. All the young folks are married at home, or rather at Arizona.

There are several young men from Mesa City at Provo going to school. They are preparing to go on missions.

What have I done that you should extol my virtues? No nor I shall never forget those.

Yes, our association was very brief. But those were the happiest days of my life. I have never had very many unhappy days.

Yes, the "stealing of that little thing," let me see, it was a ring, was it not? Amounted to a great deal more than I thought it would that night.

I think the moon was not shining on that particular night that I heard the sweetest story of my life.

No, she has never come to the conclusion that she made a mistake nor she never will. I am glad he is not sorry of making the proposition he did.

Geo. and Agnes seem to be very happy. George thinks Agnes

is the prettiest sweetest girl he ever saw. That isn't saying much for Nellie Miner and Nellie Lawsen is it?

Ellen and Andrew, Philinda and Petie, are married. It was a surprise to me that Will and Minnie should step off together.

Had a letter from John, Prof. Sundwall, a day or two ago. He had not been teaching for some time. The small pox was at Kaysville. So they closed the schools.

No, you did not ask too much, when you asked for my photo. But there is no photographer at Manti that can take good pictures. There are two of them, but they are both beginners.

Christenson's gallery is at Mt. Pleasant. I won't have time to go down now. Will wait until I come back home, to have my photo taken. That will be alright with you will it not?

The words of the song are beautiful. Isn't it a shame I am not little? It would fit the case completely if I only were. I shall commit it to memory and never forget it

I dream of you. . . ("my sweetheart" written in Morse code). . .often. I dreamed that you returned.

Oh, how happy I was. Think I will not be more happy in reality than I saw in my dream. I thought you were going away again, to be gone three years. I cannot describe how I felt. But I smiled and said I would wait. So I would. But you will not go away when you come back will you?

I will wait to criticize you for quoting the song, "some other time."

Wouldn't people laugh if they knew what is in this envelope?

> Mama sends best wishes. I am yours forever.
> *Nellie*

Baltimore, Maryland
June 11, 2009

Dear Nellie,

Like me, you are a big girl. Tall and sturdy. You stood close
to six feet in height. Yet, you still look delicate in most of
the old pictures, crisply dressed, with your hair pinned up
and soft curls falling down the sides of your neck. You look
practical, without a lot of fanfare or artificial sparkle, a face
content to breathe without make-up or cover. You remind me
of your daughter, my grandmother, and your granddaughter,
my mother, and maybe, me-- destined to be both mother and
lover, the girl next door and the woman down the street.

I never minded being on the big side. In some ways, I think
it helped to propel me past some of the contemporary
female issues. I knew I could never be a size 4, strutting
along the runways or flaunting a string bikini. My role was
not to be the next fashion queen. My clothes and body were
always an afterthought, a distant second behind my eyes and
mind. It was kind of nice to be able to face the boys at their
level, literally. Fully grown before the end of elementary
school, my mature body felt comfortable before I even
entered adulthood. I was already used to my size 10 shoes
while the rest of my classmates continued to stretch well into
their late teens.

There is one annoying issue, though, when you are a tall
woman: pants. Pants tend to be either too short or too long.
They never seem to fit right, and if they do it is only for a
month or two, after which the washing machine or dryer
always warps them. But you didn't have this issue. It will be
a few more decades before women will slide their legs into
trousers on a daily basis. Your legs will stay hidden under
skirts and dresses. Your height will be measured by your head,

not your legs. Your eyes will never look up at Peter, only across, evenly, right back at him.

Related,
another tall woman.

Vesteras, Sverige
New Year's Day, 1901

Sweetheart Nellie,

Your letter of Dec. 2nd came to hand the 18th. Glad to see
that all is well with you. I hope all may be well with you
continually the new year through and as this is New Year's Day
I want to express to you a little of the hope I have that your
life may be blessed the year through and that your path may
be blessed, happy and prosperous. Am sorry circumstances
have not permitted me time to pick out some appropriate
token to send you—some little token of my love and esteem
for Nellie. You perhaps begin to think that I am failing to show
you the consideration that a worthy Sweetheart is deserving of
her lover, but I hope Nell will overlook this failure this time.

I hope you had a good time of it during the holidays. A Merry
Christmas and a Happy New Year. I hope you will tell me all
about how you celebrated.

I just came into town this evening from Sandberg's, a family
of Saints some 6 Eng. Miles out in the country. We have had a
most pleasant time out there. The family consists of parents, a
daughter, and another widowed daughter who has a spirited,
happy girl of 17 or 18 years of age. There were also 3 merry
musicians from Eskitstima—a city of 21,000 people—with
us. The two of them—girls sing well and handle their guitars
nicely. The 3rd, a young man, plays the mandolin, a veritable
"funny man" he is—i.e. comical, and did much to amuse the
company.

The girls had offered us their services, so we availed ourselves
of this opportunity and arranged to have them over for last
Sunday's meeting. We put in a special announcement in the
Newspaper and as a result had a well filled hall, and our
meeting, as a whole was good. In the afternoon we drove over

to Sandberg's, in the country, for the purpose of holding an evening meeting. Sleighing was nice so far as roads and snow are concerned, but when the weather is 15 and 20 degrees below zero, sleighing isn't very pleasant. Especially in the little Swedish rigs, and besides the drive so slow—the "kusken" (driver) does. But I suppose they have to do that because the sleighs are so narrow between the runners, something like our little hand sleighs at home. So you see it wouldn't take much to tip them over. All the sleighs (and wagons, too), as a rule are "one horse" outfits. They don't drive here like they do at home, they go slower and the people, especially the men laborers, make a favorable comparison with the Americans.

As for the "tjenst flickorna" (working girls and women) they are ahead of the men—quick, industrious, and fully as independent as the men. Every girl of the common class has to hustle for herself it seems, when she gets to be 15, 16, or 17 years old. As a result a girl will adopt herself to some trade, or vocation. We have in the city a young lady who does ironing and laundry work (We are to baptize her next week), and another lady who is a baker (investigator of our doctrines she is). The one of the two lady singers that I before referred to is a dress maker, while the other one is a factory hand. While they work hard and the year through, they don't make anything more than their living, hardly. That is what they all tell me that I have talked with. One lady told me that she thought it impossible to save enough out of 10 years hard, steady work to take her to Utah. Wages are so low that the working class, instead of being able to save anything, has to live in the simplest manner and on the simplest food.

Now, I am off the subject. We reached our destination in the country and held an evening meeting. Everything went off nicely. The next day we enjoyed ourselves in different ways and in the evening we had a few dances, in rural fashion, they were, yet enjoyable. We stayed until after the midnight hour that marked the advent of the New Year 1901. The next day (today) our Eskilstma friends departed for home, and we back to Vesteras. We had a most pleasant time (considering my circumstances you know.) The Swedish girls are hearty laughers and it doesn't take much to bring them into a fit of laughter. Needless to say that I thought of you while spending my New Year's Day with my Swedish friends. I do that often anyway. Often have thought to myself—and particularly on Xmas and New Year's Day: "How nice if some Magic wand could bring Nell here so that she could see the people, the country, and join in a Swedish "Kalas" (party) and then I try to imagine what her impression would be.

You once referred to Rosy cheeked Swedish girls. I want to say that this cold weather brings the color to the Swedish maid's face—a deep rosy hue. Rosey cheeked they are in the fullest sense of the term. I doubt there is a land outside of Scandinavia that can show up a bigger percentage of pretty girls than can this northern land.

Don't think Nell, I'm infatuated with them or any of them. Have no cause or reason to be. There's one girl home that "takes the cake" (if you will excuse homely expression) and whom I wouldn't be afraid to compare with the best in this land. Were you here, I wonder, how 15-20-25 degrees below zero would act on you. A suitable model you'd be to pose as a Venus or one of the graces, I am sure. No flattery Nell. I assure you. Wish I was a painter and could do work such as I saw in Stockholm and other places. I wish Nell could have seen them. I have never seen a nice piece of art but that I wished at the

time that Nell was there to see it also—have never looked
upon a pretty landscape scene, but that I wished Nell was also
there to enjoy the scene with me. Never read a pretty beautiful
thought but that I wished Nell was with me to share it. But
certainly a time will come when we can indulge in these
pursuits—or some of them at any rate, together. I hope, Nell,
you won't work too hard. Be careful about your health. Don't
deny yourself too many pleasures for sake of him whom I
believe you love. Join in the parties. Show your sweet, virtuous
traits and dispositions, and continue to develop those virtues,
qualities and faculties that are inherent in you and that will
make of you a beloved and much thought of girl. You may not
have the means to accomplish yourself as completely as I am
sure you long to do or that one of your mind deserves, but
you have other qualities and virtues that can make up for this
lack of other things.

How do you thrive at Manti? Was a little disappointed a few
times in not getting your long looked for letter, but your

apology for the delay was sufficient. Am now looking for a letter from you every day but it fails to come. Tomorrow I go out in the country again and shall, it appears go out without your letter. There are now two letters due me—one in reply to 10th of Nov.—about 7 weeks ago and one in reply to mine of the 25th of Nov. My Elder companion wrote to his wife on the two above dates and answers to both letters have come. But my Nell is busy, I suppose, and I can hardly look for prompt replies.

With love,
P. Sundwall

(Note to pen and ink drawing on one page of letter: This picture represents a Swedish maiden. In summer time she wears a pretty costume and cap that is red. The married women use a white cap to denote their station.)

N.B. I received a letter from a friend of mine some time ago, in which he asks me to confess, saying: "Confession is good for the soul" and goes on to add that there is nothing he "would like better than to have me for a cousin." He goes on to make a confession on the strength of the "confession" that he hopes I will make, saying that he will this year marry a girl. Now, I don't know how he heard or guessed all this, but I suppose some young people must have told him of our relation or of our going together before I left and he guessed the rest. Now, there's nothing I would like better than to admit to him the facts and make the desired confession, but the time is hardly ripe for that. I do not know that I can answer his request in any better way than by asking him if he thinks it would not show a little "gall" or if it would not be a little premature on my part to ask for the hand of the lady whom I had known or kept company with for but 2 brief months or so and ask her to wait 2 years. I should much like to use 3-4 or more adjectives just before "lady" that would be expressive of all that I think of Nellie, but of course that then would be a "dead give away"—

That gum came alright along with your letter, but there is a little more history connected with it than you think. Have not space enough to tell you now. Forgive me for going against your orders and sending you a letter to Milburn. I hope you got it O.K. Best wishes to your mother, and Vina. Best New Year's wishes to them—happiness and everything else desirable. Who is fortunate enough to be Vina's beaux now? Is all her relations with Bro. Clement suspended?

Next time your mother offers you a good night X (something that rhymes with bliss) have her give you an extra one and suppose it to be another who gave it. At any rate play it was the unlooked for climax of a joke so that I can take all the blame.

Yours, *Peter*

Baltimore, Maryland
June 20, 2009

Dear Peter,

I penned love letters to my boyfriend when I first went away to college, when I was the same age as Nellie is now. I drafted lofty verses, 2 to 3 pages at a time, longing that dripped with clichés and ridiculous metaphors. Sometimes, my boyfriend sent back store bought cards with a brief line about missing me. Usually, however, he just hopped in his old Chevy and drove the two hours south to see me in person, his love much more easily expressed in kisses than in words.

Later, I would find out that he barely made it through his high school English classes and struggled with writing the way I struggled with Science. After watching my son's frustration with language over the past few years, I suspect my boyfriend-now-husband also had reading and writing disabilities related to focusing and comprehension, the painful pressure of illogical letters coupled with an inability to slow down and process.

So, eventually, I gave up on the letter exchanges, realizing they were just not going to happen in the way I imagined. The romantic pages of passion would eventually only be found in my own journals. You can't force anyone to become a good letter-writer, or to do anything you want for that matter. And sometimes, I think it wise that there is only one writer in a relationship. We are a bit challenging: moody, independent, and so often unsatisfied. We always want more, get easily bored, and constantly change jobs and habits when most ease into the comfort of routines. We are an anxious breed, temper-ridden, looking for ideals instead of reality.

Deep down, both you and I know we need someone stable, with at least one foot on the ground, to keep our vision both above and below the clouds, someone willing to let us dream and wander past the usual vantage point, but also willing to yank us back down when the storms start forming and we are too busy examining the way the sky is deepening to a pungent purple, to notice.

I now take my love letters anyway that I can get them. Some are Post-It reminders or lists that underline "Don't forget Q-Tips" on the refrigerator. It is what it is, and I embrace my own journals each morning for the rest, letting my own hand make up the difference.

> With love,
> *Kathy*

Fairview, Utah
December 30, 1900

My dear Peter,

I will not try to imagine what you think of me for not writing
for so long a time. I cannot tell you how very sorry I am that I
have not written. The reason for my not writing is—I will tell
you some other time.

I have written ever so many letters to you—and then not sent
them because—I won't tell why. If you will forgive me this
time Peter I will never—no, I won't say I never will wait so
long again, because I may, but I hope I will never never do so
again.

Jan. 2, 1901

Your letter came today written the seventeenth. I cannot
express how glad I was to get it. Still when I read it it made
me sad. Your letter caused me to realize that a letter from
me might help you in your labors. When you said it was so
unpleasant to leave for your country tour without getting a
letter, it made me realize more how very unsympathetic I am.
I know I ought to write you often, when you have nothing to
cheer you, only that you are laboring in the good cause, and
the letters you get from home.

Wish I could express my thoughts and sympathy as I would
like to but I cannot. My thoughts are of you always, and you
have my deepest sympathy at all times. Especially when I think
of your cooking mush.

Now I think Br. Anderson's idea of cooking mush is not quite
right. I have let you make mush in that manner for a long time,

when a little suggestion from me might have helped you. I will tell you how we make mush here.

Let water boil, salt to taste, then stir in cereal, a little at a time, until the right thickness. Eat with sugar and cream, or milk. Try our idea of making mush and see if it does not taste better.

This has been such a dull Christmas for me. Suppose it was because I am so lonesome. I am here alone, Mama, Vina and the children have gone to Mammoth. I will go over there sometime next week. Go when Bro. and Sister Christenson (Anna and Oscar) go. Can go as far as Springville with them. John is at home for the Holidays.

I have been at three dances as yet. Did not enjoy them very well, as I have been suffering with a very bad cold. You know what it is to have a cold. It isn't very pleasant is it? We have been having very cold weather. No snow to speak of. They say it is too cold to snow. We were all in hopes it would snow for Xmas, but it did not.

John called this evening, wanted me to go out to the Sunday School dance, but instead of going I am doing something far more pleasant, writing to you.

There is to be a masquerade ball next Friday, the fourth, think I will go. If I go I will represent Priscilla. Wish you were here to represent John Aldin. Two years from now you will be here, and then how happy we will be.

I was at your home Xmas evening. Spent a most pleasant evening. Talking and looking at the many beautiful presents each of the folks received. I received two very nice presents because they were from your Mother. Anna and I each got handkerchiefs alike. We are going to see which can keep theirs the longer.

You ask if Gibson's drawings appear in the Journals. The

drawings on the front cover of this month's number is by him. It is of a party just leaving the opera, very pretty indeed. There are two artists drawings in the Journals. A.B. Frost and W.C. Taylor. There has been a series of eight drawings by Frost. They are called the "Country Folks," the last is in this month's number. They are so natural too. The first of Taylor's drawings appears in Dec. No. called the "Traveling Shoe Maker." There will be eight of his drawings also. I do enjoy the journals so much. So many pretty stories.

How dreadful it must be to have to light a lamp at three. We think the days are very short here. What would we think if they were as short as they are there? I received your letter written the 10th of Nov. the day I came from Manti. The day I met that gentleman from Arizona. I read your letter on the train. I told Bro. Le Bearn, the gentleman, of the event. The first experience of yours of attending an ordinance of baptism. He said he had had the experience. Said no one knew, but the Elders and those whom were baptized, how grand it was. Said he could not describe the feelings they have. How grand it must have been that night. Then to have the moon shine for just the length of time you were there.

I am more than sorry, but I haven't as yet gotten my photo taken. I will just as soon as I can. Then I will send one. Why I haven't had them taken,--I will tell "some other time."

I have sent no little present to you as a token of my love. Some day I will. But remember you have all I can give. My heart and hand. I will take your love in return. Indeed our love is not the kind that requires to be fed by presents.

I am so sorry I did not send a letter in time for you to have received Xmas time. I hope you had a Merry Christmas and a Happy New Year.

Thank you Peter for your well wishes. I wish you the same with all my heart.

I think no one as yet suspects our relationship. Every body that I know teases me quite a good deal, but you know how the people are. Really I do not like to leave Fairview, but I will come back someday.

> I remain ever true to you.
> Lovingly,
> *Nellie*

P.S. I will do better next time.

Baltimore, Maryland
July 4, 2009

Dear Nellie,

Your letter has shadows of sadness. Your sentences are
short and to the point, quick answers that provide the two
dimensional responses that Peter desires, but do not give
him anything more. I picture you, struggling to write on the
page, the words like little shovels deepening your emptiness.
Unlike Peter, you are not able to lose yourself in the artistic
distractions around you. You do read the journals that Peter
has subscribed for you, but they are not a true literary escape
for you, the way Peter understands them to be. Unlike Peter,
monetary obligations hold your shoulders down, as well
as constantly changing living arrangements of your family.
Inspiration is much harder for you to attain. Peter does not
seem to realize this. Perhaps it is due to his more privileged
upbringing, his stubborn perspective, his youth, or maybe
all of the above. He wishes you enlightenment and passion,
when most days all you are looking for is a break from work,
a moment to sit down, someone to talk to, or a good night's
sleep.

My relationship with my husband is the reverse.

"Why don't you want to take some art courses? You are so
good at drawing and sketching," I suggested to him over two
decades ago, when he was your age.

I couldn't understand his vague response: "I don't think it
would work." My parents were helping to pay a good portion
of my tuition, and I was majoring in English. In other words,
I was a kept girl. From a very young age, my parents had
supported all of my creative decisions and, when possible,
helped financially with them. My husband, on the other hand,
had started his independence soon after birth. Born in the

Bay area of California in the late 60's, his childhood consisted of a lot of temporary homes and not a lot of clothing. He started working very early after moving to Maryland and was fully supporting himself by 18. School was never his escape. It was just an annoyance in the way of full-time work and compensation. His inspiration never came from desks, books, or acrylics, but from hours spent dismantling engines and reconstructing their own oiled language of body and breath. While I saw the realm of enlightenment in the arts, he saw it in the carefully kept plugs of a '55 Chevy.

While I will always score better on any standardized test or report card, he is the one keeping our lives financed and operating. Without him, our house would probably fall in on itself and the bills would arrive: "Overdue: Third Reminder." But without me, the glass would quickly become half empty and the windows and doors would become only windows and doors, not the openings to the soul that I point out to him each evening.

I am the book smart one, like Peter, and he is the street smart one, like you.

"I don't like the real world," I cried one day in my late twenties, when my idealism had finally been broken and burned to the ground.

"Nobody does," he replied. "I've been trying to tell you that for years."

> Some other time,
> *I will be your great-granddaughter*

Vesteras, Sv.
Feb. 3, 1901

Dear Nellie:

Your letter bearing dates of Dec. 30 and Jan. 2 and post
mark of the 6th awaited me when we came home from our
long tour of 3 weeks. I had written you a letter while out
"pa landet" telling something about our country & saints but
carried it with me to town intending to mail it here, but now
I will write you another one instead and for present anyway
let the matter or subject of the country and Saints pass by. The
13th of last month we 3 of us departed from town. Of course I
had to go away disappointed again, as Nell's letter was delayed
again, as very near 4 weeks had again elapsed since receipt of
the last letter. Well, we left that day, the 13th on skates going
over the Meloren Sea, some 20 miles to Eskistima. I shall not
detail my trip to you this time. For one not used to skates,
I think I did well. So my friends tell me. Of course, I didn't
"sail through" like an expert nor did I get through without
some few falls. Spent a week in Eskilstima most pleasantly.
A big branch it is. Next to Stockholm and a lot of nice saints
there. Eskilstima is the Sheffield of Sweden—is a city of many
factories and iron works. Her razors, scissors, & cuttery are
celebrated the world over and much of the wares imported
into the U.S. Thousands of girls have employed in these
factories. From Eskilstima my partner and I went out in the
country visiting Saints & holding meetings. We have held some
6 meetings. The one meeting was in Koping where we had the
largest gathering that it has been lot to preach to—300 or more
people were out. The hall was jammed.

Last night we came to town—it was about like coming home.
We were glad as we walked along the highway and nearing
our home. The moon was shining bright, the night was pretty,
but cold—but we were warm from walking. The rime was

collecting on our overcoats and hats. My partner had a white mustache and eyebrows. The snow that stretched across the field looked beautiful—the snow flakes glittered like diamonds.

Peter Sundwall Jr. Missionary in Sweden, 1902. Inscription reads "Out on a little skating trip. Vasterås, Sweden. Winter - 1902"

We were thinking of all our letters in letter box on our door—for surely there must be quite a few now that we had been away for so long. Anderson was happy. He was sure there were 2 letters from home—from his wife. I was sure of letters from home and at least one good long letter from Nell. So you see we were reveling in anticipations of reading sweet letters. We came to town—I found, sure enough the looked for letters. I read my letters—they were sweet—good—yours was refreshing, sweet, etc. I also got a photo—Annie and Oscar. I enjoyed looking at it. With Bro. Anderson the situation was different; his wife's letter not so refreshing, so sweet. He was not glad or happy as before. He trembled in his hands as also did the letter he was reading, and he began to cry as he related the news of the death of a child of his. Many reflections have passed through my mind. I read the letter. I admired the style in which the wife breaks the sad news, because in it there was also consolation, and it showed her courage—her strength. You see, Nellie, how the unlooked for happens in this life. How our Great Master, the giver of all pleasure to man also takes away. Life is not without its trials, its sorrows, its disappointments, and, as I reflect on the matter it comes to my mind more vivid than ever that this life is nothing more than a preliminary one, a preparation for an eternal one that follows, and I think how extremely little, small, is not after all, that mortal who is vain, absorbed in his earthly pleasure and enjoyments to that extent that he scarcely recognizes a providence or God.

Am sorry that you could not stay in Fairview. I fancy that Robinson will not have much to offer one of your inclinations or tastes. I fancy it will be dull for you there so far as social advantage is concerned. Fairview of course was dull enough, but at the same time, I imagine, the social atmosphere is more clean than one will find it at Mammoth.

Sorry you have had a cold to contend with and that you did not enjoy the holidays so well. You surprise in telling me of the little present you rec'd from Mother. You and her, it seems, must surely have established a bond of friendship between yourselves. It seems that all the barriers are already cleared away. I cannot quite understand it. She was so partial to girls & people of her own nationality,--of course, that is only natural,--and she has been somewhat prejudiced against her American bred friends. Yet you have already won her good-will and esteem, and I can hardly see how it came about so soon. But, when I think of it, Nell has that faculty for showing or exhibiting her honor, her virtue, etc. in but, a few, minutes associations. I hope Mother's goodwill and friendliness to you will continue and increase. I remember the time of our parting—Mother and myself—She couldn't approve of my calling to see Nell so many nights just before leaving to fill a sacred mission—she thought it inappropriate—much out of order. But now that she has found out Nell and knows her as

I know her she will surely hold no aught against me now. She writes me good, sweet motherly letters in her Swedish—and I have every reason to believe that she has entirely forgotten or overlooked that which once she could not approve in me. Praise to Nell's diplomatic-or-what-shall-I-call-it tact.

In one of your letters you ask if it is not a shame that you are not small so that you would fit the song, "Little darling," etc. or it fit you. Let me say here none of the fair sex of the small variety or type ever impressed me or appealed to my sense of what constitutes a beautiful woman. Under the circumstances it is fortunate, very fortunate that Nell is large and strong—for next year some fellow will come along and take liberty of "free press" and want to practice "freedom of the press" to the fullest extent. How unfortunate then if Nell were small, how unfortunate if she were frail. Don't you see? Now, it is perhaps peculiar that I should look that far ahead of me to a time when I can embrace Nell or (if the word isn't too homely) hug her. Keep this a secret.

Don't waste any sympathy on our cooking mush anymore. Your kind recipe came too late for we have quit cooking mush for we concluded that the class or product was not quite good enough or palatable to commensurate us for our troubles and pains to produce it. We cook potatoes—that goes easier. No cereals, no salt, no stirring—nor scorching of fingers and consequently no aggravations nor provocations. We eat "Sel" (herring) and potatoes instead. Thanks for the recipe, but it came too late. I hope Nell will write promptly after this. She will save other provocations and aggravations if she does. If she will I shall not delay my writing as I have done this time, but instead write regularly on the 10th and 25th of the month, if I can but get letters between those dates from Nell.

What do you say? Hope you enjoyed the masquerade and that "Priscilla" was a success as no doubt it was. Please tell me all about it. Tell me how the young folks are faring—the two Nellies, Sadie, and Emma. Who takes them out, etc.? How about Vina? Has anyone else of the young men had to suffer misfortune of meeting with the same consideration that Bro. C. did? Wish I could read some of the Journal with you. So rich in literature and illustrations—reproduces but the best. You say Gibson's, Frost's work appear in the journals. That is good. I can perhaps see them some day. Work from Frost and Gibson are so inspiring, so suggestive, so natural. I have run across a good deal of their drawings. Wish I could point or draw. How I would revel in such work. Ah if I only had the art, to draw out all your heart. But thank goodness, that's already done. No cause for worry on that scene is there? But then:--

"I'd turn from all my studies

To study you, Sweet Girl

For love with his divinest art

Has drawn your picture in my heart—"

Excuse me Nell for coming out plain won't you. Perhaps tw'ere best to keeping thought and sentiments to myself, but I can't always do it. Sometimes imagine that maybe you would prefer to get letters descriptive of Sweden, her people, customs, society, etc. etc., instead of such as I write you, but writing the mere "instructive" kind wouldn't be so interesting to me. I can tell you about them some other time.

     P. Sundwall
N.B. Excuse bad penmanship. Will try to do better next time. Blame part of the writing to ink, paper, & hurry. I used to enjoy the reputation of being able to write fairly well, but this don't look much like it. Does it? Did I tell you of our baptizing 3 new members?

     P. Sundwall Jr.

Baltimore, Maryland
July 19, 2009

Dear Peter,

"But writing the mere 'instructive' kind wouldn't be so interesting to me," has also been the justification of my own work. It seems, in some ways, it has been the justification for all of my decisions and choices—always gravitating to the "more interesting," "the new," "the unexpected" over the predictable or prescribed. Throughout school I always picked the "choose your own topic" option for each required essay, purposely ignoring the teacher's suggestions every time. I wanted each writing assignment to be completely original, and often paid the price with final grades and comments like "B, due to not following directions" or "A-, good writing, but you digressed from the topic." I loved my creative writing classes, but never warmed up to my literature ones, feeling like the research papers and thesis statements were made of cold sleeves of grey metal, unbendable beings without any consideration of beauty or variety.

Writing an instructional paper about the history of Maryland government was about as interesting to me as a paper clip. Instead, I scribbled poems inside the empty pages of my binder. I met the trade off of slightly lower grades in exchange for enlightenment with external grace, but fostered much internal resentment. Like you summarize, the critical material could always be presented "some other time," while my life could not wait for its own unraveling, each day ripe for more digging, more conjecture, more observations and secret documentation of what I saw going on around me.

Later, after college and a few years of teaching, I realized that in my rebellion from critical information, I had actually been making it an oppositional component of my work. In my fight against theory and the masses, I actually magnified their importance. My poems and stories were philosophical, political, and historical, though I didn't know it at the time. I didn't see their connection to the past or the future, though it had been there all along.

Nothing, though, could have prepared me for the years that soon followed, including a miscarriage and challenging pregnancy, as well as the years spent worrying about my sister's drug addiction. Add domino deaths of extended family members, and I finally saw the pages of my first full-length book turning through my head: my first instructional book into the world of transition, exploring the themes of fear, addiction, and death. It was the term paper I had been waiting to write since high school. Suddenly, everything I had learned about writing came together and for close to three years I woke up from nightmares and vivid dreams, sentences swarming in my brain like disturbed bees, the links finally exposed that bridged my life with words. I kept a pen and journal next to my bed, for the dreams would often disappear a few seconds after I woke. Sometimes, all I was given was a phrase, such as "nothing outside mattered," while other times it was a thematic image, like an imaginary miscarried baby. It was the draft before the draft that I was dreaming, the initial impulses of my life during those years, and I knew, at my gut level that it was my truest story, my most "interesting" story.

Nine years after writing the first section, I received my book contract from my publisher for *Halfway: A Journal through Pregnancy.* I stared at the 6 page document for over an hour. For a moment, I considering sending a copy to my 10th grade English teacher, the one who gave me a C- on my Ethan Frome paper because I recounted the details out of order, but then I realized that even most English teachers haven't braved writing below the surface, and most cannot teach longing or sacrifice, which is just as vital for writing as mechanics. They can grade grammar and thesis statements, five paragraph essays that read like retired recipes. They can't grade love, blood, the pulse of fear or desire. Those things, born from under the page, are beyond rubrics.

Without a grade,
your great-granddaughter

Robinson, Utah
January 27, 1901

My own dear Peter:

Well I have waited a long time again before writing to you, but it is because I have been ill. It is either the change in the atmosphere or the changeable weather that has not agreed with me. I am much better now. Think I will be alright soon. Your letter, written New Year's Day, came a day or two ago. I cannot tell you the good it did me. Did me more good then all the medicine I could take.

I am selfish I guess, I long for your letters, and when they come, I do not answer them for such a long time.

My head is a little heavy tonight, so you must not mind if I ramble.

It is three weeks to day since I came over here. Do not like this place, wish I were back at Fairview. We had a jolly time on the train the day I came over. There were besides Anna and Oscar, John and I, two boys from Manti, Silvia Anderson, Ottie and Hirum Terry. We entertained the rest of the passengers by singing and music. Anna had the guitar with her, and Ottie Terry had his mandolin. I was sorry I had to stay at Springville. Had a pleasant time while I had to stay at Springville. Called on Aunty Myra. Had to stay there two hours. Anna gave me their photos. Think it is nice of them, don't you? Anna told me she sent one of them to you. Guess I will have to wait now until I look a little better before I have my picture taken. Well I don't mean to say that I could look better, but I do not want to look as if I had been ill.

I won't promise to have it taken at any special time, but will send you one when I get them.

Indeed I do not think you are failing in your consideration of me. It is I who is failing to show consideration. What must you think of me? I did not think I ever would be as negligent about my writing as I have been. Hope to do better after this date. As I think I will.

I cannot imagine myself, how it would be to see the people and country where you are. I only know that I would enjoy it very much. How grand it would be to be there where you are, to be with you. How I wish that I could come, but I cannot, so I won't think of it. It grieves me. Yet I am glad you are there. Don't wish I were there now, I need a rosy hue in my cheeks.

Hope you have not inferred from my letters that I thought you were infatuated with the Swedish maidens. Do not blame you if you did. Judging from the sketch they must be beautiful. The sketch is fine. The snapshot is also. There are a few Swedish people here. I have showed this picture to them. It seems to delight them very much. Reminds them of days that have passed.

Peter if confession is good for the soul suppose I must confess. I wrote to Lois some time ago and told her of our relationship. After promising I would tell no one. Don't know why I did it. Just had to tell someone. But I ask her to let it be strictly between herself, I, and the "gate post." Suppose she has mistaken Perry for the "gate post" and told him. What do you think of me? I did it though without thinking. I told her if she wrote to anyone at Fairview not to say anything about our engagement as no one knew of it as yet, on account of our short acquaintance. I am sorry I did it. Would not have done so, had I thought Lois would have told. Lois has not answered my letter yet. Am glad Perry is to be married. Wish him all the happiness possible. Wonder if Lois is doomed to be an "old maid"!

Vina has to defer all claim to Bro. Clement now as he is to be

married soon to a Mt. Pleasant girl. Do not know her name.
Have not seen Miss Lundquist since Nov. I came away from
Fairview in such a haste that I could not call on anyone,
besides she was at Milburn so I could not see her. Would like
to have seen her and asked about her family.

Am so sorry Peter that I did not send you some little token of
my love for you. But I was so busy that I did not get time to
select something in time. The time will come though when
we can give each other presents and not have so far to send
them. Am so glad you had such an enjoyable time Xmas and
New Year's. Hope you may always enjoy yourself. I enjoyed
the holiday very much. Would have enjoyed them much better
had I been with you. Mama and Vina send best wishes to you.
Must go to bed, I am tired. Remember that I love you, and
think of you always.

Mama gave me two XXs tonight. I imagined one was from him
whom I love.

> With love I am yours,
> *Nellie.*

N.B. Take good care of your health, so you won't get ill.

Baltimore, Maryland
July 20, 2009

Dear Nellie,

So, there were blabber mouths back in 1901, too. When I look at the black and white photos of your time, it makes me mistakenly think that life was less complicated: the lack of color in the prints takes away the intensity of both pain and pleasure—no hot reds or oranges, no weeping blues or rotting yellows. The black and white presentation shows pause, stoicism, strength, un-moving, so distanced from my living three-dimensional, Blu-ray, hi-def world.

The unfocused quality of the black and white prints suggests you couldn't feel the same pinch from the sun, or the same flinch from a deep cut, which is obviously not true. Yet the difference, the lack of realistic representation that we are so accustomed to today, creates that false reaction. The pictures of you are dulled, and it is easy to imagine your life in that same lack of definition, time stopped and paused in some other dimension.

You will remain forever on another continent, one that cannot be reached by any mode of current transportation: a land not quite real, with carriages pulled by horses and lamp light as the only glowing interruption in your night.

I wonder if my life will seem as intangible to my great-grandchildren in the year 2120. In another hundred and ten years will my words describe a world that my great-granddaughter will only understand in theory? Will our cars look like crude plastic play toys, our JC Penney portraits capturing propped comedies of families in unexplained matching outfits? Will she be able to step back into my shoes, or will she see my life as a distant closet, forgotten and full of old and unwanted things?

Maybe she will see something that will remind her of herself, some similarity in my facial features. Perhaps she, too, will have squinting eyes that disappear in the light. Perhaps, she will prefer looking down, at the ground and her own feet, as opposed to an open and never-ending sky.

Perhaps,
A great-grandmother

Bertosdal, Sv.
March 4, 1901

My Dear Nellie:-

I suppose your klock is ticking away like all other klocks
and that the hour hand points to something like 1 or 13
o'clock AM. Monday morning. Whether you are in the realm
of dreaming among faeries, etc. or whether you are yet up
entertaining friends or friends is, or course, a matter I don't
know or at any rate have no cause to worry over the matter.
I shall suppose she is dreaming. Don't want you to think
that because your time is between 1 and 2 o'clock AM at this
writing that I have been enjoying myself at a "colos" (party)
or that I have allowed one of those blue-eyed rosy cheeked
maids to entertain me. No, the time is something like 9 am this
morning. Not so long since I arose from an enjoyable night's
rest. Am 2 Sv. miles from Vesteras which means about 13 Eng.
miles. Came here to meet with the local "Syskon" (brethren and
sisters) in their meeting that was held yesterday. Am stopping
with a Bro. and Sis. Sundquist. Good saints they are. Have just
eaten breakfast consisting of Rogbrod (Rybread), pankaken
(pancake) och limpa (another kind of soft bread)—Rog Brod
och limpa. Am quite used to the Rog Brod and quite like it too.
It is the bread universally used throughout the country here. It
is a thin round pancake—like bread, a little thicker and larger
than an ordinary dinner plate, dark in color for reason that it is
made from rye—It is baked and dried with a hole in it usually
in the center of it. When the "gumman" (the woman) bakes,
she bakes a big lot of them—enough to last the family 2-3 or
4 more months. When the bread is baked, she slips the bread
on a long smooth stick—from 6 to 8 ft. long—and seeing her
do this suggests the scene of one in act of stringing beads. This
stick with all its bread is hung up under the ceiling where it is
supported on some cross pieces. I see our Sis. Sundquist has
a stick well strung with Rog brod, up under the ceiling—some

75-100 cakes and she says they must do her until May. They have baking apparatus for ways of baking this bread much different from that in vog at home among you people. I shall try to get a photo sometime showing the Swedish woman engaged with her baking affairs. I think it would interest you.

Bro. Sundquist works at a Herrgard (a master's farm). The most of the land in this country seems to be controlled and monopolized by the wealthier people who, very naturally have to employ many hands to keep things in order on the farm. A farm hand is called a "statare" and lives in a stuga (a log lumber cabin) which is located on the master's farm and, of course, belong to the farm. As a rule every Herrgard has a large conspicuous white house, the master's house, and not far away from the house are the hay barns and "logarn" where the stock is kept. The "logarn" is kept in clean and neat trim as well as the stock therein. I have seen some logarns with as many as 125 cows in. The stock are kept tied up in their stalls both summer and winter, with exception, perhaps, of a short time in the fall when the stock, on some herrgards at any rate, are allowed to graze on the field. As a rule the farm hands' wives do the milking in the "logarn": getting up in the morning at about 5 a.m. to attend to this work—spending from one to two hours in milking, getting from 15 to 30 oren for her work according to amount she milks which means from 5 to 8 cts. So you see that a woman with a family of children toiling hard and late the day through has no pleasant job when she has to get up around 5 o'clock and sometimes 4:30 to do milking. Bro. Sundquist here, gets unusually good wages. His proceeds for his work is something like 500 krowns per year ($160.00). Counting off his Rye, wheat, potatoes, etc. he gets yearly 300 kr. Some "statares" get only 150 kr. and 200 kr. outside of their rent and products which means about $45 to $55 a year. Quite a sum with which to clothe a family, buy groceries, and the other incidentals that are bound to come in the family way. As a result of low wages the work man has no easy task to get a living here in Sweden, and I think that Sweden represents the situation of Europe.

Vesteras, Sv.

¾--10 pm—1901

Wrote the above this morning. Have since walked to town going a distance of some 13 miles. Rec'd your good letter the 14th of last mo. Sorry to hear that you have been ill, but also glad that you are over your illness. No, I should not think that you would thrive well in Robinson, I suppose it being a mining camp it has some of a rough mining camp's characteristics that to you are objectionable. Yes, it was good of Anna to give you hers and groom's photo. I rec'd same and am delighted with it. I hope you will contrive to get a good, creditable, photo Nell when you are in a position to get yours taken. Hope you will find a first class photographer to do the work. Wouldn't mind it for the occasion. I could be the manipulator of affairs in the gallery, if I could only do things up in the shape that the particular subject in this particular case merits. How is the situation in Robinson, with regard to religion? Do you have Schools, Y.L.M.I etc? You no doubt have these organizations. Hope you are associated with them, so that you can or will be,--though the ward may be small or obscure one,--a blessing,--a light, a benefit to your friends. Of course, I need not fear on this score. I hope you will tell me about how you fair, etc. You will pardon me Nell if I again ask you in regard to my letter of credit. I don't mean a money letter of credit for it,--the paper I mean, is worth more than the biggest money credit letter than ever was drawn up. You know what I mean. It's the paper that trusts the holder as a full fledged citizen in Christ's true Church. Not because I doubt that Nell is worth such a distinction. You know yourself that that is not my motive for asking. But I ask, because you in your circumstances need such a certificate it being necessary for you to move about occasionally. You see the paper is indispensible if you are to have accorded you the rights and recognition that you are entitled to. I took liberty of asking you this question in one of my letters last fall, but some how you did not answer. I suppose you overlooked or forgot about the perhaps, simple query. The time is 11:35 pm. I shall now go and retire for the night. Since last I wrote you we have had our Stockholm president out with us for the week and we have held meetings in both the city and country.

Yours,
P. Sundwall

P.S. Must laugh at your demand for a "confession." You say rumer has it that I'm to return to the girl the pleasure of whose company I enjoyed for some time prior to leaving home. So this is the assertion of Dame Rumer. I was about to leave off the "e" from Dame and say dam, but I am not so badly provoked as to want to say that. But don't be disturbed at such rumers, Perry. I have also heard such rumers to my amusement. To have taken a spurt of a sudden and completed such arrangements as you say rumer intimates I have done would not only have been bad policy and impertinance on my part, but also, I consider would hardly reflect good judgment on the part of your cousin Nellie. I hope you don't entertain any such thing of your cousin or of me, or put any reliance in the rumer. Will say, though that Nellie is a lady with a character and virtues that commands respect and admiration. It may not be her fortune to come from a home with the environments and advantages that the most of our girls have. She may be minus a father's devout influence and parental affection linked together with that of her good mother. She may not, either, have a home that she with her mother and brothers and sisters, can share in and say is their own—nor have the means that she would like to have with which to complete her education etc. Yet, not-withstanding she hasn't the chances and opportunities of others, she is a lady of faculties, a beautiful piety and a character that isn't the fortune of all girls to possess.

I don't think it would be proper to ask a girl to wait 2 or 2 ½ years for me even though I liked her and held her in the highest esteem and thought she would consent to it—and, besides, Perry, I have a few other problems, after my mission is through with before I can devote myself to a serious consideration of a matrimonial problem.

P.S.

N.B. The foregoing is a p. script that I added to your cousin's letter. I write for your benefit so that you may know exactly how I answered him in regard to his question. I don't claim that this is word for word as I wrote PS. in his letter, but it is nevertheless the sum and substance of it & about as well as I can remember it. I was a little surprised to learn of your telling Lois, but I hope this PS will quiet Perry so that he or she either will say no more about the affair. You can see from the PS that I am making no denial of our supposed relationship, but as you will see it is only a scheme I have of answering his query without saying "Yes." It will of course, hardly correspond with what you said to Lois, yet it isn't a denial either—nor do I think that Perry will accept it as such.

Would prefer that for awhile yet we discourage friends in belief that anything more than ordinary friendship links my Love to Me.

Hoping you will not mind that we let the matter rest on this basis or status, I am truly

>   Yours,
>   *P.S.*

Mi Sa Godt (Fare thee well)

I hope you will write me a good long letter and tell me all you know. Excuse my hurried careless writing. P.S.

Baltimore, Maryland
August 15, 2009

Dear Peter,

You are quite the persuader. Your effort to disguise your true
intentions with Nellie is impressively crafted and layered, as
you find the slippery ground of admitting your admiration
for Nellie without every really saying it. In fact, you turn the
argument back towards your accuser, almost making the
accusation Nellie's cousin's fault, for even considering the
subject, which you defend is one too inappropriate to suggest.

You would have been a good lawyer, Peter, as you are quick
with defense and have the ability to justify your every action
and thought. Turns out, you will become the president of a
bank one day, the Sanpete Valley Bank in Mount Pleasant,
Utah. Your six children, too, will all hold leadership positions.
Your first child, Nellie, will become a nurse and your second
born, Peter Valentine (born on Valentine's Day), a medical
doctor. Anna, your third child, will become the regional
representative of the Children's Service of the Department of
Health, Education, and Welfare. Katherine, your fourth child
and my grandmother, will hold various church positions and
secretly write poetry in a small white journal that she will
censor with the help of dull scissors when she gets older.
Virginia, your fifth child, eventually becomes the Educational
Director of the Bay Area Cooperative in Berkeley, California.
Florence, your last and sixth child, will marry a medical doctor
and become the mother of ten—I imagine this leadership
position to be the hardest of them all!

Today, only your youngest two daughters are still living.
Virginia sounds feisty as ever from the Christmas cards she
still sends to us from Northern California on recycled cards
from last year. She has started the process of weeding her life

of material things, sending my mother old letters and cards that she wants to pass on with coherent explanation, before it is too late. Florence remains the grandmother of many and great-grandmother of even more. In Florence's Christmas card picture I can see my grandmother Katherine's face, the woman after whom I was named. Similar wrinkles and sags are on my mother's face now too, the path my face will also take over the next two decades. My mother, at 60, is now a grandmother herself, heading strong into the final third of her life, while I continue to stumble through my middle one.

Your daughter, Katherine, will die of pancreatic cancer when I am in middle school. It will be a quick diagnosis and death, over before it almost began. Her husband, my grandfather and your son-in-law, will remarry soon after her death, then divorce, and then remarry again. He won't be able to erase your daughter from his life, though he will try —by bringing in new wives, by cutting her face out of every picture frame in the house. But she will never leave.

My Grandmother Lives in the Laundry Chute

My grandfather does not know
that my grandmother is living
in the laundry chute,
that she squeezed her death-body in
just before they took her life-body away
and she is watching.

Sometimes, she slides up
to the top of the chute on all fours
and peaks out into the upstairs bathroom
to watch him shave,
to see the metal razor pinch over his chin,
the shaving cream strong
like when he was her man.

Sometimes, when she is lonely
and he is in the den watching golf,
she bends at the sharp metal corner
and sticks her toes out
into the laundry room in the basement.
The pink fabric softener tickles her toes,
and she flutters them
before listening for the echo.

She has made the webbed grey walls her home.
She is happy here.
After all, my grandfather put her here,
nailed her in tight one Thursday afternoon
when he realized she would never come back
and could no longer bear the pain.

> A brief letter and poem telling you a few things that
> I know,
> *Kathy, your great-granddaughter*

Robinson, Utah
Feb. 20, 1901

My dear Peter:

It has been nearly three weeks since I wrote you last. It seems
as if it has been six. I have been staying with a lady that has
the rheumatism. She is almost helpless. If they could have
gotten anyone else to stay with her, I should not have stayed
there, but they could not. It is very confining to be a nurse. But
it is much worse to be the one afflicted with the disease. I can
not tell how thankful I am for being blessed with such good
health, then I see so many girls that are going astray and with
ill health.

It makes me more and more thankful for the many blessings I
enjoy.

I have just been rereading some of your letters. How I enjoy
reading them. But there is one that pains me a little to read.
The one written on the seventeenth of Dec. It isn't because it
isn't just as dear as the others, but I much rather it need not
have been written. I hope you will not need to ask me the
question, "What is wrong with our correspondence?" again.
Although I fear you will if I am not more punctual about my
writing. But it seems if something prevents me from writing.
Do not know what I would do if I were placed in your
position. I suppose I would think I did not have time to write
at all.

We had most of our winter this month. It began to snow
the second of this month and continued for several days in
succession until the snow was over a foot deep. The people
enjoyed sleigh riding while the snow lasted. We could see
sleighs flying in every direction and hear the bells ringing.
It has been thawing for the last three or four days, so the
snow is nearly all gone. Now we can hear nothing but people

complaining of the muddy weather.

There are great streams of water running all in the roads. It will be as I heard a lady say at Sunday school, "We will have to travel in boats if it does not begin to dry up soon." Quite a modern Venice.

We have very good Sunday schools and meetings. They hold meetings at night.

Apostle Grant's brother spoke last Sunday. He has been in the church but five years. He told of his past life. Has led a very wild life, but the light has come to him at last and he is very thankful for it.

I will tell you about our letter of recommendation to join the church. I wrote for it before you left you know, but it did not come until just before I came here. The Bishop had overlooked my letter, and did not think of it until, when he was making out reports he came across it. I showed it to Bishop Peterson at home. He told me to bring it out here, as I was coming so soon anyhow. When I go back to Fairview I can take one from here.

In the last letter I wrote you from Fairview, I did not tell you why I had not written for so long. I will tell you now. I had arranged to have a dress made for Thanksgiving because I knew I should not have time to do any sewing after I came from Manti, before Christmas. After getting a few presents for Mama and the children and a few other things I had just barely enough to get a stamp. After that I say that I could get one at least if I could not get more. I tell you this because I think you might think it was something else that caused my delay.

I am going to have my photo taken at last. I will be nineteen next month. I want my picture while I am yet eighteen. My! I am getting so old. Still I almost wish it were this time next year, and that it would not be so long until my lover would return. Suppose you get all the Fairview news from the folks there. Hope you are well, and getting along successful in your labors. We are all well, but Mama, she has not had very good health for some time. Vina and Mama thank you for your well wishes and send best wishes in return.

With love I am ever,
Nellie.

P.S. May I send you some more gum in my next letter?

N.B.

Baltimore, Maryland
August 29, 2009

Dear Nellie,

How did you deal with your health worries? Not on the page,
but in your actual day to day life? I am one of those people
who always rush to the doctor, constantly afraid what I have
is fatal. I can't imagine how I would have been in your day,
when smallpox and fevers hung over towns like menacing
fogs. Even the way you casually mention that people have
been sick shows an acceptance of illness as a part of your
daily life. In 2009, there is more of a sense of illness as the
enemy, the foreigner, and we wait, armed with heavy duty
antibiotics, hand sanitizers, and pain killers if it dares to intrude
into our houses. We have so many cautionary screenings and
tests that it often feels like we are constantly headed towards
something terrible, an inevitable diagnosis, as opposed to just
appreciating that we are well. There is even a sense of "failure,"
on our part, if we miss a yearly blood test or check-up.

My first mammogram, at age 35, nearly caused me to have a
nervous breakdown. The day after my initial screening, the
office called my house to say I had to go back so they could
get more views of something in my left breast. That was all
the woman on the phone would tell me. It turned out it was
just a bad picture, overlapping tissue and a blurry shot. In the
meantime, I spent the weekend in bed, unable to function,
petrified that I was surely dying from breast cancer, the disease
that took my father's sister when she was in her early 50's.
After I recovered, I wondered if it had been worth it. Had my
anxiety actually caused more harm than the actual screening?
I only see the stacks of medical bills, the never-ending
appointments penned into my Franklin Planner, the stress of
leaping from one "OK Results" to the next.

Sometimes, when I am sitting in the ob/gyn's office for over an hour, exhausted from reading yet another pamphlet about a new and improved birth control, I see the people from the generations before me, like you and Peter, laughing at our obsessions with screenings, wondering why we would spend all of our time and money sitting in doctors' offices, especially when we are not sick.

In many ways, ignorance is bliss. In your letters, people are either "in good health" or "ill." There doesn't seem to be this in-between, this waiting for the next problem, this transitory state between youth and decay that seems to start, at least for women, with the first pap smear in the late teens, the first dodge from the bullet called mortality.

I am sure I am being idealistic about your perspective, for the sake of my own desire to picture a time and place without the anxiety that hijacks my life. Perhaps, when death holds such a heavy hand above your life, when one breath or move can welcome its passage into your blood, and there is no set of miracle drugs waiting on the sidelines, you learn to treat him like a friend. That way, he might just miss you. He might, on a whim, decide to keep moving past your bedroom door, your house, skipping your family and set up shop, instead, in the tiny cabin down the hill.

Anxiously,
your great-granddaughter, Kathy

Robinson, Utah
March 10, 1901

My own dear Peter:

I was so glad to get your sweet refreshing letter. Your letters always refresh me so much. I sometimes wonder if I could endure life here without them. I would do as I did last year this time probably. Having a gay time but how glad I am that I do not spend my time so idly.

All the spare time I have I spend in reading, writing, and sewing. Besides the Ladies' Home Journal we take the Young Woman's Journal, and the Deseret News. So you see we have some very nice reading matter.

A neighbor of ours has kindly lent me all the church books that I haven't read, so I may read them all. I enjoy reading very much. Do you get the Deseret News? If so you will read of the death of Bro. Maeser. I always thought so much of him. He came to Arizona so much, for Sunday School conference, and to organize the Religion Class.

When I thought of going to the Academy I always thought of him and longed to go because I knew he taught there. But now I cannot go while he teaches. Sometimes I wonder if I shall ever go. May go next year. Hope I can.

The social part of life here is very dull. I do not go out at all. I haven't even seen a girl friend with whom I can associate. The girls here are of the sporting class. "In for a good time," as the boys say. If it were not for being at home, and attending Sunday School, meetings, etc., life in this place would be almost endurable. Should dislike to stay here very long.

Hope I can get out to Fairview for a few months this summer. But no summer will be as pleasant to me as last was. Until you return, no matter where I may spend it.

John said he would come over here when he goes home, and he and I will go down together.

The time is passing quickly to me. Does it pass quickly where you are? Suppose it does, engaged in the work that you are. I do not realize that it is hard for you to keep from getting homesick. Do you? I hope not.

Just think Peter it will be a year soon since you left. Hope next year goes by just as quickly as the time that has passed has gone.

If you always have good health, and you will, how you will enjoy your mission, and the time will soon come for your return.

My sympathy is with Bro. Anderson in his bereavement. How sad it must be to get such sad news and he so far away from home. It must be hard for his wife to endure it all, without her husband. What a blessing it is, that God has given them strength and courage to endure. I suppose those that have never had the experience of parting with a child cannot realize what it is.

Your opinion of this life is beautiful. It causes me to think how small those of us who are vain are, and I imagine they think they are attaining everything.

Wish I could express my thoughts and opinions as beautiful as you do Peter. But I cannot. Won't we have many beautiful things to talk about when you come home? You say I probably would prefer letters descriptive of Sweden, her people, etc. I enjoy them very much, but I much prefer the ones with your thoughts and sentiments expressed. If it had not been for that little sentence in telegraphic alphabet, in your friendly letter I should not have liked it very much. How glad I am that we are not writing letters of just friendship. It is as you say Peter, you can tell me all you see while away, when you come home, or "some other time."

Am so glad you are getting along so nicely. What a large audience three hundred people would make. Do you speak the Swedish language well enough to preach four hours yet? How I wish I could hear you preach. Well I will some other time, all I will have to do is to wait patiently.

I too am sorry that we could not stay at Fairview. And Mama is not contented to have me away from her long at a time.

Yes Peter I too hope that the bond of friendship between your Mother and myself will always exist. I always enjoyed going to your home because I was always treated with friendliness. Let me assure you Peter that I took no extra pains to your mother's friendship. The first I seen her to speak to her was at Anna's wedding reception. We were friendly from the first. At first she called me Miss Brady but after a while it was Nellie and since she has always called me Nellie. I did not call at the house as often as I should probably because I thought maybe they would think I was trying to gain their good will.

The day I left Fairview, both your father and mother wished me well wishes, and were so friendly and kind.

The masquerade was a success. I enjoyed it very much. Haven't heard from Fairview for some time. It is said that Frank and Emma are to be married in the fall. Sadie and Silma are all destined to be old maid school teachers, no one has taken them out for some time. Guess they are waiting for some of the missionaries to return. Nellie L. was going out with Manuel Alred. Thinks she has the "swellest" fellow in town. Nellie N. does not go out much since her mother's death. Andrew has discontinued his calls on Nellie. She thinks more of some other fellow.

No other fellow has had to suffer misfortune from Vina. I am quite surprised in her. She thinks very little of the boys now. While last summer she thought of nothing but boys. She gets letters from our cousin Rosethia in Canada, but she does not even mention Lois or Perry, and Lois has not answered my letter that I wrote her in the summer. Wonder if Perry is married yet.

Am so glad you like Gibson's and Frost's work. Are you acquainted with W. L. Taylor's drawings? I think they are fine. So natural. Yes we will enjoy reading and looking at the Journals.

I will try and write more promptly. For I do not wish to provoke or displease you in the least, and it is such a pleasure for me to write to you when I have time.

I cannot be small to fit the song and large to accommodate the "free press" both, so I am glad I am large and strong so I can endure the pressure. I can always think of the future. Never before in my life have I looked into the future, so far ahead.

Do not try to keep your thoughts and sentiments to yourself. They are so beautiful. Love has the art of doing many beautiful things. It has done a great many things for me. I could write on for a long time, but you will be weary long before this.

Mama and Vina send very best wishes. I am so glad you are baptizing so many members.

> With love to you,
> Yours,
> *Nellie*

Baltimore, Maryland
September 12, 2009

Dear Nellie, It is. . .

5:45 A.M.
In another house,
my father raises the cigarette
before he even wakes,
the movement from hand to mouth
a fluid line, like blood or breath,
the urgency grown past crutch
into undeniable instinct.

Next to him, in another bed,
my mother's fingers intertwine
into the woven slates of a tiny roof,
her hands gripped into prayer,
begging for guidance this day,
as the fleeting darkness of the night
stays closed tight within her palms.

In my own house,
the remaining caramel drops shimmer
in my husband's tumbler,
warm licks across the coffee table,
the sheen of escape still peeking out
from behind the glass—
the hint of flight, a passage through.

Yesterday's picture still hangs
crooked on the refrigerator,
miniature skulls blending into daggers
and arrows, little bits of violence
that only my son can make,
proving again and again

that he will have the last word.

And I am left with only the sparkly pen
with the silver feather on the cap,
all other writing instruments
either eaten by the dog or carried away,
barely a chance left
to find what it is I am looking for,
somewhere here
under the unmoving lines of the paper.

    -Unsigned.

Vestgothegatan 3
Vesteras Sv.
April 5, 1901

Dear Nellie,

Today is Long Friday which is observed as a sacred day
through Sweden. All the churches have their usual Sunday
services on this day in commuration of the crusification of our
Saviour. The coming Monday is observed as a sacred day, as
well as Sunday. I take opportunity now to write you in answer
to your two good nice letters which I rec'd last month. Many
thanks for them, Nellie. Quite a surprise you spring on me
when you write this second letter. You see, Nellie, I didn't
look for this letter, but let me assure you an agreeable surprise
it was to get this last good letter of yours. Very good of you.
Nothing like getting that beam with the estimation I put on
your letters. You last letter was good,--excellent and shows
to me the high sense and seriousness with which you regard
the future. You show all the earnestness in the matter. Don't
deprive yourself too much of enjoyments or associations with
other people of your age. Of course, if there is none in your
town whose company you think would be congenial, I cannot
blame you,--but I regard it as a little lonesome for you to be
deprived of social recreations altogether.

"Don't keep your thoughts and sentiments to your self," you
say. My letters particularly some of them I allowed myself to
say something almost cross, that have pained Nellie some,-
-I have not been considerate enough for her tender feelings.
But because I have done this, or that I have been seemingly
reserved in some letters I don't want her to think that there is
in me a lack of those motives and feelings which a young man,
in his letters to his "Sweetheart" should exhibit. I have at times
been far too reserved in writing you my feelings etc. to suit my
own self, but through a modesty something of the kind that

sacred mission is responsible for, I am to hold myself bridled to some extent at least when writing to my "Sweetheart." A time will come when I shall be under different circumstances, and when I can, with good grace, be as profuse in the expression of thoughts, i.e. love, as my Nell will allow me to be. Among a number of ?s you put to me is one in regard to how I like Taylor's drawings. I can say that I admire them very much, Nellie,--I remember one in particular that he executed for the L.H. Journal—perhaps you have seen it. "Minihaha and Hiawatha"—representing that exquisite part of Longfellow's poem where the two Indian lovers emerge from the dark forest. So natural was his drawing. It fits exactly Longfellow's descriptions of them in his poem. The young Indian lover has just been up to the old chief's tent (wickiup is better) to ask for the hand of his sweetheart. He was fortunate and now Taylor represents him as leading her away. I think he leads her by the hand—she follows modestly after. There is much couched in the drawing of "Minnehaha and Hiawatha." Where these two lovers are going to, now, I don't quite remember, but am inclined to think that they had no definite place—or home—homeless, they were probably under the blue canopy of heaven. Minnehaha and Hiawatha's career is reduplicated in early career of lots of young lovers of today in that lover and sweetheart agree on an alliance, leave their parental wickiups and go out into a world and on their own hook try life in its new phase. You no doubt have observed many such cases yourself wherein lovers have joined hands and gone out from home to try life's luck together with practically nothing of the world's riches to bless them or encourage them. I could continue this subject of Taylor's drawing of Minnihaha etc" and see a future application of her and his leaving home of minds in—if you will allow me to say—myself and Nellie. What do you say? "Don't keep your thoughts and sentiments to yourself"—be free Nell in your comments. You speak of the summer or part of the summer we spent together as so pleasant. You also look forward with happy anticipation to time when I shall return. I thank you for your compliments. I, too, look forward to the fulfilling of a successful mission and my going home to Nell. Yes, time goes quickly here—far more quickly than I anticipated. Am glad it goes so fast for you.

Yes, I get the News, as well as Pyramid and other county papers. Was surprised to hear of the good man Bro. Measer's death. You say or wonder if you shall be able to go to school next winter. How nice if you could do so. Not because you need to. Not because I shall like you or love Nell better for it— No--. But because I am sure she would find much pleasure and contentment in the pursuits of studies that she may like. Am a little sorry that she should be deprived of means which she could use to good advantage. I was pained to hear of your not having a stamp with which to mail a letter—the one that came so late, and for which delay I took liberty of complaining. A little unpleasant that you are deprived of money and means, which in one sense are of little value and mean little yet are big advantages to one in life, if rightly used.

Regarding the P.S. to your cousin's letter which I sent you with my last letter. No doubt it pained you to know that I had not come out and said "Yes" to your cousin's demand for a "confession"—under the circumstances, I don't consider it just the right thing to do to say "Yes" to such a query or like queries from my friends for the present. I don't want Nell to think or imagine that my faith is defective or that I am insincere in my pledges. I hope she would or could not allow such fancies to find their way into her mind. Hope that she, because I said to her cousin that I have some other problems besides the one he wanted to accredit me, to solve after my mission will cause no bad impression or disturb my Nell.

Well, Nell, I close, wishing that you shall prosper, have it pleasant and possess good health,--and will say—continue in the exercise of your good talents and graces which you by nature possess,--be a blessing for good among your friends and companions with whom you associate, win and make friends and the esteem and good will of all even as you have won the esteem and good will—I am glad to know—of them at home who once did not know Nell. I subscribe myself as

> Thy own,
> *P. Sundwall*

P.S. You might if you will, if it does not make too much trouble for you, enclose a single chew of Gum for benefit of a young member here who has never seen a chew of Gum—i.e. that is before it was "chawed"—Don't send more that one chew. They are likely to tax me for it at the PO. I enclose you a blue print of some swans. The original photo is much better, but will retain to show my friends here. It was down in Copenhagen I saw them when in the park and pleasure grounds of Trivoli.

P.S. Am well and O.K. Sunday I go out to a place in the country to hold a meeting at a place where the people are practically ignorant of our doctrines and who had not heard Mormons. The family whose acquaintance I formed last fall when out on a country trip, tracting, have offered me their house to hold a meeting when I please. It isn't often we get such invitations from strangers.

Baltimore, Maryland
September 30, 2009

Dear Peter,

It has been about a month, now, since I started my Ph.D. program and over a month since I last wrote to you. I have had a lot of reading and writing to do, as one would expect with a doctoral program in English. I am attending Morgan State University, a historically black college that was known as Morgan College in 1901, a Biblical Institute founded in Baltimore in 1867 that eventually broadened its mission to educate men and women as teachers. It is now a full fledged university with over 6,000 students and many graduate programs.

After I was accepted into the program, I went in to meet with the director. She asked me what two areas I wanted to concentrate on during my studies.

"I think writing and American literature," I told her, trying to sound more confident that I felt. "I want to understand my role as an American writer. I want to examine my writing influences and learn more about the literary history of our country."

"Do you think you have what it takes to be an Americanist?" she asked, looking me straight in the eye.

"I think so," I replied. "Maybe," I repeated in my head.

I look back over your letter today, and add Henry Wadsworth Longfellow and Peter Sundwall, Jr. to my mental list of American writers. Where does my literary influence actually start? How far back should I go, and where do I stand in all of this? Unsure at the moment, *A great-granddaughter*

Robinson, Utah
April 12, 1901

My dear Peter:

The reason I have not written before is because I have been waiting for my photos. I expected to get them every day. I had them taken before I received your last letter, but did not get them until today. I had to go from here to Eureka, a distance of three miles. My hair and dress do not look so well as they would have done, had I gone from home immediately to the gallery. Hope you will like the photo. I had disappointed you so much about my photo, so I thought I would not write until I could send it. Had I known I would have had to wait so long I would have written sooner.

I was so glad to get your letter. I enjoyed reading about the Swedish people and their customs very much. What an odd way they have of making bread. Doesn't it get very hard before it is eaten up? Keeping it such a long while. I should think it would. How very funny it must be to watch the "gumman" bake their bread. I imagine I should like to see them. Hope you can get a photo of a woman engaged with her baking. It would interest me very much. One can get a much better idea of how things are from a picture then they can from a description. A description is necessary also.

I wonder if the Lundquists there are any relation to the Lundquists at home. There is a friend of ours, a Mr. Lofgran who has relatives in Southern Sweden. He has lost trace of them. If he writes to the mission president do you think he could find any trace of them? Do you know the name of the southern mission president? If not would it trouble you much to find out what it is. Thank you very much if you will, and let me know what it is, as Bro. Lofgran is quite anxious to get trace of his folks.

I am very sorry Peter for overlooking that part of your letter, where you asked me about my letter of credit. I will try not to be as careless again. You have received my letter no doubt telling about our recommend, so will not be necessary to explain again. Yes Vina and I are associated with S. school meetings etc. We enjoy them very much.

I can not tell you Peter how very sorry I am for telling Lois of our relationship. But I did it on the impulse of the moment. Had I taken another thought I should not have done it. Seemed as if I just had to tell someone besides Mama. Hope you will forgive me this time! I will try to remember what the organs of speech are for after this, to keep from talking as well as for talking.

I received those Swedish papers alright—enjoyed looking at them very much. Wish I could read them. Maybe I can some day. Get you to teach me the Swedish language when you return. If I cannot learn it before. I also received the card with the relief on it. It is very beautiful. How beautiful it must look in marble. I will be very much pleased to get "Day" the mate to "Night." I admire those marble statues. But I have never seen anything that would compare with those at Thorvaldsons Museum. Would like very much to go through a Museum of that kind.

The snap shot is just as nice as it can be, so natural of children. They look just like a group of American children. I thought their dress would be very much different from that of ours, but it is not much different is it?

Mama and Vina send best wishes to you. Excuse this poorly composed letter, Peter. I will try, and do better next time.

Your lovingly, *Nellie*

Baltimore, Maryland
October 6, 2009

Dear Nellie,

It wasn't until fifth grade that I became aware that last names
were related to immigrant backgrounds, after a new music
teacher arrived at my elementary school named Mrs. Lindquist,
and I heard all the parents and teachers gossiping about her
tall, blond Swedish husband and their days spent singing
opera across the stages of Europe. She was a breath of fresh
air—young, energetic, thin, with narrow features, soft light
brown curls, and a brazen confidence that I had never seen
in a woman, at least up-close, in person. I didn't know where
Sweden, or Europe, was for that matter, but I did know it was
a place where I wasn't, past an ocean across which I could
never swim. And, I knew that she was different. She saw me,
even when I tried to hide behind the other students.

She was nothing like the rest of my teachers, all old women
with crispy perms and bright magenta lipstick that they applied
religiously, with the help of their compacts, before recess. Mrs.
Lindquist broke out her guitar without any warning, just when
she felt like it, even when it wasn't on our daily schedule. She
was loud and moved all over the room, unlike the rest of my
teachers who grew cobwebs behind their desks. But the best
part about her room was that she did away with all of the
desks and chairs that had been clogging up the former "Music
Trailer." The year she came we shuffled through the portable
trailer door expecting to find the usual dusty vinyl floor tiles,
and instead found a soft and fluffy rug under our feet and a
colorful musical theatre poster on every wall. It didn't even
seem like we were going to class. It felt like vacation, with the
lack of dittoes, pens, and Scantron forms, the latest computer
aged trend in the Baltimore County school system that year.
Music class was yellow and bright and was over before it even

began, compared to the never-ending ticks of the rest of my classes.

Even when I was staring at the weaving threads in the rug, avoiding Mrs. Lindquist's eyes, I could feel her eyes. But, they didn't look back at me in blame. It was exposure, like she could see right through my skull; my usual curtain of downcast eyes and bitten nails no match for her x-ray vision. When I knew an answer, she knew I knew the answer, even if I didn't raise my hand. I was and wasn't surprised when it came time for our spring musical and she cast me as Kate, the lead in the play about a girl who has trouble making friends at her new school.

The two most popular girls in my class, the blonds with the perfectly winged hair, were mad at me for weeks for getting the part they both wanted. But, luckily, I didn't have to worry about retribution. I hadn't even tried out for the lead. I had signed my name next to "student (female) in the class," hoping to hide myself in the background of the auditorium's grey stage curtain. Mrs. Lindquist had made the final choices for the roles, she told everyone, after much thought and consideration.

There is a bad VHS tape of the play somewhere in my parents' house, shaking up and down from the forty pound camera and a tired set of hands. I am the girl in it, at the front of the stage, trying to remember to speak loudly and clearly to the audience, not faking the tears that were prompted in Act II, Scene III.

A few years ago I was surprised to hear that Mrs. Lindquist had divorced her husband and remarried another man. She is still teaching music at the same elementary school, but only part-time, and I imagine she must be close to retirement now. I am curious if her trailer classroom is just as comforting to her current students as it was for me. Do they look forward to her class, like a glass of cold water in the midst of a parched day, or has her aging taken away her magic?

Her new husband is a plumber, and her new name is Mrs. Ay. Mrs. Ay doesn't sound like a woman who could make magic and see through skin. Mrs. Ay isn't soft and capable of quick costume changes behind a dark and polished wood stage. Mrs. Ay might have a sparkly purse, but it would have a bottom to it, unlike Mrs. Lindquist's bag of infinite possibilities. I wonder if her old opera albums are hidden in her attic now, the Swedish influence of her ex-husband erased as she now makes room for PPC pipes and caulking in her large, brick colonial. It seems an unexpected change, but then again, she was anything but expected. In my mind; however, she will always remain the new music teacher, Mrs. Lindquist to me. And Sweden, a land that grew vibrant and artistic men and women from different seeds than the gardens I had seen in Maryland.

What I remember—
Kathy

Vesteras, Sv.
May 4, 1901

My Dear Nellie:

I take this opportunity of writing Nell in answer to letter and photo which was on hand at the office on arrival from trip in the country. Thanks for same. Thanks for the photograph. Nell, it is good. You ran a big risk when you sent your letter in with the photo and sealed the packet besides, and fired it across the continents and ocean with only a 2 cents postage stamp. You violated the laws of the postal union when you cheated the government of 23 cents postage. You laid yourself liable to a fine of something like $200.00 or a taste of penitentury life of a number of months. Now I should not have liked to have come home from a mission to find Nell serving out a term in jail for having violated the laws of the land. It wouldn't be quite so much satisfaction courting her behind the bars, besides, the jail guard may be, would not allow it. I don't mean to scare you Nell. Take what I have said in the light of a joke. Yet it must be acknowledged that Nell has committed a penitentury act in what she cheated the government out of 23 cents—though, of course, she did not do it knowingly. Well, about the photo, it is nice, it is good. Yet, allow me to say that the pose or position isn't just exactly that I should have preferred. But I shall not complain at all. Nell, it is good. Perhaps, because I regard Nell as ideal, I regard that her picture, too should be ideal—perfect. It lies with the photographer to make a good picture, i.e, good in all respects, and all photographers cannot do that. But your face, eyes and features are good, and, of course, that is the greatest or most important consideration of a photo. Well, Nell, I want to say that I am glad for the photo, I almost feel like I had Nell with me. I feel like "I see her bright bewitching eyes, shine with beams from paradise," (If you will allow me to quote a poet). The photo shows well "Your looks of glances bright, Skin of purist lily white, underneath whose melting

snow, Roses and carnations grow—" If Nell, will please pardon
me for citing the above, I shall quit, if she will grant me liberty
to say:--"Ever dearest, tender'est best, Reigning Empress of my
breast"—Nell, may not regard it as exactly sensible in me to
express all what I think best, but she must remember she once
said: "Don't keep your thoughts and sentiments to yourself."

Came in from my long trip to Norberg last week, tracting,
preaching etc, also, since went out on another 3 days jaunt out
in the country a distance where I held a meeting last Sunday,
having a well filled room and ante-room of people to talk to.
Shall likely go out for another trip out to Koping, Kolsva, etc.,
in a few days to visit Sts. Also expect to go on to Sinde, about
75 miles from here to visit our neighbors, Sindquists folks. At
the last of the month we shall take a boat ride up the lake
and canal to Stockholm. The scenery along the route will be
beautiful, such a variety of it. I do not know of a place where
nature is so rich in her variety of landscape, forests, small
islands, hills, water, etc, as along this canal to Stockholm. If
Nell could only be along to enjoy nature's beautiful, interesting
panorama. All Sweden will be beautiful in a month from now.
It is so now, but will be more so then. You should hear the
birds sing these beautiful sunshiny days. They fill the air with
gay, merry songs. May 1st, of course, was May day. The Swedes
welcome May day with delight. The night before, the public
was treated to an excellent display of fireworks and music at
one of the popular parks, and for a couple of days previous,
again, the public was treated to most excellent music from
the military band, which played in a park, a few steps from
here. You see the park on the blue print here attached. That
the music was appreciated was evidenced from the throngs of
people that filled the park and sidewalks about. People of all
classes were out. The swell & girls of the city were much in
evidence as well as the pretty girls. Straight, erect and proud
they are, as much so as girls of England or America, and take
all the girls as a whole—working girls and all, I think they are

more proud and dignified than the girls as a whole in America. Their dresses fit them almost without fault and they look well in their little caps which don the back of their heads, and locks & curls which dangle in their foreheads and the long braid of hair which extend down their backs.

If our girls at home did not have the dry, burning weather to hinder them they too then could with the girls of the North bear title of "fair faced, Rosey cheeked girls" etc.

In regard to your friend who has relatives in Southern Sweden, I don't know how much he can do (Mission Prs.) in the way of finding trace of them. My friend Bro. Nielson is laboring down in Skone or S. Sweden. He perhaps could do something to help Mr. S. if he can furnish particulars and send them to me, rather in separate letters from Nell's because I want Nell to write as much as the 5 cent postage stamp will admit of. Should Mr. S. prefer to write direct to the pres. he may direct his letter to P.V. Bunderson, Kornetgatan #9, Malmo, Sv.

No, the Lundquists here are no relation to friend Amanda. I hope you will have something good to tell me in your next. Write me a good long letter, tell me what you are doing and how you feel. Don't fear as to composition, write me as you feel and think. A spontaneous, letter written as one would speak is the best kind of letter. You see it mirrors one's natural self, and one feels about as though the writer was talking personally to him. My mother's Swedish letters I enjoy immensely well for she writes exactly as she speaks and her words on paper come to me with the same effect that they do as when she speaks. "Don't keep your thoughts to yourself," Nell. You have no reason to do so Nell, but I have some reason for restraining myself to some extent, and considering my spiritual calling, should even, restrain myself and express less of my thoughts or sentiments, yet saying, what, so far, I have said in my letters to Nell I cannot see should occasion any reproach. Do you?

Am glad that you are associated with S.S. and meetings etc. Continue so Nell, also turn a little of your attention to singing or music if you can develop yourself in that simple art in your S.S. work etc. or at home. I had once said that a proficiency in singing or music to some extent must be an essential quality in the "makeup" of my ideal. But of course, when I saw Nell, this consideration was not a paramount consideration, because Nell had other qualities which over weighed this. Yet there is no reason why she should not have a faculty for this other art. You see a little proficiency in this other go wonderfully for to help one to forget the stern realities of life and conduce much to make life pleasant. It requires no gift or natural endowment to acquire a little proficiency in singing or music and I should not like for Nell to be deprived of these things altogether, as, sweet, young and good as she is. She certainly has a right to possess a little accomplishment in these things as well as be fine for a recreation. Nell, with her friend. . . may find many occasion to join in a refrain or song. Mr. S., self, manipulating the alto notes, while she manipulates some other notes, or how admirable it would be if Miss. B. or Mrs. S. rather could take her turn at that instrument the name of which begins with a P and do her share to entertain her friends. I dare not hope, nor want her to think or hope that she shall be so fortunate as to possess such a thing, but never the less, she no doubt may some day have some neighbors or relatives that would delight to have her come over and give them a selection or so. Glad to see that you are interested in our church works. To have a good knowledge of the gospel of our doctrines and know why we are here and what awaits us if we are faithful is of all things an accomplishments the best. Nell, what is better than having a sweetheart who knows what is couched under that, perhaps, unbecoming name "Mormon," who knows and feels that she of all this world full of vain, proud, pretty wealthy girls is herself the best off and who values the prospects she has for a fortune heritage to that extent that all this world's glory, honor, and wealth could not induce her to forsake her religion.

You say that perhaps you shall be able to go to school next winter. How much better if you could. Bad it is that Nell should be handicapped for means. Don't it strike you that with a winter's schooling or even a part of a winter's schooling you could take out certificate that will entitle you to handle or manage school the following winter. It strikes me that this would be not serious trick for a girl of your faculties. But perhaps you have no taste or inclination in this direction. To get a school would be no trouble for you. My bro. who, I am proud to know bears title of Ph.D. would help you to get position. I may find it to my advantage to spend fall and part of winter 1902 in England if home and Nell will permit and providing I can restrain my longing for Nell and home. Don't know yet. You see, Nell, I want to fill a mission, so will cancel my intentions I once had of spending my time in Stockholm and for present let my ambitions slip in to the background. To fill a good mission, Nell, will bring me more satisfaction and inheritance and will be of more worth than all the cultivation or accomplishment I can acquire in an art. So will first seek the kingdom of God and do my duty in its establishment or helping the same. While I should thus be engaged in England (should I decide to go there) you at the same time could occupy yourself with your new temporary vocation, teaching.

Well, Nell, I hope you will pardon me for taking the liberty of making these simple suggestions. It is no doubt your ambition to accomplish in many respects. You would do so had you the money or means with which to do so. Don't misinterpret my motives in making these remarks. You see, Nell, that Nell belongs to me and I feel that I am to some extent justified in making some suggestions that are correlated but for good. Now I, too, am open for all she should like to say for my good and inspiration.

I send you under separate cover my photograph. What do you think of it? Am, I believe, some poorer than usual. Held my own during winter but now that spring is here I am not so heavy. The photo in all respects, fails to come up to yours. Small size cards are popular among the Saints and Elders here. We are continually exchanging photos. I shall have a variety of Elders photos, also photos of our Saints including a number of our good Sisters and girls to show you when I get back.

Now, I have spent all forenoon writing some 13 pages of reading matter for you and I'll be "danged" if I couldn't say lot, yet, but I had better quit now, for this time and say write again next month. Again I thank you for your photo, for your good letters---write more in your letters if your time will permit. I enclose a miniature bouquet of flowers, the first that have appeared in our Swedish forests. "Boa slipper" they call them. The flowers here enclosed are the first ones my eyes chanced to spy as I walked through the romantic forest. My thoughts as I gazed down upon these flowers wandered to my Nell. So I picked them and now enclose them, though they have lost their original beauty, though only a simple flower it was or is. Nell, when will there be but 25 words in the English Alphabet? This is a simple riddle that may some day find its practical application in you. Guess it will you and let me know the answer. Love to your Mama and Nell with most reserved for Nell.

      Yours,
      Peter

Address me at Hornsgatan #80. Stockholm.

Baltimore, Maryland
October 24, 2009

Dear Peter,

I am now two months into my Ph.D. program. Would you imagine you might one day replace, "My brother who, I am proud to know bears title of Ph.D." with "great-granddaughter?" It has been difficult to get to your letters lately, trying to stay on top of my doctoral work, teaching poetry online for Johns Hopkins University's Center for Talented Youth Program, as well as keeping the house from crashing down on us.

I have been brainstorming about dissertation ideas and am considering a focus on American Love Letters over the past 100 years, sparked by reading your letters. My dissertation has to be research based, so I am thinking about looking at a variety of different letters from the past century, and perhaps the evolution from long distance epistle to today's instantaneous twitter. Yesterday, it occurred to me to look at the role of metaphor in the letters. After all, it is the comparisons that continue to drive my imagination and writing.

I did some quick searches on love letters on the computer and came up with some possibilities to present to my advisor next week: President Reagan's and President Truman's letters to their wives, Jackson Pollock's lines to Lee K., and Elizabeth Taylor's and Richard Burton's confessions. These are all people who will become famous in a few decades, either for their political positions or for their art. I realize they are just names to you now, in 1901, words that do not have faces yet, the same way I am only air to you at this point—the wind behind your ear.

I am intrigued by the love letter form because of the desire and the unrevised quality in which it operates, which is so often discouraged in the professional world: the urgency on the page, opened up in raw form, usually without the smoothing layer of editing.

The love letter is a bit of a hybrid genre, too, which I like, as it isn't exactly poetry, and it isn't exactly prose. The pen becomes the mind and the body, creating palpable tension and tangible marks, acceptance of a lack of control over one's own life that is exhilarating and frightening at the same time. And doesn't that sound like a much more interesting dissertation paper than 250 pages on the theme of mortality in Moby Dick?

Ph.D.-in-training,
your great-granddaughter

Robinson, Utah
May 1, 1901

My dear Peter:

It has been a week since I received your dear letter. But have been so busy that I could not write before. Mama has been ill for some time. Is not able to be out of bed. There is much sewing to be done, besides the house work that keeps Vina and I quite busy. The work isn't anything, it's the worry of having Mama sick. I think she will soon be well. The Elders administered to her last night, she has felt much better ever since. The Doctor said she would—with good care—be well soon. I believe it is too high here for Mama. Wish she were in the valley. Wish we were where we were this time last year.

If we were only where we could see the trees and grass. There is only one place here, that we can see anything but sage brush, cedar and pine, and sun-burnt houses, that is the yard at the Mammoth Hotel. There is a lawn and a few trees growing there. When I go past there I always feast my eyes. You know "green is good for the eyes."

The only pleasant part of the weather now comes in the evenings. From sun rise until sun down the wind blows constantly. But the evenings are warm and balmy. I enjoy taking a stroll in the evenings. Haven't had much time to stroll since Mama has been ill except when we go to meetings. They hold Sunday meeting in the evenings here. We had to miss "Young Ladies Meeting" Monday evening because Mr. Pritchett was at work and we could not leave Mama alone. I enjoy our meeting very much, almost as well as I did at home.

You say that my letters are good—excellent. Ah! Peter they are nothing compared with your good sweet letters.

Maybe I am selfish, always thinking and planning for the

future, or after you return, and not thinking of your mission. But you know Peter that I know you will fulfill a successful mission, so when I can be with you and see you again is what I think of most. I don't mean to be selfish.

I know that one in your position can not be so expressive of their thoughts and feelings, as they could under other circumstances. That is alright. I know that you love me, and you know that I love you. That we know. Don't for a moment neglect your work to think of, or write to me too often those fond sentiments. But don't be too reserved in all your letters for there isn't anything that gives me more pleasure than to read one of your letters where you express sentiments of affection.

Yes I have seen Taylor's drawing of "Minnehaha Hiawatha." Think it is beautiful. As are all of his drawings representing Longfellow's poems. Evangeline, The Shipbuilder's Daughter, The Children's Hour, The Hanging of the Crane, The Village Blacksmith, and Priscilla and John Alden. They are all shown in the Journals. Anyone of them could have been gotten for one dollar. But they are all gone now. I should have liked very much to have gotten them all. But I could not.

Peter I will close, because I want to get this letter in today's mail. I will write very soon. Excuse this poor written and composed letter, but I have been interrupted several times since I sat down to write.

> Mama is some better now. Vina and Mama send best wishes. With love and best wishes, I am yours
> *Nellie*

Baltimore, Maryland
October 29, 2009

Dear Nellie,

I marvel at the attention that you and Peter give to poetry, from the magazines that you mention, as well as within the internal lines of your letters to one another. You both allude to poets and artists like we reference movie and television stars, but then I remember that you do not have movies or television. Part of me envies your lack of TV, radio, computer, and phones. My world is smothered with visual and auditory stimuli, and it is often hard to even want to bring another "distraction" into my life, even if it is just a few more quiet letters. Sometimes, I wonder if I am just adding one more piece of unnecessary information to the overwhelming cacophony of images and sounds that are already aimlessly circling around the globe.

Sometimes, I see the world as a cyclone of noise and movement, composed of tiny bolts and arrows swirling above everyone's heads. I know that you had different challenges, and fears in compartments that I will never open, simply because I am living now, in the early years of the 21st century, and not the early years of the 20th century. You will never experience the frustration of a computer crashing and deleting all of your saved material for the past two years, but you will also never know the comfort of an email from a relative in Australia saying "I'm fine" mere hours after an earthquake.

SEND
Kathy

Vesteras, Sverige
June 3, 1901

My Dear Nell,

About a month has passed since last I had the pleasure of
writing my sweet-heart out in what she calls the dreary place
of Robinson. I have since that time I wrote, rec'd two good
nice letters, which were indeed welcomed and appreciated as
are all the letters I get from you. Your last letter was handed
to me just a minute or two before one of our meetings were
called to order down in Stockholm. Glad that you are well,
and to hear that your mama is up again and over her sickness.
It pleases me to learn of your interest in S.S. work etc. It is
evidence to me of your interest in the gospel, and that you
have more than an ordinary conception of what is or means.
Your S.S. work and lectures etc. suggest to me that Nell is
actually engaged in a good missionary work. What if Nell
should be asked to extend her good work out beyond the
confines of our own Utah into some other state in country.
Then I should come home and wait for Nellie. A Sister Booth
(Josie Booth of Provo) was with us this last conference. She
talked to the people through or by means of an interpreter.
She has now fulfilled a two year mission and will soon return
to Zion. I cannot blame your mama for not assenting so readily
to your going into the city. I cannot blame her for being
sensitive or cautious over her girl or girls. She has reason to
be proud of them, and for you to go into the city will give
her cause for anxiety as to your welfare. She well understands
the dangers and snares that Nellie cannot comprehend. For
my part though (Should I be allowed to express myself) I
should have no particular objections to Nellie's going into the
city for a time, for I believe that Nell, as well as being pure
and virtuous is possessed of that odd character and made
of such metal that she can and will avoid the dangers and
unwholesome things that beset a girl's pathway in the city. I

have faith or every confidence in Nellie, yet I cannot blame your mama for being a little anxious or cautious over her girl, Nell's and my sweetheart's welfare.

I think of the girls that leave this country to go to Utah—a trip of between 6 or 7 thousand miles. You know that as soon as they embrace the gospel the people want to gather with the saints in America, consequently many of our young sisters who are dependent upon themselves only—i.e. have no parents that are so situated that they can help them, manage through persistence and work to get to far off Utah. The most of them usually go to Salt Lake, where they find work and help and contribute to their parents' immigration. You see, such things as that is what a living faith in the Gospel will impel a great many of the young sisters of Scandinavia. Of course, they are warned of the evils and vices that even abound in the so called "city of the saints." But, however, the most of them avoid these things. It seems, and of course, is true, that they on embracing the gospel are infused with a new life and a strengthened character.

In your "Song without Words" you say "tis not my gift to sing in tuneful words" etc. but close by saying that "in whatsoever way we sing in deeds or words let but our song be true. True to the highest wisdom we have grasped. True to the good within us placed" etc. Yes, so I say Nellie, "One may sing in works that which shall longer last than words." True Nell.

The "jar" like objects, you see in the blue print over the water are but some of the many Chinese lanterns that illuminate the park and water at nighttime. I shall send you a better copy, in the near future, I hope.

Did I say one night that it had been or was my desire to get or have, or marry a girl of wealth? A lady with a wealth of $ or cents. If I referred to the latter kind of wealth, then, as Nell knows, I was jesting. Nellie is wealthy. She has no occasion to wish she were the heiress I once might spoke of.

As you perceive, I am back to Vesteras, to labor during the summer in company with a Bro. Sundell.

Well, I shall close and go out in town and see what success I can have selling tracts and having conversations.

What our prospects are for the season I can hardly say or judge. We have friends and cultivating new acquaintanceship, but what the future will bring I cannot say. A couple of women who are subserving the interests of Satan have been holding lectures in Stockholm and other places exposing as they say "the Mormons and condition of affairs in Zion" etc. We have not as yet had the privilege of meeting the distinguished individuals here as yet but look for them. I shall likely take a month off and go to my mother's birthplace in Vermland. I also want to take a trip up to Sundsvall, my father's birthplace and boyhood home, but will likely leave that until next summer. Just rec'd photo and letter from Bro. Nielson. He is doing I believe, OK—looks well in photo. We shall likely arrange to see each other during summer sometime. I want to tell you Nell, that a Swedish summer is beautiful—beyond the comprehension of them who have not experienced a summer here. The beauty of nature with its variety of sceneries and views is at this time at its Zenith. The many different trees and bushes with their varieties of flowers,--fragrant flowers—are beautiful things to see. Our sail to Stockholm was grand and delightful. If I was a poet or could use language, I should try to, through medium of pen and paper, to portray or express to you how grand and beautiful a Swedish summer is, but I must for bear, for you see, I can't. Just a few steps from here is a park which is beautiful with its pretty trees, grass, and attractive fountain. During the night the orchestras have their place on the stand and treat the public to sweet music.

Well, good bye. My Sweetheart be good to yourself. With love
and best wishes I remain

> Your
> *P.S. J.*
>
> Adr__Vestyothegatan Z.

Baltimore, Maryland
November 20, 2009

Dear Peter,

The day my brother, your great-grandson, received his mission calling was bitter sweet—dark semi-sweet chocolate my mother would hide on the top shelf of the pantry closet. My sister and I had long since given up on church by that point. My brother was the only one who remained by my mother's side on the pew, putting up with the itchy button down shirts and ironed dress pants each Sunday, watching the Sacrament trays go up and down the aisles in reverent silence.

My brother, like my father, barely made it through school, his mind focused out the window more than on any textbook. He shuffled his way through the special education system, what they called "learning disabled" back then. My mother helped him graduate from high school by practically writing his senior English research paper for him. I can still see her up until midnight on the old Smith Corona typewriter, clicking away in short bursts, bags under her eyes, muttering, "I am going to get this kid to graduate even if it kills me!" I, meanwhile, had coughed my senior paper out within a few days, without any extra help or guidance and was a bit annoyed when I only received a B+.

My parents were smart enough to realize that further education was not the right move for my brother after graduation. It would have been a complete waste of his time and my parents' money. So they supported his current interest that year: guns. I realize now that it was not the traditional senior year choice for future advancement. But at the time, it seemed like a completely ordinary progression for him. Instead of going to automotive or electrician school, my brother flew to Denver and moved in with my father's sister and began an eighteen month gunsmithing program. There, he learned how to make and repair guns. I remember the excitement when he came home for Christmas and brought his first crafted rifle—a smooth body of wood and metal that gleamed like a new bike, or a new bible.

My father was working for the FBI at the time, and not so secretly wanted my brother to go into ballistics. My father started pressuring my brother to interview in D.C. after my brother graduated and moved back home, though my brother never seemed that interested in pursuing that path. He went to one interview as I recall, and when he didn't get the job due to lack of "experience," my father shifted his obsession and found new objects for his attention: collecting new reading glasses, polishing his work shoes, and building a food storage shelter in the old cellar, though I can't remember if this was the correct order.

Then, one day, against the still-unpacked suitcases and gun parts that furnished his room, my brother announced he wanted to go on a mission. My mother smiled with Mormon-mother pride, which resembles the smile when a child brings home his packet of school pictures, and they all look good. The rest of us half-smiled, smiles that looked more like the reaction of when pick a White Elephant gift and after opening it, you realize you really wanted the previous gift that was picked. But we all supported my brother. We always supported one another in our family. I think because we knew no one else would.

Even my father, a non-member of the Mormon church (whereas my sister and I were, and are still considered to this day, inactive members), spoke at my brother's mission farewell, a special Sacrament Meeting devoted to his departure into the mission field. There wasn't a dry eye in the pews as my father recalled his own father's surprise and lack of understanding when, during his rebellious junior year at Towson University, he had announced he was becoming a Republican.

"I don't understand it, son," his father had said, "but if it's what you want, I'll support you."

We lived our lives that way—no one completely understanding each other, but there in person, spirit, and some shared mental wiring. I always felt an unconditional support from my family that surpassed difference and didn't hold to any particular trend or affiliation. Every decision and new direction by a family member seemed to be defined by the question, "Who says I can't?" as much as the desired interest or goal. Even in the midst of my sister's addiction issues my parents were always there—sometimes beyond frustrated and distraught— but still there, loving her as a person, even if she was running away from the daughter they once knew. My parents never waivered in their faith in their children.

My mother helped my brother to re-pack his suitcases with enough clean socks, underwear, white shirts, and blue suits to tide him over for the next eighteen months. We all cried as he boarded the plane to his "calling," the last place anyone expected the Mormon Church would send him for missionary work: Utah!

> Bon Voyage,
> *A missionary's great-granddaughter and sister*

Robinson, Utah
May 31, 1901

My dear Peter:

I received your letter some two or three days ago, but wanted to wait until I received your photo before answering. I enjoyed getting both very much especially your photo. I can not tell you how I enjoy looking at it. As I said to Mama wish he could speak to me. It is so natural. It is fine of you. Thank you very much for your photo. I am so glad to have it. It is so refreshing to sit down in the evening and look at your own dear face again. Sometimes when I look at your photo it seems as if you are looking very serious, then again you are smiling. It must be I who is serious when I look and find you looking serious. I get lonely sometimes. I then get so serious that one would think me to be quite unsocial. But I am not so always. Don't think me to be of a moody temper either.

I am learning to be a Telephone girl. Do you mind Peter? They promise me a position and thirty dollars per month, after I learn thoroughly. You see by doing this I can go to school next winter. And then next summer I can secure a position in some of the settlements where they employ telephone girls. Because one who has had the office here can get a position even at the main office at Salt Lake. I have all the main points learned now, and answer all the local calls. The lady whom I take lessons of said I was doing well. In a week or two I will be able to do all the work. I like the work very much. Hope you won't mind me taking it up. Through this I can come nearer being your ideal. For indeed that is just what I want to be—in the fullest sense.

How I wish we were in the valley where we could see the trees, grass, and flowers. We will appreciate those things much better when we do see them, being deprived of seeing them for such a long time.

I remember one night, about this time last year, when a young man and myself enjoyed an evening under the trees, and breathed the sweet perfume of the flowers. Yet I look forward to a time when I and this same young man may spend a much more pleasant evening—or evenings under the trees. Do you remember the evening I speak of? It was the twenty fifth of May I think, the evening after our stroll in the meadows. Wish I were out home to have another stroll in the meadows.

About me cheating the government. I should have explained to you before, I told the postmaster about it and he said it would go as printed matter. I am sorry that I did it now. I won't tell you what I did when I read the first page of your letter. I thought you would think me selfish or ignorant. But it was neither. I take what you said as a joke. It was quite hard at first, but when I read the rest of your letter I felt much better. Am glad you received the photo. It nor the letter either were worth 2 cents. I did not loose any sleep over cheating the government. I should not say this. But it seems to be as if they get enough. Suppose I would not talk like that had they found out what I did.

Had they found me out, and I could not pay the fine, you should not have had the privilege to court Nell behind the bars. Even if the guard would allow it.

Thank you Peter for saying those beautiful things about me. You may have the liberty to express your beautiful thoughts just when you choose. They are so sweet to me. Wish I could express my thoughts as beautiful as you. I too do not think the position in my picture is well. Wish I had sit over as I contemplated. But everybody said "O! you won't get a better one." I feel as if I should have gotten a much better one had I sat over. I know I should have just what we wanted if you had been the manipulator of affairs when the picture was taken.

You once said you should liked to have been. I wish you had been.

I am glad you are enjoying yourself. Sweden must be a very beautiful country. I should like very much to be along with you to enjoy the beautiful scenery. Suppose I do not half imagine how grand it all is. Thank you for the snapshot. It is very pretty. How I should enjoy to walk along those walks with you, and gaze into the water. What a beautiful river this one must be. If I did not know I should think it to be a lake. This park is surely a beautiful place now. Thank you for those pretty little flowers. It is so nice to know that they grew in Sweden, and were picked by you Peter. We have no flowers here. But a friend gave Mama a few roses. I ask Mama if I may have one. I will send it to you. You will—I hope, get a parcel through the mail. The chain is of my hair, and the handkerchiefs are not a fair sample of my needlework, because I did them just at odd times and did not get them so well. Will make some better, "some other time." Accept same as tokens of my love for you.

Thank you for your suggestions, Peter. I will profit by them. I shall not become Mrs. S. until I can play the piano. For that I can do with study, but as to singing I can not say. I will do my best to accomplish myself worthy of him who will have fulfilled a sacred mission.

Do as you choose about remaining part of winter 1902. As for me I can wait. As much as I should like to have you come.

It is just the other way about, my photo does not come up to yours in any respect. I rather like the smaller sized cards, I shall be very glad to see the photos of the elders, sisters, and girls.

I will try to solve the riddle and send answer next time I write. It is time for me to go to my lessons now.

I am writing the paper for conjoint and have to do some more writing on that. I went with Vina and her fellow for a "buggy ride" last night. The first since I came over here this time. We all enjoyed looking at your dear face. Mama said it did her such good as it did me to get your photo. Mama sends best love. My love to you always.

Nellie.

Baltimore, Maryland
November 28, 2009

Dear Peter,

This week, I spent hours reading about mission work for my
graduate class, Multicultural Literature for Adolescents. We
are reading *The Island of the Blue Dolphins* by Scott O'Dell,
and I am in charge of presenting the background of the story,
the history of the Native Americans in the coastal islands of
California, and the role of cultural authenticity in terms of
the author and the text regarding the fact that the author is a
European American and the story is from the perspective of a
Tongva girl.

The missions that I read about were Catholic, as opposed to
Mormon, lead by Spanish Franciscan padres and sounded to
be about as close to hell on earth as possible for the Native
Americans who were taken from their lands and into the world
of forced labor. The history reads like it could be fictitious, but
it is not. In fact, it is a repetitious story: one culture thinks it
better than another, one religion forces itself onto the others,
an entire people are or are almost erased.

The whole idea of a mission is to convert "others", to show
"others" the "true" way, to bring the "ignorant" into the "light."
I wonder, Peter, did you ever see past the "other"? Did you
ever, even for a moment, see yourself as the "other" on your
mission or in your life? Is there some physical difference
between a member and a non-member that I cannot see?
Maybe that would help me to understand missionary work. Is
there some aura that you can point to on a non-member-- to
say, "Here is the one who needs redemption?" Is there a dotted
line that travels through the world, marking right from wrong,
good from bad? Maybe it is my near-sighted eyes, or perhaps
my own distracted mind, but I have never seen it. I only see

people and notice this invisible and unnamed virus that seems to sometimes possess them, making its rounds about the earth each century, causing the drawing of swords, arrows, guns, and bombs to swipe across the surface at sudden whims.

You were a smart man, Peter, with accurate eyes. Did you ever look out into an audience of listeners during your mission and just see women and men, regardless of their religion? I imagine, deep down, you did, even if it was just for a fleeting moment, in-between your Swedish translation and the slow shift of your weight from your right foot to your left foot. It probably appeared as a mild stutter, a motion no one would have picked out as unusual, a nervous tick that emerged as you searched for the right word, the converting word you knew, deep down, you was lacking.

> What is the word I am looking for?
> *your great-granddaughter*

Vangsta, Sv.
June 24th
1.30 oclock AM

My Dear Nellie,

I take this opportunity of writing you a letter on this
midsummer day. Am sitting by the window and writing by
day light, beginning my letter at half past one oclock. During
the darkest part of the night which was just before midnight
I read from Christ's sermon on the Mount. I stood outside of
the house and read, of course, by daylight. My companion
was up for awhile or until 1 oclock when he concluded to go
to bed, two members of our good family of saints with whom
we are stopping are up. We have decided to see the sun rise
at 2:34 AM. In a house in the edge of the woods close by have
the young folks been celebrating the advent of Midsummer
day in the way of dancing—an accordion being the source
of the music. They (the young people) dispersed and went
to their different places of abode a short time ago, the merry
talk and laughter of the boys and girls on their way through
the neighboring barley fields and woods, we could hear. I
have been amused to hear of the many methods that on this
midsummer day the young people of Sweden resort to to
settle question of who she or he is to marry. Midsummer day
probably rates after Christmas in importance as a holiday.

Your letter of May 31st arrived day after my departure for a
trip out in the country, and of course laid in the letter box
for a whole week until my arrival home yesterday. Thanks
for same, Nellie. I enjoyed it immensely well. I was sorry that
I had pained you so much with what I meant as a harmless
simple joke, which I hoped would in no way affect you in the
way it did. But when I think, "cheating the Gov." "jail" "fine"
and "courting Nell behind the bars" etc. were certainly hard
and inappropriate terms to associate with sweetheart Nellie,

however much well meant and innocent the impulses were
that prompted it. Don't think Nellie that I thought as you say
that you were "selfish or ignorant." No, indeed, No! May I ask
what my sweetheart did on reading the first sheet of my letter?
I wouldn't want to occasion Nellie any pain or hurt her for
anything and I beg pardon for what I have occasioned her.
I was wholly and purely jesting but I must have been a little
awkward about it and consequently my Nellie misinferred
what my motives were. And Nellie is learning to be a
telephone girl Eh? I wish her success. I had not dreamed of
such a thing. Though the work be responsible it is no doubt
pleasant at least when compared with a great many other
things to do. How nice if my Sweetheart could operate or
control a long distance telephone, a line that stretched from
her to Europe or Sweden and how nice if I should or could
then have the pleasure of "ringing up" the "telephone" girl and
say "Hello" together with some other desireable things to my
sweetheart. Again, I wish you success in your undertaking. It
is amusing to hear the Swedish girls say "Hello" when they
are at the telephone. The telephone is responsible for the
introduction of the word into the Swedish language. They say
"Hello," pronouncing the e as we would a in the word "all".

You seem to have the idea that I have fixed or established an
ideal above you and to which it is expected Nellie must attain.
Don't think so, Nellie. I meant not to write or say anything
in such a way that you should infer such an idea. My ideal
is in Nellie as she is. The other things I have mentioned, or
bits of accomplishments that I have referred to, do not go to
constitute my ideal. These attainments while desireable or little
things when compared with the real inner girl herself with her
solid character and improchable integrity together with the
charms and virtues which nature has endowed her with. Nellie,
in the beautiful verses she sent me, gives expressions to what
in her opinion we should aim, in our actions and life, to do,
i.e. in whatever way we sing,--in words or deeds or otherwise

let but our song be true, etc. It is her who understands and comprehends our mission on earth and life's object etc. that deserve the synonym name of ideal. I feel that I can regard the girl that I love as ideal i.e. Nellie.

Now Nellie, that was hardly right for you to remark that letter or photo which you sent me were not worth the postage 2 cents. Why doesn't my sweetheart put more value on the beautiful photo she so kindly sent me? Do not for a moment think that I do not appreciate it. So often when home at the office do I gaze at my sweetheart's picture for so beautifully and actually does it portray her "Lock of dark hair—glances bright, skin of purest white." True I may have suggested another pose, but that does not say that the photo would have been better, and your friends were no doubt, right when they said, "Oh, you won't get a better one." Don't depreciate your photo, Nellie. I delight in it as well as do my friends who see it. Thanks Nellie for the Rose you sent me—a very pretty token of your love. I have before me a plate of "Forget me nots" whose delicious fragrance I inhale as I write. O little unassuming flower is a "forget me not" yet pretty and rich in fragrance. I shall enclose you some pressed "forget m.n." but do not suppose they will have much of a resemblance of the fresh "forget me not," as it looks when it is fresh plucked.

My love refers to package that she hopes I shall receive through the mail. How could my love, my Nellie in a more substantial and appropriate way show her love than through a chain worked from Nell's own hair and kerchief of her own handiwork? What invaluable tokens they will be to me of a sweetheart's sincere love and integrity. While I have not received them as yet, I thank her for them. I hope they will reach me. It would be a pity should the parcel go astray in the mail. Yet when I consider that it is now two weeks since your letter came, I wonder occasionally if now possibly the articles or presents have not gone amiss. I hope not.

Yes, I remember the night of the 25th of May when I first went to see the girl that in the full sense of the meaning I loved. Yes, I remember that night when we passed the evening away trying to express our opinion of Kipling and some other celebrities, because we did not, or I at any rate, dare to venture on anything nearer. May our association which dated from that night be a source of perpetual eternal enjoyment to Nell and I. May the love which found its birth on that night be an eternal and sincere one as I have every reason to believe it will be.

Glad for the love your mama sends me, also for Vina's.

Baltimore, Maryland
December 6, 2009

Dear Peter,

I have been up a lot at night this week, too—not from the
light of Midsummer's Day, but within the deep darkness of our
shortest days. I am exhausted from a lack of sleep, two hyperactive children, graduate exams and papers, and the left-over
adrenaline from a car that started to lose its brakes while I was
taking my son to school this morning.

Several missions are calling at this point in my life: children,
school, writing, and your letters. There are not enough
hours in the day. Yet, I still read, finding new energy in your
descriptions of Nell's hair chain and handkerchief, your image
of the figurative phone line reaching from Sweden to Utah, like
it just happened yesterday.

It is hard to believe that you and Nell are so young in these
letters. Your voices reflect a maturity about life that I am
just uncovering in my late thirties. Is it the time period, the
expectations, the delay of responsibility on my generation's
part?

Immediately before my car lost its brakes, I was screaming at
my son for his lack of responsibility, for only wanting privilege,
for taking, taking, taking, and never giving back. Then, after
my adrenaline subsided, and I knew we were okay, I wanted
to hold him for the rest of the day.

This weight is tiring, Peter, feeling so many jobs to be done—
callings that keep us from sleep, distracted throughout the day.
I am coming to terms with living a solitary mission, without a
helpful manual or a living prophet to guide me. My converts
are my poems, my stories, my journals, my essays. My mission
is for the articulation of the moment in between the invention

and the reaction, the second before the first Swedish girl tilts her lips towards the mouthpiece of the telephone and says "Hallo." My mission is the need for something else, a new word, sound that will feel like it has already been in the language for years, even if it has only been here for a few brief seconds.

Calling,
Your great-granddaughter

Vesteras, June 27, 1901

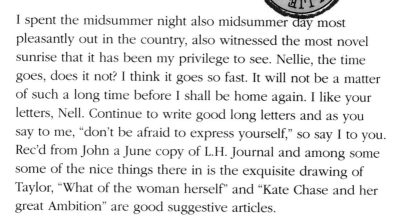

Dear Nellie,

I spent the midsummer night also midsummer day most
pleasantly out in the country, also witnessed the most novel
sunrise that it has been my privilege to see. Nellie, the time
goes, does it not? I think it goes so fast. It will not be a matter
of such a long time before I shall be home again. I like your
letters, Nell. Continue to write good long letters and as you
say to me, "don't be afraid to express yourself," so say I to you.
Rec'd from John a June copy of L.H. Journal and among some
some of the nice things there in is the exquisite drawing of
Taylor, "What of the woman herself" and "Kate Chase and her
great Ambition" are good suggestive articles.

In a letter from Anna, I learn that your cousin Perry is coming
to Utah with his bride to marry. Perry hasn't answered my last
letter as yet. I had ought I think, get a wedding invitation or
some thing of the kind from my old time friend Perry. Perhaps
er you get this letter Perry will have come to Utah and is
visiting his friends. He is likely, or will call on you and family.
Anna tells me also that Lois is to marry a cattleman who is
quite rich but a "Non-Mormon." My cousin Heber Olson has
returned from his mission and a Bro. Hanson, a good friend
is also released and, consequently, will soon be home. You
perhaps have read my brother's article in June Era. He certainly
is doing well and making a most excellent start in life. You, no
doubt, know that he now has a degree of PhD, a title which
not many young men in the country at this age earn or acquire
under the circumstances he did. He is likely now at Provo and
I hope he will find a convenient time to go and take a trip
down to see my sweetheart.

Now, I have written a long letter, and have not said anything in
regard to me and my work etc. Will say that I am well and feel

well in the work of God—though the work does not progress as fast as I should like to see it. The people of the country are so shrouded in prejudice that it isn't so smooth a sailing as perhaps we should like, but smooth sails and tranquil waters are things that an Elder does not look for.

If the symbol or signs attached to my signature do not just strike your fancy or you regard my action in so doing as a deviation from laws of good breeding or etiquette, I in explanation of my conduct, refer you to Mr. Shakespeare who once said: "Love is blind and lovers cannot see the petty faults they themselves commit." I do not take the liberty of making a dozen as I have seen on some letters, but for this time, just two, thinking perhaps that is all you will allow me.

As Nellie's happy lover I subscribe myself with love to her, Mama, and Vina

Affectionately,
P. Sundwall Jr. X X

Hope you have rec'd some photos I sent you some time ago.

Baltimore, Maryland
December 15, 2009

Dear Peter,

Funny how Mr. Shakespeare has always been utilized for
love letters—his quotes continuing to be passed through the
centuries like open secrets. Funny, too, that my son and I went
over to my parents' last night for dinner, and there sat three
female missionaries across the table. I am not sure why there
were three, as they usually travel in pairs. But, even still, they
seemed like one large unit: one body with three very different
sets of arms and legs. They would have made a very attractive
PR poster for today's Mormon missionaries: three young and
intelligent women: one African American, one Asian American,
and one Polynesian American.

My mother made a wonderful spinach salad with blue cheese
and pear sauce, followed by green peppers stuffed with rice
and ground beef. She is a much better cook than I am. A fancy
meal for me includes a frozen pizza with a side of Rice-A-Roni.
I didn't inherit your granddaughter's domestic skills, Peter. I am
more like you, burning my fingers on the hot stove.

"Congratulations!" my son said the other day. "You didn't burn
my Pop-Tart!"

The missionaries were chattier than usual, and one even
mentioned that she liked my tattoo, and then elbowed the
Sister to her left, "Sister Norris has some too!"

"Hush," Sister Norris said, with a thick Texan accent, "I'm
a convert." "I'm a convert" is the phrase most converted
Mormons use to explain any unsavory former activities they
participated in prior to joining the church. It always seemed
a little unfair to me. The rest of us had been given the
expectations list since birth, without an "I'm a convert!" card.

"Are you members, too?" the Sister in the middle asked my sister and me, sitting on the other side of the table with our children.

"We used to be," my sister said, cutting up the green pepper into little pieces for her one-year-old. "We grew up in it." And the missionaries smiled their smiles that said, "We do not know what to say. We just don't understand members who would prefer to be non-members. We just don't understand why someone would pull away, as opposed to toward, the church."

I stepped away in my head and saw that it was the opposition, really, that holds us all together. Missionaries are opposed to non-members, and non-members are opposed to members. Children are opposed to parents, who are opposed to their own parents. All are slight turns of the magnet, swinging back and forth in generational rhythm. Turn to one side: attraction. Turn to the other side: repulsion.

> What happens if the magnet never turns?
> *Kathy, your great-granddaughter*

Vesteras
July 20, 1901

My Dear Nellie:

Am looking for a letter from you, as I have not as yet received reply to mine of the 1st of last month. It is now more than 5 weeks since I heard from Nellie, and consequently it seems like a great long while. I suppose though, that Nellie is busy so that she cannot answer so promptly all my letters. I went out on one tour in the country and thought that when I arrived back in town I should have a letter awaiting me from Nellie, but it did not come. I then went to Gefle for a week, a beautiful city of 30,000 inhabitants, some 100 or more miles north from here. I thought that surely when I returned back my sweetheart's letter would be on hand, but I was disappointed. How are you prospering, Nellie? Have you good health? I suppose you are busy at the Exchange now answering the many hundreds of people who greet you with "Hello." I wish you success in your new undertaking. Do you not take my share in some of the season's enjoyments? How did you spend the 4th of July? I could perhaps give you a little interesting narrative of how I spent that day, but will let it pass for the present until "some other time."

As I said I was up to Gefle went up to see the fair, which was a credible successful one. The exhibits there were good and interesting to see and well worth the trip. My friend Bro. Nielson was there also. It was previously decided that we should meet there. Bro. Nielson together with his partner comes from southern Sweden. We had an excellent good time together with the 2 elders that are laboring in Gefle. Later Bro. Swen Nielson together with his partner (whose name is also Swen Nielson) came from Stockholm and made us a visit to Vesteras. We had a most pleasant time during their stay, seeing sights, rowing, etc.

It is just a year now since I left home—since I called at your home to say "Good bye" to my sweetheart. You remember we didn't say much—too serious we were to speak much, and you (so thoughtfully & good of you) gave me your photograph. I often think of your home on the corner by the depot and even wish you still lived there. Reason because my memory so often reverts back to the home you then had, is because my first love experience and the cherished object of my love—Nellie, are so perpetually linked with that home. Time goes so rapidly. So far as returning to my Nellie is concerned it cannot go too swiftly. I want to fill a mission first, want to do my duty. The serious-ness of my call, and work dawns more and more upon me. I have the privilege of devoting part of the time to other avenues, but for a while I want to as near exclusively as I can devote the time to my divine calling.

How happy we shall be when we meet again. I shall then have reason to value Nellie and appreciate her to the very fullest extent when I consider that for 2 years and longer she has been true to her love she pledged me. We shall then at some opportune time take a stroll back to your home environed with its trees and shrubbery, where a year ago I humbly asked for and you modestly gave.

May "angels around you their silent watch keep" and may our All-wise Creator—our Father bless Nellie and me. I believe we can with good, clear conscience ask this of Him for it is a pure love, and nothing less, that unites Nell and I.

July 22, 1901

Penned the above last Saturday. Yesterday we went out some 3 or 4 Eng. miles into the country and held two "open air" meetings, both in new parts. It is very warm these days and not so pleasant to travel the "land's vaggen." At the present it is fully as warm here as at home.

Your parcel which you more than 6 weeks ago referred to has not yet come to hand. I hope you did not send it at the time you wrote as one might almost infer from your letter—for had you done so, the parcel has undoubtedly gone astray in the mails, but I hope it will "show up" not because I am selfish to get the presents for their intrinsic value, but because they are from Nellie. I take it that Nellie is or has been very busy so that she hasn't been able to complete or send the gifts er this. How I shall cherish the Kerchiefs and the chain made from Nellie's own hair when they come.

May Heaven's choicest blessings rest on Nellie and I close for this time awaiting every day for your letter and parcel with love to your mama, Vina, and yourself.

> Affectionately
> *P. Sundwall*

Will probably go up to Stockholm the middle of next month. Please address me at No. 80 Hornsgatan—Stockholm.

Baltimore, Maryland
January 8, 2010

Dear Peter,

I leave you pining for Nellie today, yet holding tight to your mission calling, your heart caught between your mind and your soul. Has there ever been any other true dilemma? Already, your first love "meeting" has moved into the realm of nostalgia, a picture no longer tangible or real: only a memory.

I remember the day my mother got the call from my brother three quarters of the way through his mission. He told her he was leaving his mission. He had met a girl. The true love turned out to be a woman he met while pounding doors in Ogden, Utah. He brought her back to Maryland. She was a beautiful red-head, but turned out to also be beautifully unstable. Within a few weeks her issues started to surface and she eventually returned to Utah, alone, and my brother returned to life, alone, without a woman or a finished mission.

He assimilated back into life, slowly, in small steps, as one does when moving from one extreme to another. He got a job in the private sector, bought some new clothes, and purchased an old row home downtown that he spent the next few years restoring. He was quiet about the whole thing. He didn't ruffle any feathers.

Did he regret leaving early after finding out that the love of his life was not the love he thought her to be? Did he feel tricked, pulled by alluring legs away from his spiritual calling?

"He can't leave. He still has four months left!" the mission president demanded in his separate phone call.

My mother spoke back, with defense in her voice: "I know, but he is. He's coming home." It sounded like they were talking about someone in a war, stationed overseas, ready to desert in the middle of a strategic operation. My mother had the guilt of aiding a fugitive in her voice.

Leaving early is not acceptable on a mission, especially if it is for love. A life-threatening illness or serious injury might constitute coming home, but not love. Love takes away from the mission goal, as it distracts, distorts, and causes all sorts of mayhem that can't be allowed. Love makes missionaries come home early.

The church hopes to nip Love in the bud before it has a chance to affect one's mission, to keep the opportunity for temptation so small that Love cannot nest its complicated claws into a young missionary. But, as I see from your and Nellie's letters, as well as my brother's mission experience, love usually wins out. It is too strong a need to deny. Sometimes, just walking by someone is all it takes. Paths collide. Roads open that were not there minutes ago. Detours announce themselves in new intersections. Even with its often risky consequences, love wins out. And what a horrible world it would be if it didn't.

Love,
Kathy

Robinson
July 7, 1901

My Dear Peter:

You will think soon that there is not much use in writing to
such a neglective girl as I. You will think if neglective now, she
will be in the future. But I won't Peter. I am tired to-night. That
does not sound well to say I am tired on the Day of Rest does
it? But it has not been a day of rest for me. Peter I have been
so busy for the past week that I had scarcely time to eat the
cold meals that have been brought to me. I have been the only
operator at this office for the last week night and day both.
I did not think there would be so much work to do, when I
came, as there is. But I have gone through the worst of it now
so I should not like to give it up now, for something just as
hard and maybe harder. The worst is that it is so confining.
But I can have Vina learn and we can relieve each other. I am
getting so I really like the position. There are so many nice
girls along the line. For two weeks before I came to work
here Mama was ill and I was kept quite busy at home. On
the fourteenth of last month, there came to our house a dear
little angel brother, but because Mama will again be restored
to her health Mama and baby are doing very nicely, now for a
name. There isn't one of us that wants the same name. I like
Hugh, because it means "spirit." Vina prefers Carl. We all rather
like Frank. Suppose we will all decide upon some nice name,
when the time comes for us to name the little darling.

Sunday the fourteenth. Isn't it dreadful, but I have just been
so busy the last week that I could not write. I wrote you a
letter the twenty fifth of June, but did not send it. Will tell
you some day why I did not. I received your last dear letter
yesterday. Peter will you forgive me for my neglect? Little did
I think just a year ago when I promised to wait, that I should
be so neglective in writing. I am afraid I do not realize and

appreciate the blessings I have. I aught to be—and I am the happiest girl alive. I am more than sorry that I wrote you as I did last time, I was a little down hearted. But why should I be, so, when I have so much to make me happy. I cannot tell, yet I sometimes feel a little "blue." Perhaps it is because I am not situated so I can accomplish some of the nice little things that I should like too. But your dear good letter encourages me, and it is as you say Peter, I am wealthy. And I aught to be very thankful for it. I am. So will not complain anymore.

This has certainly been a very dull summer, for Vina and I compared with last. Our Fourth celebration, the dances, wedding receptions that we enjoyed last summer are recalled with much pleasure. I never imagined that I should ever spend such a Fourth as I did last Saturday here in this office all day. This was the dullest place on earth that day. Most every body went down to the valley. I was kept busy straightening up the checks and bills for the past three days. I came in on the first. The toll line was down for two days before, you can imagine just how busy I was for the first two or three days. Really I hardly knew where I was. I almost gave up in despair. I didn't and now it is quite pleasant. If it were not for the scoldings I get when I cannot get the stock brockers just when some of the mining men want them. But then I don't mind when I can't see them. Then again I wish I was where some people are, that I talk too. Was talking to Mt. Pleasant night before last. How I wished I was there, or driving from there to Fairview.

I am thinking of the night I had such a pleasant drive with one I love, and we invented a little joke. How I should like just such another drive. Maybe I will some day with this self-same young man—only under different circumstances. O how grand it will be.

The 19th. Peter you will never forgive me. I have been so neglective of you dear. It is a year ago today since you left Fairview. I shall never forget just how I felt that day. I am so glad you are well. Forgive me Peter for not writing more.

I received the pictures alright. They are just lovely. And the moss and relief card are very nice Peter.

Hope you receive the parcel that I sent you. I will write you a long letter Sunday in answer to your two dear letters. Sundays are the only days that I have anytime at all. If you were here Peter—I should allow more than two of what those signs represent, attached to your signature. Put in two or more in every letter. A dozen if you like, but that isn't necessary.

With my love and best wishes. I am livingly yours.

Nellie X X

Baltimore, Maryland
February 1, 2010

Dear Nellie,

You wait so patiently for Peter's return, more patiently than I could ever wait, within the clatter of your switchboard office, holding in your breath through these long days. I see you there, perhaps myself a little too, taking on your small world of paper and wires, trying to connect others' lives through your own voice, scampering to meet all of their needs.

What do I really know of waiting? I no longer need to even wait for the mail, as all good news comes in email form and the mailbox (before, a designated spot of anticipation) is now only the dreaded birther of bills.

My pregnancies were probably my longest periods of waiting, 9 months felt like 9 years at the time, though I know they were nothing compared to the burden your own mother must have felt while on bed rest, waiting for the son you mention was just born.

Do we miss something these days with our lack of waiting, when the click of a button brings a person's current status into view within seconds? Waiting is almost obsolete, on the top of the endangered list, an endearing condition of the past. "Now" is the standard, not "when."

Perhaps, waiting has just gone into remission, quietly waiting to rear its inevitable head when I least expect it to return, when my life check-off list is almost complete and what I have left are the thoughts I don't want to think about—the only things that truly wait, until I finally have to face them.

> *Your great-granddaughter, in-waiting.*

Vesteras, Sv.
August 20, 1901

My Dear Nellie:

Thanks for your good letter bearing postmark of July 19.
Would have answered before, but as you said you would
write again on the following Sunday. I thought I would wait
for your 2nd letter as it would only be a matter of 3 or 4 days
of waiting. I perceive that you were not able to get the letter
off as you intended. Your many new duties hindered you
from doing what you intended to do. Perhaps I shall have a
letter from you awaiting me at Stockholm when I go up next
week. Our conference was postponed until the 27 or 28 of
this mo. Instead of 18th. Huru harligh skulle det icke vara
at ha min fostmo med mig da vi till Stockholm ga Seglande
ofer Molorens glansande vatten. Huru harligh det skulle vara
att mad herme skada fran botens dek den harlig skona kring
liggande nature—A little Swedish for you to grapple with—
Forward my sincere congratulations to your Mama, Vina and
yourself on the arrival of your young brother. Glad to know
that both are doing nicely. Hope that he will grow up to be a
blessing to his mama and papa and that your mama will be
restored to her normal health again. Those most appropriate
gifts you sent me are probably lost. Sorry that such a package
should go astray, a package with such presents that I should
have devotedly cherished. It grieves me when I think of those
presents, that it should happen that they should go astray. I
have made enquiries at the P.O. here regarding the matter.
The authorities say that it is the sender's duty to first institute
a search for the missing parcel. So Nell you will please inform
your P.M. of the matter and have him send out a "tracer" or
investigate the matter. I suppose you did not register the
package. When did you send it? And did you address to me
at Stockholm? Perhaps Nellie will not object to enclosing a
little lock of her hair in her next letter so that even if the mails

have cheated me out of the tokens of my sweetheart's love,
I shall have some substantial keepsake in addition to what
I already have, i.e., her photo, letters, etc. Since last I wrote
you I have been on a number of "land turer". Last Sunday
we held meetings here in a pretty forest or grove outside of
town. Mayor refused us privilege of using a popular grove that
belongs to the city—consulted another party who offered us
use of his grove, but later through influence of some of the
dignitaries, he went back on his promise. Our 3rd attempt was
successful though the place was not so suitable or attendance
so large it otherwise would have been. I enjoy the work and
am contented and feel that the Lord is with me and have seen
his power manifested in different ways.

How are you getting along? With your work at the exchange?
Glad to hear that you are beginning to enjoy the labor. You no
doubt must have been rushed the first few days, and no doubt
your time is well occupied all the time. Hope you shall enjoy
your labor as long as it may be your wish or desire to pursue it.
Over 10 days since I heard from home. Hope to get letter with
news of home and town. Has your cousin P. been to Utah yet? If
he has been down to Zion he probably did not go to Fairview.
My cousin Heber-also H.P. Hanson and Fred Christiansen are
home from their fields or labor and, I am informed go with
girls as follows—Heber—Helena A.; Hans P.—Selma Ny.; Fred
C.- Vina Brady. The last name probably is either your sister or
your relative. Bro. John has taken May C. out occasionally while
Carl goes with May Bon. Jo Hanson, I am informed will move
to Idaho, in connection with some of his brothers, and operate
a fruit farm. Now Nellie, please give my regards to your Mama
and Vina. It would please me if Vina would "drop a line or two"
in with your letter sometime. Excuse my hurry and consequently
poor writing. I doubt you can read it.

> With love to Nellie
> *P. Sundwall Jr.*

Baltimore, Maryland
February 15, 2010

Dear Peter,

It has been days that I have been stuck behind the wires, too: my sick daughter whining for water and stomach rubs, my graduate books closed and winking their guilty eyes at me.

"Try coloring for awhile," I finally told her when I couldn't take another minute of a purple dinosaur dancing and singing around the cheap, cardboard television stage set.

When she thumbed through her new blank coloring book of colorless girls, I decided to try out my own informal variation of the doll's test, a test about racial preference in children that I just learned about in one of my doctoral classes, which shows that most children pick white dolls over black dolls, regardless of their race.

"Find the prettiest girl," I instructed. She eventually found the page with the prettiest girl, at least in her opinion, which meant a cute mini-skirt and long, curling eyelashes. I pulled out three markers—one bright yellow, one red, and one brown.

"What color hair does the prettiest girl have?" I asked her. I, honestly, thought she would pick the yellow hair, to crown her girl with the soft curls of sunshine and shiny gold, the yellow of her Barbie's unattainable scalp. Or, perhaps, she would pick red, the fire of the Little Mermaid's locks, the red of adventure and a life of scales and underwater breathing. I expected her to go right along with the rest of the doll's test results.

"No, Mom!" she snapped. "None of these are the hair of the prettiest girl!"

She huffed. "Mom, she has blue hair—that's the prettiest girl!"

Then she looked at me like I was the stupidest person on the planet.

"Of course," I thought, as I quickly searched for the blue. How silly of me to think she would fall for the three colors I had placed in front of her, instead of the ones that were out of my view but not her imagination.

Her answer has stayed with me through the rest of the week, as I waited on her, received an email from my son's math teacher, strongly suggesting an in-person conference, and felt the weight of trying to do everything while accomplishing nothing.

Blue hair, I tell myself: the choice not given. How many other choices do we miss simply because we are only looking in front of us? Tonight, I think I will color a strand of my hair blue with a magic marker. So I won't forget.

> What you don't see. . .
> *me!*

Stockholm
August 31, 1901

Dear Nellie,

How is my Nellie getting along? Well I hope. I hope her health
is good and though she is busy at the telephone post she
enjoys life and feels O.K. I had hoped to hear again from you
er this, but you probably have been very busy so that your
work has interfered. Maybe you sent your letter to Vesteras
so that it is lying in the box down there. We have just held a
conference and have had a most pleasant time. Ap. Lyman has
been with us. I leave in less than 3 hours for the docks where
I shall take boat for Orebro. I shall spend a few days in Orebro
after which I shall go to Varmland to my mother's birth place
where I expect now to do missionary work for some months.
We probably will have our quarters in city of Karlstad which
is not such a great distance from the borders of Norway or
city of Kristiania the Norway capital. Hope to get see Norway
and Christiania and also Bro. Larsen who is working in the
conference. Orebro, you well remember was the place where
I was first sent to on arriving in Sweden. I shall be pleased
to again see the city and good saints who kindly received
me when I came as a stranger to both the country and the
language.

The Swedish summer is no more nor the long bright lights that
characterize the Swedish summer. Our evenings are more like
the nights we have at home, and the bright moon shines down
upon the Swedish landscapes as serenely as it shines upon
vales in Utah. The moon for 2 months or more has scarcely
been visible on account of the long days. Now it shines as it
did some more than a year ago when I was home and spent
my most enjoyable nights with you. The moon's reappearance
after its summer absence makes me think of those few but
happy occasions when I was with Nellie. To night I sail down

the lake and beautiful canal to Orebro. Will be sailing all night. The moon will probably smile down on the deck passengers and make nature look beautiful. The moon rays will probably stream across the dancing waves. To night I shall allow my thoughts to revert back to the beautiful moonlight nights of a year ago. I shall make no effort to restrain myself, but just think of those pleasant, happy occasions that once were and of the prospective occasions that sometime will be.

I shall not say much more but will close for this time. Hope I shall not have to wait long before I get a good, sweet letter from Nellie. Most refreshing things they are and when there is a delay in coming of the letters I don't feel just right. Time goes fast—I hope it does for Nellie. I look forward to time when I shall have filled a sacred mission and when I can with a good conscience and with the blessings of the good saints here leave for America or Zion to my folks and sweet-heart Nellie. I hope you receive the Ladies Home Journal. I ordered the magazine to be sent to you for another year. Well Nellie, please accept same as a little token of my sincere love for Nellie—Love in fullest sense of the term. May Heaven bless her and protect her. Hoping that she will not have too much trouble in reading this so-hurriedly written letter. I remain with love to her, Vina and Mama but most for her—(Nellie)

> Affectionately
> *P. Sundwall Jr. X X*

P.S. Address me for present Hornsgatan 80 Stockholm

Baltimore, Maryland
February 25, 2010

Dear Peter,

I understand your words, "When I came as a stranger to both
the country and the language," though I have always felt like a
stranger in my own land and with my own language. Each day,
I wrestle with my language like it is a slippery serpent trying
to wind its way out of my grip. Each day, I open my eyes to a
place that could be familiar, but isn't quite. Becoming fluent in
another language is impossible for me to comprehend at this
point in my life.

There is now a Language Training Program incorporated into
the Missionary Training Center in Utah, for young missionaries
to get crash courses in languages before they venture out into
the field. I always picture the young missionaries-in-training
wearing silver helmets, wired up to a central computer that
recites declension drills directly from God. As with everything
in religion, languages can be learned in mere days with divine
intervention, spells can be undone, but alas, my brother was
even too-focused challenged to receive a calling that required
a foreign language. The only language he needed for Ogden,
Utah was a crisp "Good Morning."

When I was younger, I could almost see the spiritual power
coming down from Heaven, straight into the high seats of the
row of priesthood men at the front of the Sacrament Meeting.
God's invisible rod tapped each one of them on the head,
transferring the mission callings for that year. The Priesthood
men were his extended fingers, the words for his silent
commands. I figured God was supposed to look something
like the Priesthood men, as they all looked like cleaned up,
conservative versions of other people's grandfathers, certainly
not my father's father-- who chewed tobacco, told dirty jokes,

and was always dribbling brown spit down the front of his
shirt.

> A stranger,
> *your great-granddaughter, Katherine Cottle*

Robinson, Utah
August 25, 1901

My Dear Peter:

I do not know what you are thinking of me this morning. Yet
I am very happy. The reason is because I am at home and
have time to write to you. Every day since I received your dear
letters I have thought that not another day would pass until
I would write to you. I have been at the telephone office to
close. One would think that I have plenty of time there to do
all the writing I wish to do. When I am not at work I have to
make out the bills and enter every day's work into a ledger.
The work is very confining. I get so tired that I doze to sleep
just as soon as I get home at night. There is so much to do
at home. Feel as if I aught to stay home. Yet I can not earn
much at home, and as you know Peter it is hard for a girl
to accomplish much without a little money. I asked if I may
have this afternoon off. Because I would not let another day
pass without writing to you dear. And then the children and
Vina are not well and I could not leave Mama with all the
work to do. We all have colds but Vina is not able to sit up
hardly. There is ever so much sickness here. I think this is not
a healthy place at all. Wish we did not live here. I tell Mama
if I get away from here once I will not come back. Mama said
she would not let me go, because I will have to leave her soon
enough. I will stay if it is Mama's wish.

I had a nice letter from Lois. Perry is married, and Lois is soon
to be. Sent hers, and Roseltha's picture. Look just like they
used to only a little older. We heard that Silma Lawsen and Jim
Calston, Nellie Lawsen and Manuel Alred, Maud Anderson and
Cris are to be married. Maud must have forgotten her promise.
Do you remember? My I should like to go to Fairview. I think
there is no place like Fairview. Did you know that Roselpha
Nottstrom was married? She and her mother came out here this

spring. Meet a young man, and within a few months they were married. The name is Betts. They seem to be perfectly happy. Hope they will continue to be so. Mrs. Voo is separated from her husband. Their wedded life was not very long.

I will tell you just how I spent the holidays. We all stayed here. I sat in the office. I thought of just a year ago and of the pleasant time we had. I started to write you on the twenty fourth of July, but did not finish my letter. I don't think that I could count the letters I have started and not finished. Every time I would start anew and think nothing would prevent my finishing it. But something would and I would lay my letter aside.

I spent the Twenty Fourth very differently from what I did last year. You remember I had the honor of representing Utah. I was happy that day yet I was sad too, for it was so soon after my lover's departure. I realize more fully now what going on a mission means. Am so happy to know that he whom I love is on a mission, and that it will not be long before he will return.

Oh! How glad we all will be Peter to receive you. Do you remember the night of Oscar Hansen's reception? I remarked something about how nice it would be to receive you when you would have returned from your mission. In my heart I secretly wished that it may be my lot to receive you as I hoped to, and will. Yet I did not think I ever should. I dreamed of you last night dear. But it was different from what I usually dream. You were with me, but this time you came and were not pleased with me. Yet it was through my neglect that you were not. I asked you to forgive me but you were not willing to do so. I cannot describe how I felt. I am so glad it was a dream and not a reality. But you will forgive me won't you Peter?

The dream impressed me so, is the reason I tell you of it. I think it came to me as a warning. That if I continue to be so neglective, my lover will come back very much disappointed in me. And that would break my heart. For you know Peter how I love you. I will not make any more promises for I do not like to break them, but I think I shall not be so heartless again.

Your letters are so sweet and good. I should like to read them and answer all the questions, but I haven't time. Must go to work at noon. What a beautiful place Gafle is! How I should like to walk down one of those beautiful streets with you. Am so glad you meet Willie Neilson, or Elder Swen Neilson and those other dear Elders. I can remember Bro. Neilson quite well. It will soon be time for him to return will it not?

Peter I want to mail this letter today so you will pardon my hurry. Yes, Peter, our Father in heaven will bless you and I. With health and every blessing that we desire. Hope you are well my lover. Take good care of yourself.

I hope you will get or have gotten that parcel I sent you. The pictures are just fine. And Peter to have your photo to gaze on is such a comfort to me.

Mama and Vina send best love and wishes to you.

I close hoping you will forgive me Peter. With all my love I am

Ever yours.
Nellie

Baltimore, Maryland
March 14, 2010

Dear Nellie,

I had nightmares last night, too, one vivid one in which I was
on the top level of a cruise ship, playing a silly game where
the cruise director sent everyone scurrying to one side of the
boat, making the ship tip and flip completely over, turning
itself all the way under the water and back up again. I grabbed
a hold of a pole and held my breath as soon as the water hit
my ankles, the cold tongue of the sea swallowing then spitting
me out like a bad meal. My husband and children were all
under deck, scattered in different rooms and places; the kids'
club, the arcade, the bar. I found myself frozen, not knowing
where to go first. The other passengers screamed and tripped
over one another, while my feet remained bolted to the wood
planks of the deck.

I woke then, my hands clutched around my torso in a hot
sweat. I touched my daughter, fast asleep next to me in the
bed, feeling her skin rise in unworried rhythmic breaths.

This has often been the pattern of my dreams: fearing one
thing after another, my feet frozen, first because of childhood
monsters, then devils I found out were sometimes real,
sometimes just in my head. During my school years my
dreams usually included long hallways with rusty lockers that
I could never unlock and classes that started before I could
find their unnumbered rooms. Somehow, the credibility of
my life depended on my responsibility to get to these places.
If I didn't figure out a way to un-glue my feet and get to the
needed destination, life would unravel and everything would
be a complete waste, all because of my one mistake.

I have good dreams, too, but they are usually forgotten, as
all pleasant things are, while the sharp and painful ones nest

themselves into the back of my mind for years.

I still remember one particularly frightening dream of a horned devil-man who broke into my childhood home and tried to kill all of my family members with an ax (this was coincidentally while I read *The Shining*). Perhaps, that is why I gravitated to scary movies as a child, as they brought these monsters to light for the whole room to see and showed ways to defeat them. And, usually, the child in the movie is the only one to make it out alive.

I've read that a lot of writers are attracted to horror movies and books at an early age. Horror creates that transitional landscape that is part imagination part realism, a blend of past and present for the child. Horror tales credit the true nightmares children often feel swarming around in their heads. This was definitely the case with me and Stephen King. I broke into *Carrie* in Junior High School and never looked back. King's words carried just enough violence and sex to keep me interested, yet also enough plot and character development for my early teenage mind to understand there was craft involved in the literary process. King could do anything in his books and never end up in jail. He could injure an annoying character, kill the enemy, sleep with the prettiest woman, and then decide to throw everyone over the bridge to the starving alligators, all with just a few sentences and periods.

I pushed an onion skin paper through my dad's typewriter when I was twelve and tried to write a page like one I had recently read in *Cujo*. I included at least five uses of "fuck," some bloody wounds, and a skinny blond woman with big boobs and high heels who always forgot to wear her underwear. I read the selection over a couple of times and stuffed it into the back of my desk drawer so my parents wouldn't find it.

A lot of professors bash Stephen King. He isn't usually

included in the literary canon. But, he was much more influential on me as a young writer than any author from a literature anthology. He allowed me the rebellion that I needed, without the ramifications of actual actions and consequences. He provided the outlet and the escape for my restless and dark thoughts. Honestly, if it wasn't for him, I don't think I would have ever considered publishing my writing. His books grew past the structure of "books" for me: they weren't just words, pages, and a spine to me. They were places where I wasn't allowed to go in my real life, people with whom I would have been forbidden to associate, yet they were there, sitting on the sale shelf at the local mall Waldenbooks. King wasn't just writing stories for me, he was writing me from his stories.

And to this day, I don't really picture what I am writing as poems, essays, stories, letters, or books-- just paper and words that allow the daydreams and nightmares a place to go, a papyrus room where they can run around in play-penned safety: an invisible zoo where they can live in cages without bars.

Awake,
Kathy

Ana-Frykerud Varmland
Sept. 19, 1901

My Dear Nellie:

Rec'd your good letter yesterday. Thanks for same. I do not think I can attach any blame to Nellie for not being able to write. She is so confined to her work that I can perceive that she has not the time. I hope that she will get a change or that her present duties will so moderate as to allow her of more freedom. If I have anything to forgive Nellie for I freely do it.

Hope you are well from your colds at this writing and that your mama and the jr. member of your family are O.K. On this last trip—first for me in these parts—we went into a district where Elders before had not trod. We came to a good lady's house who recognized us as Zion's Elders for she had seen us in a dream. We held a successful meeting at her place to an audience of over 40 interested listeners. We return to the place the 13 of Oct. to hold another meeting and baptize 3 souls who believe us to be the only messengers of the gospel of Christ in its purity and completeness. A lady in the house here in which we are staying will probably embrace baptism. Thus you see the Lord is blessing our efforts. In a letter I rec'd yesterday I hear again of marriages. It is getting to be an old story. C.O. and Maudie and you mention prospective weddings of Selma and Nellie also Ros. Nordstroms. They tell me of the boom Fairview is favored with. They have it appears discovered gold and petroleum there in the neighborhood. I hope Nell will some time in the near future find opportunity of going out to Fairview and renewing her acquaintanceship with some of the people there—particularly with our folks.

Yours with love, *P.*

Baltimore, Maryland
April 2, 2012

Dear Peter,

Your quick letter today is just the right length for me to read, as I have tons of school work waiting for me on the dining room table. I don't know if I am biting off more than I can chew by working on these letters, as well as all my other critical and creative projects. I am on a bit of a treasure hunt without a map, trusting my mind to point me in the right direction, though its compass isn't securely in place. I am scared, too, of failure, of the responsibility of beginning two large projects at one time. I think, however, that I do not have a choice.

It occurs to me how much my life is one of the mind; creative and academic endeavors that push and pull me into new landscapes, much like yours do too, Peter. I often forget my body is even there; arms and legs dangling down, feet in shoes, and underwear on somewhere below my pants. Sometimes, I look in the mirror and do not recognize myself. Not that I think I look different, better or worse, only that I forget a face is there, as well as two eyes, a mouth, and a few pimples that continually replace themselves. My perception is skewed, I am sure, too tilted inward than is healthy. I visualize currents and tree branches, waves and small knots on my external self, more than lips or a nose, bushy eyebrows or grey brown hair. I expect to see haystacks or dripping icicles coming out from my skin, not yellowing teeth or a new brown mole on my cheek.

Meanwhile, my husband, like your Nellie, scrambles through days of long labor, hours driving on the road to document damage from car and truck accidents. He takes pictures in the rain, in muddy tow lots, in impound yards, in back fields and driveways. He sees vehicles full of crash and injury, lights broken, necks broken, fenders smashed, lives smashed and stolen. He meets anger face-to-face on the front door steps, sometimes finding bullet holes and blood in the seats, sometimes smiles, sometimes lies, sometimes just a scratch on the bumper, sometimes tears. And then, he works on the computer well into the night, plugging in his numbers, emailing the body shops, the insurance companies, digits clicking from screen to screen in numeric blurs. His weekends are packed with the household chores I never volunteer to do: mowing the lawn, replacing broken pipes, fixing the water heater and the cracked windows.

"Don't you want to work on a creative project?" I asked while we watched a crime drama in the basement.

"When would I do it?" he said. "There's no time."

The next day he pulled out his old unfinished models from before we had kids—a WWII airplane wood kit that contained a collage of toothpicks, a fragile pinned backbone.

"Don't you want to leave your mark on the world?" I questioned him. "Something for your descendants to see?"

"I'm not like you," he stated, fitting another wood splinter into the arch of the plane's spine. "I'm only here for a lifetime."

> Temporarily,
> *your descendent*

Robinson, Utah
September 20, 1901

My Dear Peter:

Your last dear letter came some time ago. Am so glad I am
able to answer it. I have had the Typhoid fever, and am just
able to get around again. Was ill for nearly three weeks.
My hands shake so badly I can scarcely write. The only
nourishment they gave me was milk. I can assure you I did
not gain much on that diet. They all laugh at me, I have gotten
so poor. I could not read your letter for several days after it
came. It did me so much good to get it. Peter I cannot tell you
how sorry I am, that you did not get that parcel I sent. Very
foolish of me, but I did not register it. I was quite hurried the
day I mailed the package and did not think to register it. Just
as soon as I can get to the office I will do my best to have the
missing package found. The chain is what I cared for most. It
was quite pretty. And I did so much want you to get it. This
will teach me to be more careful hereafter. Mama and Vina
wanted to write while I was not able. But Vina had to take
my place at the exchange, and Mama was so busy with all the
work to do, and attending to me. Am so thankful to be able
to get around again. I can more fully appreciate the blessings
I enjoy. How grand it is to enjoy good health. I should dislike
very much to be ill much of the time. Think I will be able to
go to work next week. I will have all the bills to make out and
all the work to enter into the ledger. I will be busy for some
time. One more month at the exchange and then I will leave.

Mr. Pritchett has decided to go to Arizona. Mama and the
children will go out home the first of next month. But I will
remain here for another month to instruct someone to do
the work. I shall be so glad to go out home again. Hope we
will not leave there until you return. Mr. Pritchett intends to
have Mama come to Arizona in the Spring, but I hope she

can stay until fall. Mama knows that if she went with her husband now she would have to leave her girls in Utah, and that Mama could never do. Mama is such a hand to worry about her children. I am glad she worried about me enough to have me come to Utah from Arizona. For all I had so many more advantages there. Suppose I will not get an opportunity to attend school. I had planned to stay at the exchange until Xmas. I could have gone to school from then until spring very nicely. But this move that Mr. P. is to make will keep me from carrying out my plans. And to remain here I will have to pay so much for the board that it will not pay me to do so. To live here with the folks is bad enough. After they are gone it will be hard indeed. Hope we will never come back to Robinson.

I have accomplished so little of what I desired to, that I sometimes feel a little discouraged. Yet I should not when I have so much to be thankful for. I may yet have an opportunity to accomplish some of the things I should like to most. I have promised Mrs. Frank Pritchett that I will spend this afternoon with her. It is just about time to go. It will be the second time I have been out since I was ill. I went to the station last night to get a box of flowers that a girl friend of mine at Lehi sent to me. One day this summer we had a Sunday School conference, and went to Lehi. I went down. The only day I got off, and the only time I have been to the valley since I came over here. I tried to get Vina to go but she did not care to. I enjoyed the day ever so much. There are many nice girls there. I became so well acquainted with the operator at Lehi through the telephone, so I thought I should like to see her. There is a family of five girls, and they are all operators but the youngest. They are just lovely. I think so much of them. It was one of these girls who sent me the flowers. We appreciate anything like flowers because we see so few of them.

I will finish to-morrow as I must go.

The 21st.

I feel much stronger tonight. There has been so much to do that I did not get at my writing early.

George Young called in for a short time this afternoon. Tells us that he intends to go home soon to prepare to attend the L.D.S. Business College. So glad he has decided to go to school. Wish more boys would use their earnings to do the same. Sad that George's brother and father should pass away so suddenly.

George and I used to have great times when we went to school. We have just been talking over some of the good times we used to have. I enjoyed my visit with Mrs. Pritchett's cousin. They are from Mt. Pleasant. Think I shall stay with those people after Mama goes.

The news I wrote you about those people getting married came to us in a letter from home. The person who wrote it was just supposing. Because I have been told by people from home that the Larson girls had no intention of getting married. Maud must have forgotten what she promised you that night at the dance. Do you remember? I should have liked very much to have been present at Maud's and Cris's wedding. They will surely be happy in their wedded life. There is but a few girls left at home. Those that are left will be "old maids" soon.

I am so glad you are doing so well with the grand and noble work. How I should like to be present at your conference this month.

I should like very much to be able to read and understand the Swedish you have written. But I cannot. Hope I will be able to understand Swedish some day.

We are very proud of our baby brother. He is getting to be such a big boy. Mama gave him the name of Frank Carl. Carl is Vina's choice. I had nothing to say about the naming of the baby. But that is alright, the name pleases me.

Am glad you were successful in getting a grove to hold your meeting in. How selfish those other people were not to let you use those groves that would have been more suitable. You could not help but enjoy the work you are engaged in. I know the Lord will bless you as you should be blessed.

Yes, Perry came and was married, and has returned, but did not come to see us. Aunt Mary said they were detained by a washout on the road and had to get back at a certain time, is the reason they did not get to see any of their friends and relatives.

Yes I should like very much to see and hear the returned missionaries talk. They say your cousin Heber is a fine speaker. I shall have that pleasure sometime this winter I hope. The Vina that Fred C. goes with is a relative of ours. Her father is a cousin of ours. I asked John to write to me, but he has not as yet. Suppose he has been very busy.

Carl and Miss Barker seem to agree very well. They have gone together quite a long time. They were going together before I left Fairview.

Peter I subscribed for the L.H. Journal for another year. I received a card some two or three days ago telling me; that at your request they had entered my name for a year's subscription to the Journal. Thank you dear Peter. But what shall I tell them to do? Hold one over until next year? I do love the Journal. I could not get along without them. They are so much comfort. There is such a sweet story in the last four numbers. Vina is sitting by us now reading the last Journal.

Thank you for your dear letters Peter, and the lovely pictures and many other nice keep-sakes you have sent to me. How I shall enjoy showing them all to my friends when the time comes.

Dear I have written a long letter, but nothing to amount to much. I cannot think well as yet. I will try and write soon. Must not make promises as I did before. Vina said she would write some other time. She is tired tonight. You will think someone is tired too from the looks of this writing.

I send a small lock of my hair and some of those flowers I received. Accept same with my best love.

> Goodnight Peter
> With love I am yours
> *Nellie*
>
> (In Morse Code: I love you)

Baltimore, Maryland
April 21, 2010

Dear Nellie,

I was supposed to get up at 5 am this morning, so that I could devote an hour to writing before the kids woke up. But I pressed snooze instead, after a bad night's sleep, and now I will be lucky to get this response down, and even luckier to get a shower before I have to drive my son to school. My daughter is off for conferences today, and I am babysitting my niece since my sister's daycare provider is sick. So, in other words, nothing will get accomplished today, other than keeping children alive.

I think that watching kids is the hardest job in the world. I can't even imagine the stress that women of your generation faced with so many children, spread across so many years of your life. Your letter today mentions Frank Carl, your new baby brother, which means there was a twenty year stretch in between your mother's children. I can't imagine.

I have heard some children listen. I have heard some people say they enjoy going on outings with their entire family. I have heard of something called Sanity, and something called Patience. These are other people's relatives.

I have heard, "It gets easier." I have heard, "It gets harder." The teenage years are already carving their upcoming scars in my mind: yellow caution tape slapped around wet narrow alleys, dark rain leaving puddles across my brain.

"Enjoy it now," I tell myself, and then hear myself reprimand, "How many times have I told you not to leave your trash on my desk!" I search for a form to capture the stair steps that wind their way up my fraying nervous system:

Don't fight

(Burmese Climbing Rhyme)

Mother said, strong
in her song of
love: long hot days

where we dragged her
down, further then
further still. Not

a care, just us
and the fuss we
knew must make some-

thing come alive,
to survive hours
stuck, striving for

more than what we
were—to be her,
to see like her.

Don't fight, I say
the same way, yet
this day it sounds

like some other
voice, mother of
other children,

no magic stored
in its words, no
key curled inside

its tongue, just sound
and its grounding.
Love found, in pain.

Yesterday, while reading the love letters of H.L. Mencken
and Sara Haardt for my dissertation, I chuckled at Mencken's
annoyance at his nine-year-old niece, who comes to stay with
him and prevents him from getting any work done. She, too,
like my children, "must have a thousand legs," her physicality
in constant resistance to his stationary writing life. In another
letter to Haardt he asks about her nephew, who is dealing
with the mumps. Sarcastically, he remarks, "at least it (mumps)
keeps them quiet."

And so I see it has been this way since the beginning of
children, which had to be the true beginning of the fusion
of love and hate. It is noteworthy, too, that so many prolific
writers and artists do not have any children. Deep down, I
think I want both part-time: writing and children. In fact, I
think I want everything part-time, including myself. If only I
could have a long lunch break from myself, a mid-afternoon
siesta in which I break away from my body and mind and just
float away in blissful ignorance or escape into the solid sleep
I never get at night, my dark hours filled instead with tossing,
turning, and dreaming.

Earlier this week, for instance, I woke from a nightmare about
my son's recent creepy declaration that there is a ghost girl
living in our basement laundry room. He told me that she runs
away when I go in there, which is why only he can see her.

"How did she get in the laundry room?" I asked him.

"When you were on the operating table and the doctor took
Ellie out, she came out too. I saw her standing next to the
doctor, and then she came home with us."

I flinched at the story. "Oh, Addison, there aren't any ghosts in the house."

"You don't see her," he said. "She runs away when you go near her. She doesn't like you."

And my nightmare took up where his real story left off, and I woke up in a sweat, my second miscarriage, the one before my daughter, snarling its failed and bloody face like an angry demon.

> Do you ever dream about
> a great-granddaughter?

Ana Linedal
Vermland
October 17, 1901

My Dear Nellie:

Your good letter came to hand last week for which thanks. I
was indeed surprised to hear that you had been ill and even
had had typhoid fever, and you only mention the matter
incidentally in your letter. I can well guess you have been
severely sick although you do not say so. I hope though that
the sick spell did not so reduce you but what you will regain
your normal health, etc. Hope you henceforth will enjoy the
blessings of good health.

Thanks for the flowers and especially the other keepsake
you sent me. Just arrived from a tour in the country last
night, and among the mail awaiting us was your beautiful
chain and kerchief lying among some papers forwarded from
Stockholm. The package had arrived from what Bro. Anton
says, so tattered and torn that it could not be sent or forwarded
in through the mail in the shape it was. The package could
have been missent to or what can be the cause of the long
delay I do not know. Thanks Nell for the presents. The chain
is indeed charming. I hope to get an appropriate charm to
match and attach to same. Again my sincere thanks for your
good presents which to me are invaluable. Since last I wrote
you it has been our pleasure through the help of the Lord to
make inroads into a new socken and to add 5 souls to our
church and these together with a young lady here whom
it was our privilege to baptize last week make 6 souls that
have embraced the true plan of salvations since we came to
Vermland. Vermland has been considered a hard branch to
work in and no converts have been made here in years. So
you see we have reasons to feel encouraged and jubilant. Our
prospects for the future are also bright. While we succeeded

in reaching a few of the honest in heart we also have raised
a great deal of excitement and stirred up the adversay. We
held our second meeting in the trakt last Sunday. It was a
successful meeting. People congregated from all parts of the
surrounding country for 3 or 4 and even more (English) miles.
The house would not hold the people and we had to take our
position on the outside by the door so that we could address
both the people on the inside and the people on the outside.
It was somewhat cold and damp for those on the outside yet
they were attentive and still during the entire meeting. After
meeting we had a rather noisy crowd to talk to who had taken
offense at our remarks against infant baptism. They also had all
sorts of questions to ask regarding polygamy etc. Our meeting
however was successful and we now have a number of earnest
investigators outside of those we have baptized.

Fall is now in full evidence. The trees outside of those that
belong to the family are yellow. The nights are also long.
Instead of it being light at 10 & 11 o'clock pm as it was during
the summer it is now nearly dark at 6 pm.

And so your folks Mr. Pritchett, your mama and family
contemplate removing to Arizona again? You will quite
be without a home then in case you stay in Utah, as you
contemplated doing. Hope you will find a place which can
serve as a substitute home. Of course, no temporary or
substitute home can fill the place of the home where mother,
brothers, and sisters are to be found.

Am sorry you are thrown out from accomplishing what it
seems it had been your desire to do this coming winter.
Hope however you will have your friends with whom you
can associate and that among some of them you will find an
agreeable home. And if it may not be your good fortune to go
to school or pursue any study I hope you will make the best
of it—feel cheerful and happy. Be sociable, don't sacrifice and
hold yourself from social recreation and amusements. Don't be

too much given up to thinking of the future.

Let those good characteristics and charms which providence has planted in you and which you have developed continue to develop and win for you friends. May your bearing and conduct in society be such that none can impeach the virtue, judgment and good sense of Nellie, and may Heaven bless you. Regards to your mama and Vina.

> Affectionately,
> *Peter*

P.S. Hope you will enjoy yourself in Fairview as long as it is your privilege to stay there. Allow me to remind you that it will be advantageous for us that no one have an inkling into positions as concerns you and me and hope my folks as well as your relatives and friends will have no occasion to suspect anything of the kind until we can with good grace and formality let them know.

N.B. Have sent a postal to Phil. advising them to withhold one of the subscriptions to Journal for a year.

P.S. Address me at Ana-Linedal. Frykerud. Vermland, Sweden.

Baltimore, Maryland
May 30, 2010

Dear Peter,

My mother called yesterday to confirm that we want to go to
the family reunion in Fairview, Utah next summer. She needs
a head count so that we can start planning flights and rooms.
She is generously offering to help with the flights, which is
wonderful since we are down to the wire when it comes
to money these days. Between my Ph.D. program, the kids'
activities, fourth quarter taxes, and medical bills, it is a sorry
state of affairs. I am choosing to look the other way, because it
isn't pretty.

I am hoping to take pictures of the house where you and
Nellie will live, your parents' house, the one in which you will
eventually raise your children, the one my mother remembers
visiting each summer as a child, the one in the town Nellie
misses so often when she is away. But, there is also a part of
me which knows it will also be sad—that the actual place,
seen today, will never live up to the images painted through
your lens. It is your lives that have given them breath, not
their paint or stone foundations. What is it that I am trying to
capture? Your life? Nellie's life? The past? Some place that does
not exist today, except in these letters?

I think I am searching for something that matters, for me and
my children, for something missed, so small that I can point to
a tiny board of your old house and write: here is the splinter,
the beginning of it all. But the more splinters I find, the more
they lead me backwards and forwards in time. Perhaps, my
camera will capture a peeling window sill or the reflection of
the evening sun. The light will show a flicker of a quick kiss
before bed, before your children begged for one more story.
A corner cupboard will darken with its shadow, the long years

after you died, the ten years Nellie continued to awaken by herself.

Maybe it will all be fabricated, my own wants transferred onto the physical place, the landscape actually in my head. The pictures will just show a house, furniture, some beams, and fresh white paint on the porch.

What will I really find?
Your great-granddaughter

Robinson, Utah
October 13, 1901

My Dear Peter:

It being Sunday I have time to write. Your dear good letter
came two or three days ago. Thank you Peter for the same,
I wish I could tell just how much good it did me. I am here
alone now, Mama, Vina, Mr. Pritchett and the children left last
Thursday for Arizona. They are at Fairview now. Will leave for
Arizona tomorrow. I have been almost heart broken. To think
of the folks aging away now. Wish it were next Oct. I feel a
little lonely today. Have the "blues" I guess. I have begun, this
is the fifth letter to you, but have felt too heart-sick I could not
help but write blue letters. Would think—well, I will feel better
tomorrow night. Each time I feel as lonely, will attempt to write
today though I may not be successful.

Am still at the exchange. Will not remain longer than this
month. Life here is too dreary without the folks. Have not as
yet fully decided upon what I will do this winter. Hope I get
a letter tonight telling me to come out home. Mama said she
would tell me if I can get something to do out there. If I do
not go home I will go into the city for the winter. I would have
gone with the folks. But you know why I did not and there is
another reason why I did not go. Some other time I will tell
you. I do wish they were not going. I cannot prevent their
going, will say it is for the best. It was not Mama's desire to go.
Just now anyway. If Mama were well there I should not care so
much. But her health has not been good while she was there.

Are you well? I have gotten strong again. Do hope you keep
well this winter. Do you dread the cold winter weather? It is
quite cold here. Snowed a little some time ago. We have to
have a fire to keep warm. Am glad winter is coming. Shall be
more glad to see it go again. Then I will know that ere another

winter passes I shall see you dear boy. As I told you, I feel lonely. Should like very much to be with you to go to church together. How grand it will be.

Had a nice letter from John or Prof. J. Sundwall. To me he is our jolly John. I can't imagine his being sincere enough for a teacher. But I have only seen him at a party or at home, when the occasion did not demand any seriousness. Vina writes me the news of Fairview. News you have heard ere this.

Am so glad you will be able to visit your mother's birth place. I too hope you will see Norway Christania and Bro. Larsen. Yes I remember your writing from Orebro. Am sure the saints will be as well pleased to see you again as you will be to see them.

Does it seem to you that more than a year has passed since those enjoyable times we spent to-gether? How I should like to be with you on one of those beautiful moonlight nights when you sail down the lake. I can only imagine how beautiful it would be. It is so pleasant to think of the future as well as the past. Sometime you and I will sit in the moonlight, and you will tell me of your noble work and that beautiful country, its people, their habits. You have told me a great deal in your dear letters. But we can talk of it over again.

Yes Peter I received the journal alright. It is just fine. Will send you a copy of the Oct. No. I like it very much. "Aileen" is such a sweet story. I take very much pleasure in reading the Journals. How nice it will be when we can look them over together. Thank you again Peter. Peter I forgot to tell you that I addressed that parcel to Hornsgaten #80 Stockholm. I have sent a tracer. Hope they will find it. I will some other time send some token or tokens of my love for you Peter. Will be more careful in sending them. So they will reach you in safety.

You are holding meeting at that good ladies place. And are to baptize those people today. Indeed the Lord is blessing the Elders.

Yes there are more marriages. It is an old but sweet story.

Fairview has boomed indeed. Isn't it nice? I think I shall go out there for Christmas if not before. I hope to go sooner.

My prayer is for your success, your good health, and safe return. Also for all the other Elders who are called and those who are now in the field. It is time for me to report on the day's work. This is a poor letter Peter. Will try to do better next time.

Here is a good night X with my best love.

Know Mama and Vina send their love.

> Goodnight,
> *Nellie*

Baltimore, Maryland
January 20, 2011

Dear Nellie,

Even in your fifth draft, sadness still seeps through your words, "blues" left from being alone in a desolate town without your family. I don't think I would have coped well either.

Today, a doctor would give you Lexapro and tell you to come back in four to six weeks. I know from experience. In your time, it was the blues. Today we have many other names for it. There is no question that I come from two long lines of people who walked the fine line between genius and madness, who juggled that fragile balance of creativity, drive, anxiety, and depression.

My great-grandmother on my father's side was hospitalized for her "nerves," given shock therapy, and later, a straitjacket. I still have the straitjacket somewhere in the attic. She gave it to me before she died, tidy and folded, with a blood stain on the right tie. I knew her in-person and in voice, unlike you, who I never met or heard, and only know from pictures, letters and other people's memories.

"I told them I have a great-granddaughter who writes. I told them she'll tell my story. She'll tell everyone what they did to me. She'll tell the truth," she said after coming home from the hospital for the last time. They, being the hospital staff, the doctors, her childhood enemies, and eventually everyone who came near her.

I think about the bits and pieces of stories that I overheard as a child, and then attempted to decipher as an adult. I realize I sometimes create events with people who never actually stood together, simply because they came from the same story teller in the family or the same setting. I pieced together the demise

of my great-grandmother on my father's side was because of
a man's bitten ear, a violation, and some water. I don't think
anyone ever told me this. I just listened and saw the segments
of her life like a stuck film, the old projector burning a hole
in her history from its jammed reel. Maybe I was only allowed
to hear parts of the stories, and that is why I had to invent
the rest. I could never sit through the entire afternoons the
relatives on my father's side spent in the living room, drinking
coffee and smoking cigarettes, doing nothing but telling
stories.

As I child, I understood that alternate beginnings and endings
were not only possible but expected, and I didn't need a
timeline to see the interaction between real blood and fake
blood to know they both counted, and to realize that memory,
even if inaccurate, sometimes hurts worse than the actual
incidents.

*

What Was Told

I.

It was the left ear, some said, and it came off without much
struggle, her teeth clamping down and pulling like it was a
piece of tough beef, the gristle barely an interference as she
ripped and didn't stop until the job was done. Some said there
was a lot of blood. Others said that didn't start until after the
ear was gone, and the hole gaped open like a recently robbed
grave.

There wasn't usually the mention of any sounds, just the act.
Like it was done in slow motion, like how a kid yanks off a
band-aid, or picks at a scab until it finally releases from the
skin. No, most just remember the after, not the in-between, or
the before for that matter. It's what she did that lingered. Not
what led up to it, even though that is what held the weight
of her deed, having been hurt enough that she could see her

mouth as a sword, her teeth as shiny metal blades of defense.

II.

Some said it was on Occurrence Bridge, her leg slipping out from beneath her new cotton skirt. The deputy stepped out of his car, and she could see his gun hanging down from his belt, black and limp like a sleeping bat. She tried to tell him that she was just taking the short cut home, that she wasn't doing nothing wrong, not like those other women that walked this way often when their husbands didn't come home for days and the kids cried from being so hungry that the women thought their minds would leak out of their heads. No, she was just walking home late, and no she wasn't trying to tempt him, to laugh at him. She had just stayed too long talking to Millie and found herself here, in her best dress, in the dark, in the middle of the night.

She could hear the water trickling by under the bridge, her mother's hands across the piano, her fingers moving along the riverbed in constant practice, not needing to turn over the rocks to find the music: instead, drifting over the shapes, the smooth pockets, leaving the creatures and the mud underneath still undiscovered.

She felt the sharp pain inside her body, and it was even worse than the first time, when she was only twelve, and Layton, the sixteen-year-old up the road had told her that it would be like kissing, only better. This time, she knew what was coming, and the man on top of her was just that, a man, without the mystery, and she was already a woman, and knew that label was also was nothing like she thought it would be, way back when kissing added to her life instead of taking it away.

It didn't matter that he had a gun when she saw the ear, its curved shell of cartilage calling to her mouth like a beautiful sea find. His black hair framed it in a picture, allowing her to enter, to pass through the pain into the window. He was going inside her, and she needed to go somewhere else. She needed to run, to flee, and the ear was the first thing that she saw that made sense, that showed her there was a hidden tunnel to safety, a place she could enter, where she would be okay.

III.

Some said the water pump had already been removed by that point, replaced with the filtered ease of indoor plumbing. But others said that was where she was, her hand paused between pumps of the rusting iron handle, the bucket half full of the metallic gleam. Her neighbor Louis, drunk to the point of insanity, had surprised her from behind, grabbing her around the neck while the water continued to dribble down into the dark mirror of the wood bucket.

The exact words have been forgotten, but it was noted that they were in German and that Louis had thought he had finally captured the soldier who had haunted him since the war, a smooth faced boy who aged with him, growing wrinkles and hairy growths during his long nights filled with nothing but insomnia and drink.

She could not have translated the foreign language, nor known what it was like for him to watch the seven bullets pump slowly into the chest of his younger brother, nor the fleeting moments of his brother's eyes, as they opened past the point of safe cover, when the body knows it will be ending in a matter of seconds.

She could have felt his hands and she could have smelled the high grain of the alcohol, but she couldn't have ever made him understand that she was not his enemy, that the enemy had actually been shot in the head two weeks after his brother's death. But even that wouldn't have mattered, as Louis had created an enemy who continued to murder his brother, and himself, night after night after night. He had finally come to the realization that the killing needed to be stopped, and put his shaky hands tight around the throat that was right in front of him.

And, even though the neck was smaller and smoother than he had dreamed it would be, it was still strong enough to put up a fight, and he found himself struggling to keep hold because the soldier had tricked him, had sprung a secret weapon on him, and it was causing him to feel numb on the left side of his head, with a weird sensation that he was back on the ship, the rough seas rocking the vessel back and forth, the deck slippery from the urgent rushes of the thick salty water.

IV.

Some still swear it was cold water, while others were sure it was steaming hot, the tub filled to the top, the canvas drape roughly cut with a circle for her head. She had been in bed for 2 weeks, or 8 weeks, or three months. Each version contained a house saturated with the sweet stench of sickness and open windows that wouldn't allow the awful scent to escape.

It was before her second child was born, and after the miscarriage. Or, it was before the miscarriage, and after her first child; a still born, though no one can remember the name of the child, only the house, withering like an old weed, and the amount of blood on the bedroom floor.

She was beyond empty by then: a body with skin and blood but no soul, as it had been pulled away with the deceased child, had followed the child through the hills like a lost echo. She was left with a heart that kept beating, but no words to explain that she was no more. All of her family and friends had tried to pull the language from her, to get her to respond—to food, to light, to touch. But she was nothing but a rag doll by that point, a piece of sour blanket on the top of the bed.

The doctor had arrived with his black bag, a pouch full of slippery metal instruments and glass bottles full of green and blue liquids. Perhaps, the answer was in there, her family hoped, in a magic powder or potion that would bring the life back into her body. But, instead, he instructed them to fill the tub and to cut the cloth, as it would help to scare the demons out of her.

The doctor inched closer to her face, looking into her eyes for some response, for a blink or pupil dilation. Her breath was so scant that he even questioned himself for a moment, tilting his head just a bit, to see if he could hear her breath, invisible threads that had to be escaping from her slack mouth. She could almost taste the artificial slap of his shaving soap, like new wood and discovery, and that was all that it took, for her to open her dry lips and wake up.

V.

In the stories, there was some agreement: there was always water and there was always a man, though the slow drip of a bathroom faucet was never revealed, nor a father's shadow entering a tiny room.

> I may be lying,
> *your great-granddaughter*

Ana Sinedal Fryderud
Nov. 21, 1901

My Dear Nellie:

It is well nigh time I should answer your good letter of Oct.
12 and let you know how I am prospering. Am pleased to
learn that you are strong again and that you have good health.
Hope that it will be your lot to enjoy this blessing for a long
time to come. Sickness seems to be such a general common
feature that almost every individual more or less meets with.
To possess good health is certainly a priceless boon for which
we cannot be too thankful to our Heavenly Father.

You ask regarding my health. It is good. I do not think it ever
was better than it now is or has been during the time I have
been out in the field.

Am sorry that you will be deprived of your mama's and your
family's association and that you will be quite alone in Utah.
Hope though that the tide will not be against you, and should
it so occur that things do not just come your way, you in your
good judgment will be able to breast the situation or tide, or
surmount the obstacles. Hope you shall not be subject to "blues"
and that these temporary depressions you speak of in your
letter will give place to a more contented and a better spirit or
feeling, and I hope it will be your lot to come into association
with good people who will show regard and respect for the
virtues, character, and integrity you possess, and give you the
consideration that these characteristics in you merit.

You will be quite alone now for a time and deprived of
a mother's benign influence, and you probably will meet
with occasional unpleasant things or even temptations that
would tend to hurt your good character or reputation should
you give way to some of them. Regarding this however, I
need not apprehend nor fear for I have implicit faith in my

sweetheart, and am convinced of her unreproachable character in whatever circumstance she may come in subjection to. Just bring your good faculties into play, Nellie, as you have done and win for yourself friends. Let your sweet influence, your good judgment and virtues be brought into action wherever you are so that you will be a blessing and a delight to them you associate with.

Do not sacrifice anything in the line of social recreation or parties that it may be your privilege to attend such parties as where a healthy atmosphere pervades. It will yet be a while before my return so get what enjoyment and amusement as your judgment tells you is good and healthy.

Day before yesterday we came from a trip to German skog socken where we visited our new saints and also held some meetings. Our new members there fare valiant and patriotic and truly feel as though they have come into possession of the pearl of great price. 3 sisters and 2 brothers and 3 blessed children it is that we have there now, and probably we could have baptized another one or two this time had not the lake been frozen over. We have a number of honest investigators we feel and realize that we are the true messengers of truth and righteousness. As its natural our little degree of success through the help of the Lord, has agitated the devil to some extent. It has pleased some 3 newspaper editors to raise a warning cry for the two "Mormon Apostles" and it seems that in the socken that I alluded to before some good people have taken pleasure in spreading a few tales regarding us— my companion Elder Anderson and I—for we now enjoy the reputation of having stolen meat in a certain city by the name of Arivka and also for having been seen drunk on the streets of said city. What does my sweetheart Nellie think of him who loves her for having such rumors afloat regarding himself? It is rumored here that a certain preacher intends giving a special lecture on "Mormonism." I hope we shall be informed when the event comes off so that we can be present..

Some over 2 weeks ago we held a meeting in the beautiful capital city of Vermland with name of Carlstad (Carl City). There the priest tried to forbid the parties who controlled the hall to allow us use of same, but it didn't work and we held our meeting and we hope to hold several meetings there in the city. Thus you see that while the adversary is on the alert, the Lord is with us and He helps us. When we came to Vermland not 3 mo. ago there were but some 6 members in the branch. Now we have members and blessed children to the number of 18 souls.

Some two days we had our first snowfall, which means that winter is soon here and Sweden will be held in its icy spell for a number of months. The days are short and continue growing shorter each day. If I had you here we would tonight (or this afternoon rather) (if it is clear) go out for a moonlight walk at 4 o'clock, but for reason of its being cold it perhaps would not be so enjoyable. If I had you here we could take a promenade down to the pretty lake in the neighborhood and compare our abilities on skates. It was my pleasure when in Summarskag to do some skating and "kolking" on the pretty lake where we last mo. did our baptizing. If you were here it would undoubtedly amuse you to observe the country people as I can say interest you, particularly would it interest you to observe the women in their different vocations. It would interest you to see how they work the linen after it is harvested into soft wooly fiber and then afterwards spin into yard which they afterward weave into cloth of different kinds.

—If you were here just now, I would show you a "Mormon eater" of the red hot type, for on looking out of the window of this upstairs room, I see him out in his yard across the road. At different times has he chased the Mormon Elders from his house who have called to visit the good sister who is his wife. He has employed such weapons as his gun, clubs, sticks, etc. with which to affectively rid his premises of the elders. He is wholly a bigoted fanatic and his good and patient wife has suffered much at his hands for the sake of the gospel.

Occasionally he goes to the mill and consequently is away for some time. His wife then gives us the hint and invites us to her house where she prepares a good meal or invites us to "soft" (fruit juice) and "dopp" (i.e. dip and soak her good cakes into juice and eat and drink.)

I must bring my letter to a close. Again I thank Nellie for her good invaluable presents you sent me. The chain is a most charming present. As soon as circumstances permit I shall get me a charm to hang in the place you so thoughtfully have provided. The chain then will with the weight of the charm attached to it, hang most gracefully on my vest, and I shall find pleasure in wearing the charming tribute of Nellie's love, when occasion suggests for I can not afford to wear it all the time, for it then some day may wear out. I want it to last, as I hope Nell's love will last and as my love for her will certainly last. Such a beautiful tribute of her pure love etc. it is.

Thanks for the journal. I enjoyed it very much. I was especially pleased with Thompson's story of the sparrows. When in Vesteras, I took much delight in observing the little sparrows as they played and chirped in the public park there and bathed themselves at the fountain etc.

If they continue to send you 2 copies of the journal perhaps it would be well for you to request them to withhold one of the subscriptions and let it take effect when your own subscription has expired. However, do whatever you like in the matter.

With an ._. . (L) I close my letter and subscribe myself with love,

>Yours affectionately,
>*P. Sundwall Jr.*

>Ana Linedal
>Frykerud, Vermland

Baltimore, Maryland
January 21, 2011

Dear Peter,

Your. . . well, a story:

The Mormon Eater

If you were here just now, I could show you a "Mormon eater" of the red hot type.

-Peter Sundwall, Jr.

Ana Sinedal Fryderud, November 21, 1901

"Do you see him, Elder Anderson?" I nod towards my companion, who is busy chewing half of the stick of gum I generously gave him from my Nellie's recent letter.

"Yes," he says, not even bothering to get up off of the bed to look out the window. He is in the middle of a daydream about his girl back home. I can tell because he always rubs his thumb against the pad of his middle finger when he is thinking of her.

We have established quite a reputation, Elder Anderson and I. At least three local newspapers have dubbed us the two "Mormon Apostles." Apparently, we have stolen meat from the city of Arivka and stumbled drunk through the streets after our robbery. I think it is funny, but Elder Anderson seems a bit nervous about all of the attention.

The Mormon Eater bends over to examine a large rock in the ground, and then wipes his hands down the sides of his pants. He glances up at our window and I immediately move my head to the left, out of his view. We stay in a room above a small family with two horrible children. They scream and cry and make me want to spank them. But, of course, we are kind and polite to our host families, so I say, "Oh, how interesting," to the children's pointless stories. "Oh, they are such sweet children," I say to their exhausted mother.

The Mormon Eater's wife reminds me a bit of Nell, with her patience and beauty. She is a few years older than Nell, yet not enough to wear the drape of age. She has dark brown hair, like Nell, and a tall frame, like Nell. But, unlike Nell, she is trapped under the thumb of a rotten man. I can't imagine how she got there in the first place. I don't see one redeeming quality about her husband, other than his collection of weapons. Some nights, I look out my window and see her standing behind her upstairs window. She remains there for awhile, staring out. I cannot tell if she is defeated or longing. I can only see that she is facing away from her house, as I am in mine. Sometimes, she is up late at night. I never see her husband in the window, only in the yard. I do not think he passes by windows. He stays in the center of rooms and does not feel the need to look to either side.

"Elder Anderson," I turn towards my companion, who is still thinking and rubbing his fingers.

"Yes?"

"Do you think we should be heading out soon?" We are due to meet in Carlstad today, the capital city of Vermland, to hold a meeting. I am comfortable with my Swedish, but Elder Anderson is not so fortunate. I know he will just stand there and nod as I speak, his feet shifting back and forth in nervous rhythm. We are bound, however, for the duration that we are assigned together. I try to think of him as an extra arm, as opposed to feeling the weight of his entire person.

"Elder Anderson?" I repeat, when he doesn't answer. He is five years younger than I am. I can feel the age difference between us a lot of the time, like a thick brick of air in the room. Some days, I feel more like his father than his companion. "Did you hear me?"

"Oh, yes," he stammers, his freckled nose twitching above his nostrils.

"I'm just going to finish up this letter and then we can go, okay?" I say, picking up the pen again.

*

The first time I noticed the Mormon Eater's absence was when his wife was sitting on the porch. It was evening, darkening early as it does here in late fall. Elder Anderson and I walked by the house on our way back from a long tracting hike. We almost didn't even see her, because she usually never sits outside on the porch. It was getting dark, and we were not looking for anyone sitting on the porch. The Mormon Eater doesn't ever sit on the porch. He just scowls in the yard and disappears into his house each evening.

The wife coughed, just a little cough, but enough that we turned and saw her there. She almost blended into the porch, her face in the shadows, her dress faded into the rough wood of her chair. She was the porch for a moment, the transition between the day and the night, before it is time to enter and after it is time to leave. Elder Anderson and I stopped walking and stood there for a second, before she coughed again.

"God dag," I said, nudging Elder Anderson with my elbow.

"God dag," Elder Anderson repeated.

"Hur lange ar du har?" she asked, her body moving forward in the chair, her arm motioning towards our host house.

"En manad," I answered. Elder Anderson remained silent, staring down at his shoes.

"God," she said, crossing her ankles underneath her. "Vill du bo pa middag?"

"We would love to!" Elder Anderson suddenly blurted out in English.

"Elder!" I reprimanded, as we were supposed to accept dinner invitations with polite and reserved grace.

"Det ar for mycket besvar?" I looked over my shoulder to see if the Mormon Eater was headed our way, armed with a sharp arrow dripping with poison.

"Inga problem," the wife smiled. She got up out of her chair and walked towards us. I could see that she had a scar on the side of her face, an inch wide line that curved from her ear towards her cheek in a half moon. She was tall, almost as tall as me. When she got closer I could see her eyes, and they looked straight at us without blinking. They were darker than most of the blue eyes around the town, like they had been stirred instead of born. "Kommer in i huset."

Elder Anderson and I looked at each other. There was a moment of hesitation, mainly on my part, of knowing this was not our usual dinner appointment, of knowing the wife already knew we would accept her invitation, of knowing the meat had already been cooking for hours, its salty juices rolling over itself in hot bubbles.

But it was Elder Anderson who initiated the step forward, his nose leading him towards the old porch, the door, the dark inside that we had only seen from our window.

She opened the door and we walked into the unknown, without even realizing it was happening. The Mormon Eater was drunk over two miles away. For the moment, the yard was empty of his weapons. Our scriptures were still marked in our hands. And we followed her, because she said to. That was enough to get our bodies through the door.

Writer: your great- granddaughter

Fairview, Utah
Nov. 24, 1901

My Dear Peter:

I have no excuse to offer for my negligence. Why I have not written I can scarcely tell. Each time I attempt to write I would think I will feel more like writing tomorrow. But "tomorrow never comes," and I will never write if I don't write today. Hope I will succeed in finishing this letter.

I have been quite lonesome since my folks left, but if I can I will go to where they are. It remains with you Peter. Do you think it will be better for me to go to Arizona and come back some day? Or shall I remain in Utah?

I have been here nearly three weeks. You can imagine how I appreciate meeting my friends again. It does not seem quite natural to see so many of them married. There are just a few old maids left.

Thank you Peter for your good letter and the beautiful relief card. What a beautiful place this must be. A river is it not? I should like very much to sail down one of those beautiful rivers in Sweden.

Am glad you received the chain and handkerchiefs after so long a time. I did not get a charm for the chain because I wanted you to get one.

Am so glad you are so successful in your great and good work. The Lord is surely blessing your efforts. It shows that the people are very much interested or they would not have congregated so far away to your meeting.

It is a beautiful moonlight night. The weather is very pleasant. I almost dread to see the snow come. If I had gone with my folks, as I should have done, I would not dread the winter, as it never snows there. I am sorry I did not go. For this very reason. The people suspect that I am waiting for you. Through no act or word have I let anyone know, there at Fairview, of our relationship, only that I have remained in Utah and have come here. I have called on your folks. Spent a very pleasant evening there. People may suspect from that that there is something between you and I. I can not keep the people from suspecting. Unless I go to my folks. I can not go for some time, but even then I think it will be best. I leave it with you Peter whether I go or remain in Utah. Your folks are just lovely to me. Anna has a beautiful baby. Isn't it nice to be an uncle?

I was dancing with Bro. H. Hansen and he told me he would swing me one for you and write and tell you about it. Now how he learned you and I ever went together I do not know. I think he and Bro. Olsen look and seem just the same as they were before we left Fairview. There are so few of the boys here now that were here before I left, what few that are not married have gone away or nearly all of them.

Suppose you have heard of Nellie Miner's engagement? Is to be married next month to Mr. Fred Christenson from Colo. By the time you return all the girls and boys will have been married, and there will be another generation grown up.

Think I shall remain here until after Christmas. You will not come home until the next Christmas will you? The time goes by so rapidly I can scarcely realize you have been gone as long as you have.

Take the very best care of yourself. Hope you will enjoy the best of health always. I have fully regained my health. It is so nice to be away from Robinson. I will be cheerful and sociable and not think of the future. Let what will I will make the best of it. Yet will endeavor to have the best come.

Hope you will forgive me once more. I wish I could talk to you. I could explain why I have not written.

Merry Christmas and Happy New Year to you dear Peter.

Hope you will accept this little token of my love and Xmas gift.
It isn't much but I send it with best wishes and love.

> I shall love you always Peter.
> Goodnight X X
> Lovingly,
> *Nellie*

Baltimore, Maryland
August 17, 2010

Dear Nellie,

Instructions:

Do not open it immediately.

Take your time.

Look at it.

Turn it over.

Notice its dusty clothing,

the stamp like a crooked tongue.

See the bent corners,

the accidental slip of a pen tip.

Feel its weight,

the history of two hands.

Take your own finger,

run it across the seal.

Don't open it.

Not yet.

First, remember.

First, linger.

> Just a suggestion,
> *Your great-granddaughter*

Ana Sinedal Frykerud
Dec. 16, 1901

My Dear Nellie:

Your letter dated Fairview with a beautiful kerchief as a token of your love reached me last week. Thanks for last. Your kerchief together with the previous gifts I prize highly and for all of them I thank you sincerely. Am only sorry that I am so situated that I cannot reciprocate your affection in the way of sending you a gift or some little token of my love for Nellie. Were I located in the city where I had access to the book or stationary stores, I would perhaps be able to find some thing that would serve as a little token to send you, but under the circumstances I hope Nellie will accept my regard, my extreme love for her without a present as an evidence for same.

Hope you are well and strong and enjoying yourself among your circle of friends in Fairview. You appear somewhat worried over prospect of some of your and my friends guessing or surmising that there is anything between you and me. Don't think anything about it. If they come blank point out and ask you regarding us, say "No," though at the inconsistency of such a question or idea. It may be a little "white lie" and one that I think you, and I for that matter would be justified in resorting to. You see Nellie "alls fair in love," hence nothing so wrong in this. It cannot be anything wrong to play a little policy game on some of our friends.

As far as folks are concerned I do not think that any of them doubt Nellie's integrity, her high virtues, character, etc., but should they imagine that any attention was being mutually exchanged between us, they would perhaps doubt that I am devoting my full attention to my religion and the discharge of my duties etc. Johnny tells me that they often ask him when at home if he thinks that Nellie and I are corresponding to which queries he replies by saying that he does not know.

As to my being home by another Xmas, that is doubtful. It may not be so pleasant for you to learn that I will probably be retained here in Sweden at least 2 ½ years and then after my release it will probably be a matter of 3 or 4 months before I get home if I can have things come about as should like to and can arrange for means etc. So Nellie you see my being home in another year is very improbable. I will not be home so soon as you or my own folks even expect. They are establishing a new precedent here in the mission in the way of retaining young men 2 ½ years in the field before releasing them. Two young men that I know, Pres. Cannon being the one, have now been in the field between 3 and 4 months over 2 years, and Elder Cannon does not look for a release before Spring. Now Nellie I hope this will not pain you to hear of this. Don't think anything of this. Just go ahead and think nothing of the future but be the winsome and happy girl you have been.

Let not the young men or ladies guess that anything is between you and I. Avail yourself of every opportunity to go out in good society, and in your association with ladies and young men assert the high order of your character etc. and womanhood.

As to your remaining in Utah or not, will let you decide the matter. It should have pleased me if you had had a good family with whom to make your home and where you could have found it agreeable etc. But as to your remaining in Utah for my sake alone, don't know that that would be advisable, as it is yet a matter of more than a year before my return home. If by your staying and remaining you think the people will interpret it to mean that you are staying or waiting for my return, then perhaps it is not advisable to remain. Exercise your own judgment in this matter.

How I wish you were in a position to go to school this winter.

But a little training would be necessary to fit you to enter into a career of a school teacher, the experiences of which during my absence from home would be quite agreeable and beneficial to you. However it seems that circumstances govern us and that we are not always able to govern circumstances.

A merry Christmas to you and may the New Year have a rich store of blessings for my Nellie and may her pathway through the next year be a happy one and beset with no sorrows or trouble.

> Yours affectionately,
> *Peter*

P.S. Wish you would go into a little more detail when it comes to telling of your visit to my folks, also regarding the young folks' parties in Fairview.

> Affectionately,
> *P Sundwall*

> Ana Linedal
> Frykerud, Vermland
> Sweden

Am well with regard to health and otherwise. It has been extremely cold these last few days.

Baltimore, Maryland
September 22, 2010

Dear Peter,

Today I found myself pulling out the family history book again, thumbing through the index to find your pictures: one of a handsome young man, one of a distinguished old man. You were a very attractive man at any age. It is no wonder, like my own brother, people enjoyed just watching you speak.

There is a biography about you that Nellie provided for the family history book compiled after your death, a few years before she died:

"While in Mammoth, I saw an advertisement in the paper by a young man from Fairview, Utah, who wanted work as a display artist. His name was Peter Sundwall, Jr. I jokingly said I was going back to Fairview and marry that young artist. Soon after that my family went back to Arizona and I went to Fairview and stayed with the Clarence Pritchett family. I did meet the young artist when I was in Fairview and became well enough acquainted with him that we had sort of an understanding before he left on a mission for the church. He was in Sweden for a little over two years.

My family moved to Oakville just north of Fairview and I decided I wanted to go to Salt Lake to work and I packed for the trip. I would have been 19 at the time. I remember Uncle Lin Brady was going by our place with a load of logs and I ran out of the house and asked him if I could ride into Fairview to catch the train. He accommodatingly found room for me and my luggage on his wagon. I was back and forth between Fairview, Salt Lake and Provo for the next two years. I worked in the Utah State Hospital for a time. Some of the patients taught me to do some beautiful handwork which I have enjoyed."

-Harriet Eleanor Brady Sundwall, *Lindsay Anderson Brady Family History Book, Compiled 1960-1970.*

Somewhere, I expected to read that you continued your art, and that you did not stop with your letter writing. However, it seems that the responsibilities of marriage and fatherhood carried you down a very different route and you became the best you could be in providing for your family, your business, and your church. Nellie wrote your biography notes when my mother was a teenager, probably around the same time she met my father at the bowling alley in Silver Spring, Maryland one lazy Saturday afternoon. Nellie mailed off your biography notes just a few years before I was born and my parents would argue over whether to name me Katherine, after your daughter, or Anna Casja, after your mother. In the end, Katherine won out because my father said he didn't want me to get teased at school over an unusual name.

An unusual great-granddaughter,
Katherine

Linedal Frykerud
Jan. 27, 1902

My Dear Nellie:

An opportunity presents itself this morning to me to write you a letter. I hope you are well, that your health is good and that you enjoy yourself among your friends and relatives in Fairview. I have been somewhat disappointed these last few days for reason that no letter from you has come to hand. I have been especially desirous to know how you spent the holidays. I sincerely hope that you enjoyed yourself under the circumstances. I enjoyed my New Year and Christmas this time less than I did a year ago and by far less than I would had I been with my sweetheart 8000 miles away.

Have just reread your letter bearing date of Nov. 24. You see it is over 2 months ago since it was written and I do not think you will blame me for waiting for another letter. It will be interesting for me to learn of your circumstances and what you intend doing. How nice it would be if you could remain in Fairview. You probably by this time have decided in the matter. It had been my fond hope that brother John would help you a little to prepare for duties of a school teacher and thus put you in a position to use the time more lucratively and pleasantly. He as well as I think you need but little preparatory study to equip for the work. John was enthusiastic in the matter and assured me that he would help you. Now it appears that Johnny's ambitions have taken assent, as he intends taking a couple of years at the Chicago University, and now, will probably lay up his means for that purpose.

John says that he called on you on New Year's day in a short letter he wrote me dated same day. He says you are as good, happy, and healthy as you have been. Am, of course, glad to hear it. I hope that may always be your good lot and condition. My friends that write me take it for granted that you are my sweetheart and that you someday will be my WIFE. They appear to have guessed our secret. However, when I write them I shall neither deny or affirm their statements. Carl seems to understand how things stand between you and I. My parents though have not remarked or hinted anything touching on the matter. How much credence they put on the gossip that may possibly reach them I do not know. It is my opinion that they by this time have observed enough of the purity of your character and girlhood to not feel disturbed should they even conclude there is something in the gossip that they may hear. Do not feel disturbed, Nellie, because some may surmise our position, however, in your remarks and conversations, manifest little or no concern for me. Continue to be the happy and winsome girl you are and circumspect in your deportment so that all will come to regard you with the full respect and consideration that you my Sweetheart merit, and I assure you that it will be his aim who loves and adores Nellie to so acquit himself as to be in a measure worthy of her.

When you write, Nellie, do not be afraid to exercise yourself. Be frank and write as you would talk. Do not be afraid to tell all you know, or feel. For my part I do not consider that my letters exhibit or portray my appreciation and love for Nellie that they would were I under other conditions. My sacred mission deters from so doing and perhaps a little natural modesty is to some extent responsible, too.

Regarding our work will say that we are doing the usual canvassing and holding of meetings though not as much of late as heretofore. The priests and press are aroused against us. It often occurs that articles concerning us appear in the newspapers.

I sent a letter to the Des. News some time ago in which I related some of our experiences. Perhaps the letter has come under your notice.

Last night I enjoyed the novelty of being out to a "begrafnings Kals" (burial party). The man in the family in the neighborhood had died and yesterday was buried. After his burial the "Kalas" or party began and did not adjourn until about 3 o'clock this morning. At this party was a time of eating and drinking and merriment. No one with exception of his wife perhaps, of the 35 or 40 guests appeared the worse on account of the death of the father. Brandy, wine, cigars, refreshments, food of all kinds, both dainty and substantial was served the guests, galore. I did not partake of all these items. I shall not write all my impressions that I received at this party last night.

I am invited out again to night or this afternoon rather, when the gay festivities are again resumed. If I do I am sure I shall not stay so long as I did last night.

Well, Nellie I shall close my letter for this time. May peace and the good blessings of the Lord continue with you. I wish you were here for a little while. If you were I am sure I would not wait to devise a "hobson Salute" or a "get cider" (side her) to "squeeze her" joke or scheme, but with out ceremony take some ._..s (L's) etc.

> Yours sincerely,
> *P. Sundwall Jr.*

Baltimore, Maryland
October 30, 2010

Dear Peter,

Last night I finally typed up and turned over the first twenty pages of this collection of letters to my husband to read. You are around the same age he was when we first met, over twenty years ago. However, we don't have a trail of letters to document our early years, just blurry Rite-Aid prints from the early 1990's. We met when I walked in to fill out an application for a part-time job at a movie theatre. My husband was the assistant manager. I was a high school senior looking for some extra cash and free movie viewing.

"You looked like an angel," my husband likes to say, perhaps mistaking my new gold headband from Claire's Boutique for a halo. "I knew as soon as I saw you that I would marry you." I, on the other hand, took a little more convincing.

"I'm not getting married, or too serious," I told him several months into dating.

"That's okay," he smiled. "I'll wait."

And so, he hired me to work during his shifts and assigned me to the projection booth, a dirty and dark room full of the smell of newly unpacked film and concrete corners packed tight with dust. He taught me how to thread the projector, and luckily, how to use the phone to call downstairs for help, as I was constantly tripping over the film that stretched across the floor like a moving tongue, panicking from the "boo's" that reached me high above the audience, as the movies temporarily stopped until the repair was complete.

It was a fun time in my life. The crew of characters at the theatre was entertaining, and the 20:1 male/female ratio provided lots of extra attention, which I didn't mind. I loved being able to watch movies for free, minutes after they were released and before they were screened for the general public. My husband would hold late night viewing parties with bags of popcorn loaded with artificial topping (we had to be sure not to call it butter when working concession) that went into the wee hours of the morning.

There were plenty of aspiring directors working as ushers at the theatre, and I got talked into playing the main role in one amateur film. It was a Baltimorean take on *Alice in Wonderland*, in which an innocent girl accidentally takes a bad acid trip and finds herself trying to escape from all of the derelicts of the city. I remember diving into a trashcan at some point, skipping around the zoo, and having a pretend fist fight with one of my girlfriends from high school. *Alice Underground* was hardly an Oscar-winner.

So, besides it being the birthing center of my one and only acting stint, the theatre provided minimum wage, entertainment, and a boyfriend, so it was a pretty good deal for the summer. However, the district manager didn't appreciate my two-hour lunch breaks with my boss, so I had to quit.

Luckily, it wasn't before the *Silence of the Lambs* raffle. My name was drawn to be the proud owner of the 8 X 4 foot standee of Anthony Hopkins behind bars, wrapped up tight in a straitjacket, glaring from behind his muzzled mask. It came complete with a plug and blinking lights across the top of the cardboard jail cell.

My mother was thrilled when I brought it home. I set it up in the front of the living room bay window, so that all the street traffic could see it as they passed the house. After a few weeks, he became a member of the family, and he didn't look so menacing, as nothing does after making its home in the bay window of your parents' living room. In fact, soon I couldn't imagine our house without him in it.

One day, much to my dismay, I came home and Hannibal was gone, without a trace of his cage, any struggle, or jail break, the living room bay window bare and empty without his hungry stare.

"I couldn't take it another day," my mother said. "He had to go."

I'm sorry, Hannibal. If it had been up to me, you would have become as permanent as the old rocker, your stomach growling in anticipation of your next hearty meal.

> Serving, with a side,
> *Katherine, your great-granddaughter*

Fairview, Utah
Jan. 18, 1902

My Dear Peter:

Really I do not know what to tell you in regards to my not
writing before this. Time goes by so quickly that I do not
realize so much has gone, since getting your dear good letters.
Yes this is in answer to two good letters from you Peter. Isn't
it dreadful? It seems to be as if I get worse every day. I am
ashamed of myself. I must be like the little boy who, "frets
best when he is ashamed." Wish I weren't such a "sleepy
head" maybe I could sit up at night. I will try to get this letter
finished so that I may mail it tomorrow as I go to Sunday
School. What you think of me I do not know. I am indeed very
sorry I have not written before.

I will tell you what a nice time I had during the holidays. Had
the pleasure of meeting your friend Mr. Neilson. I like him
real well. He told me he wrote you on New Year's Day. How
we came to speak of you. We were dancing and Mr. Neilson
said, "How is Peter getting along?" I said I think you can tell
better than I. He laughed and told me about writing such a
long letter to you. I told him boys could usually think of more
to write then girls could. I went to four dances Christmas
night, Fr. Night following New Year's night and the next Friday
evening. I went to the two last dances with Jim Carston. Wasn't
very fortunate in getting an escort. Boys are very scarce in
Fairview. I shall be sorry to leave. I will remain here until April.
I think I may go before.

Spring is just around the corner, and has been peeping at us
for nearly two weeks. I am so glad it is nearly here. Yet we will
have winter weather before spring is really here. The roads are
nice and dry now. I dread to see the snow come although we
have not had very much snow this winter. I suppose there is

enough snow where you are. Wish I was there for just a few days, but I would be very much afraid to compare my ability on skates, as I never had skates on. Some day I will get you to teach me how to skate. It is a beautiful moonlight night tonight. Wish I could transfer myself into a bird. I would come over to Sweden. If it were just to get a glimpse of you.

What is the difference between the time here and in Sweden? If I should send you a wireless telegraph message. I mean one the angels will bring at nine in the morning. What time will you get it?

I have not heard from Mama for some time. They were well when last I heard.

Peter it pained me some to hear of you having to remain a ½ year longer, but I will remain true to you if it were ten years.

I must close as I am sleepy. I will write very soon and tell you more. Thank you for relief card and the bird you drew—it is very pretty. I like that work very much.

I close asking Our Father in Heaven to bless you in all things.

> Lovingly
> *Nellie*
>
> With all my heart.

Baltimore, Maryland
November 20, 2010

Dear Nellie,

I, too, am ready for spring, and we haven't even officially started winter yet. Maybe I am getting old, but I now understand the reasoning behind "heading south for the winter," like the birds. When I was younger, the cold never entered into my interpretation of this phrase, only the promise of turquoise pools open year-round and fruits that could grow past one season, unlike the fickle apples in Maryland. The kids, however, rejoice in the white playground that comes with the winter months. They dream of snowmen that never melt, tunnels that will lead them to places beyond our front yard, school cancellations that prove the importance of their wishes and prayers.

I catch a glimpse of a young girl with brown braids and bushy eyebrows, bundled up in a red snow jacket and hood, in the mirror on the other side of the room. She is so very cold, but only I know it. However, she is too busy to stop and think about herself, only of her next creation, something with ice crystals and secret compartments carved big enough for herself and one invisible friend. In seconds she becomes an old lady in a red sweater, her thickening teeth shivering from the open front door.

"What is it you want?" I ask her. She smiles sometimes, but not today. Today, her lips stay tight. She wants to keep the warmth inside her mouth. That is the only place that has stayed the same, the only place she has never left.

Shivering,
Kathy

Fairview, Utah
Feb. 9, 1902

My Dear Peter:

I have a few moments spare time, I will use them to the best advantage. It sounds rather strange to say I have spare time on the Sabbath day but there has been so much sickness here that we have not had much spare time. The children (I stay at Clarence Pritchett's) are all ill, are some better now, Mrs. Pritchett has just worried herself sick. One's time is not their own when there is sickness, I have not been able to go to either Sunday school or meeting for the last three Sundays. My I shall be glad when spring comes, maybe there won't be so much sickness. We are having the pleasure of wading in the mud down in this corner of town. I did not get one sleigh ride this last snow storm we had. I wanted to have one badly enough, but that did not help matters any.

Everything is rather dull at present. We are going to have an apron and bow dance on the fourteenth, think I shall go. There is to be a big lodge dance the eleventh. Do not know whether I will go or not; Have been to one dance since the holidays. I enjoy dancing with Bro. H.P. Hanson, we have either a two step or a waltz. I understand that he and Silna are to be united in wedlock soon. Bro A.R. Anderson and Ida Bushan were married last week. The fifth I think.

The "bachelors" and "old maids" are going one by one. O.K. and Lena to be wed also. By the time you return there will be a new generation grown up. There may be an old maid or two left. The Lawsen girls, Sadie and myself are very much concerned as to our situation.

We were just wishing some one would be so kind as to ship a car load of boys into town. Maybe we could be successful in getting a fellow out of a carload.

Don't you sympathize with such lonely people? But we live in hopes. "If it were not for hopes the heart would faint."

Will you return as soon as you are released? Or will you visit some of the principal cities of Europe before returning?

It seems to me as if I write such poor letters. I do wish I could express my thoughts better on paper. If I could but have a long talk with you Peter, but I must wait, not very much longer though. It seems long to look into the future, but the time will soon be here. Then how very happy we will be. I will know how to appreciate you more after this long time of waiting is over. Yet I could wait many years longer, knowing you would return to me, and then happy time.

I have not called on your folks for a long time, but I see and talk with Carl occasionally. He and Mary came down and played for us one evening. We had a very pleasant time. I enjoy Mary's playing very much. Clarence has a piano I can play a little. Wish I had more time to devote to practice.

The next letter I write may be from Ariz. Yet I may remain here until April. When I hear from mama I will know. Have not heard from them for a long time, a little over a week. If I should not go to Arizona what would you say if I should go into Salt Lake City and learn to be a nurse. Think I should take to the work readily. Maybe I should not speak to you about what I should like to be, but I want to know what you think of it.

I hope you still enjoy good health. I do. Feel just a little worn out on account of being up so much at night.

I hope I will be forgiven for the "white lie" I have told. The people will have to keep on supposing until they know for a surety, whether there is anything between you and I.

I have written rapidly. Please excuse poor writing and

composed letter, but I must close. May the blessing of our Heavenly Father be with you to guide you and bring you safely home.

Lovingly,
Nellie.

Baltimore, Maryland
December 14, 2010

Dear Nellie,

I write the date today and realize we are over 108 years apart in our letters. I can feel the closeness in terms of centuries, and the distance in terms of days. I could break out the calculator and figure it out in exact days, but I will leave that for my son to do. He likes to multiply large numbers on the calculator, a tiny computer we use to do math instead of using our brains. He only likes to multiply large numbers, not small ones. I think it gives him a sense of magnitude, that his fingers can create a product so large with so many zeroes and commas. He feels there must be strength in a digit that takes up most of the calculator's display screen, in anything that reaches to the very edge of a boundary.

It is a two hour delay for schools, another almost snowstorm that managed to leave only fog instead of mass inches, another week without pattern or predictable schedule, my grip of sanity weakening by the hour.

"Wade through," I remind myself. "One day it will be easier." "One day" is my Morse code for a romanticized future, though I know that "one day" is as possible as winning the lottery, the odds not quite weighted in my favor. You must have felt this same sense of suffocation when you cared for the sick children, as you mention in your letters. No one prepares you for the exhaustion of caring for the sick, especially children and elderly people.

I still remember a long week when the entire family had the stomach flu, and vomit and diarrhea seemed to be coming out of the walls. I couldn't keep the towels coming fast enough. The kids were messing their beds every other minute, and I could barely manage to drag myself to and from the bathroom.

I remember lying down on a dirty sheet at one point, resigned to the stench, my head spinning, body aching and pulsing from the fever. Any attempts of cleanliness seemed completely futile. I wondered what would happen if I just didn't move, if I continued to lay in the vomit and feces of myself and my children? I wasn't even sure which fluid belonged to whom anymore. I started to think it wouldn't be too bad, to just resign and drift off past the place where dirt and smells mattered. And yet, I saw my hand reaching for the phone, dialing the number I knew from memory, a sequence as comfortable as the pattern of the letters of my own name, the voice answering that sounded like a clean bed, a soft bandage: "Hey Mom, can you come over? We are all really sick."

Your mother is not four miles away, like mine. You can't just call her to come over when there is illness. At this point, you are living in two different states. You must have wanted to call her, not just by phone, but also by your voice. Did you simply muffle the need, burying your frustration like a chewed bone in the backyard? Did it stay silent, like a sleeping child? Or, did it yell and pound against the sides of your skull, like mine does, in pure tantrum fashion? Maybe it just waited, as you seem much more patient than me or my children, accepting the back of the line—aware of the long wait, but still inching forward, telling yourself, "One day, one day."

> For today,
> *I am your great-granddaughter*

Ana Linedal
Frykerud
Feb. 25, 1902

My Dear Nellie:

Rec'd today an unusual big batch of mail among which was your good letter from home and S. Wm. Nilson. The latter is feeling well in his labors in Southern Sweden. Bro. Nilson has soon been away from home 2 years but he does not expect a release until about next fall.

Am pleased that all your patients will be, through your tender care, restored to their health again. For my part, I am well and enjoy the best of health which I regard as a good blessing, considering that so many of our Elders do not thrive in this northern climate.

Rec'd today Wedding Card of Bro. A.R. Anderson and his bride. As you say, Nellie, there will be quite a new generation in the town when I get back. All of my friends with but a few exceptions will have embarked off on the sea of matrimony and the situation in the "old town" will certainly be quite different when I return.

Father in his letter says that "the sun is out beautifully, spoiling the sleighing for us altogether," so I presume you will not get the benefit of your much desired sleigh ride. Here we have plenty of snow and we are, so to say under the icy spell of winter and will so continue until no sooner than April. Winds have so drifted the snow into great heaps in the roads that they have been abandoned in places and instead new roads formed inside the fences in the fields to serve temporarily.

I returned yesterday from a week's absence canvassing and visiting Saints and friends. We are having a rather "hot time" in this part if you will allow me to use the expression. The priests, preachers and press are, of course, all against us, and my companion and I are exposed to a great deal of notoriety and abuse. Some time ago in the leading paper published in Vermland's capital city, Karlstad, we were called some very bad names, such as drinkers, Card players, etc., and the people in these parts manufacture all sorts of simple and petty yarns in which we figure. One of the preachers in this socken, it is expected will soon appear with a public lecture in which he hopes to announce public sentiment against us. In another socken the priest has delivered a public lecture against us. We were not there at the time, but we hope to be on hand when Mr. Preacher here, is prepared with his speech.

Thus you see the adversary is alive and is exerting a perceptible influence here. However, I hope this will not last long and that the Lord whose servants we are will bring about better conditions and that the saying "It is always coldest just before the sun rises" will have a fitting application in our case. Reports of our work done in the branch have been heralded in all the Swedish papers it appears, even in the leading papers of Stockholm. I hope the storm will blow away and that a sunshine of bright prospects will follow.

Next month my companion and I will attend conference in Norway and we anticipate having a good time with the Saints over the line.

You ask my opinion in regard to your going to S.L.C. to do work in the hospital. My opinion is that it would be an excellent experience for you and the training in that direction would no doubt be of much profit and pleasure to you, considering that you have a natural longing for such work and as you say you could no doubt after a time command good wages. You unquestionably would find the work enjoyable. I have visited hospitals in this country and have been interested in observing the nurses as they attended to the many patients. The nurses are mostly young ladies and comprise both the trained nurses and beginners. My impressions in the hospital led me to think of the importance and nobility of the office of a nurse. Having the inclination for this work as you have it would no doubt afford you much pleasure to be engaged in this calling, and I should certainly like for you to try your hand in this calling. I believe you would do well and that you would make good progress in the field as nurse. I would suggest that you go to S.L.C. if you think you can succeed in getting a place. It is my opinion that in life in the hospital and even in the city there would be much inspiration that would be of profit and value to you. The intellectual atmosphere is of a much more higher order in the city than you would find in Ariz. and you would certainly find better opportunities and chances for development in the lines you like.

Your folks may argue that how much evil lurks in the city, consequently it would not be advisable to let you go. For my part, I am thoroughly convinced of the soundness of your good and unimpeachable character and moral virtues and believe that you would be fully capable of steering clear of any or all evils that exist in the metropolis.

Whatever you do, Nellie, do as your judgment says and act according to what you deem is advisable. Do not take my suggestions as grounds for your actions. Should you go to Salt Lake and your folks assent to your going I hope you will have some friends to help you get a place in a good institution where you could feel yourself at home and enjoy your labor and where you could be sure that a good moral atmosphere pervades. I hope circumstances are such as to permit of your going to the city and engaging yourself in this field of usefulness, and besides I should much prefer to find you there on my return to Zion than in Arizona, although I would not want you to go to S.L. or remain in Utah just for my sake alone.

You ask if I will return directly after my release. I cannot say now. According to my feelings now and if I can arrange for means it will be a matter of a few months from the time of my release until I get home. However, it is not at all certain. My longing for Zion may perhaps be too strong when my release comes along. It would be much to my advantage to stop off, probably in Chicago, not to visit cities as I had, perhaps, previously stated, but to take a course in school and get a training that I hope would put me in a position to better meet the little problems, that it will be my experience, probably (and some one else's too) to meet occasionally in the pathway of Life.

Johnny has said that he would settle all financial matters for me, should it be my desire to go to Paris and take a thorough course in training in my favorite line that you know I have a weakness for. I have not the inclination to go there and grapple with the problem of learning a new language, and besides, I do not regard myself as sufficiently endowed or gifted by nature to justify me in such an important and serious move.

With best wishes for your success and continual happiness, I extend to you a respectful salute—a hobson salute if you know what that means, and remain yours most truly

P. Sundwall Jr.

Baltimore, Maryland
February 14, 2011

Dear Peter,

Today is Valentine's Day. You do not know it yet, but you will have a son with Nellie, born on this same day in 1907, five short years from now. He will be your second born, two years after your first daughter, named after Nellie. You will name your first and only son after yourself, followed by the romantic holiday: Peter Valentine. After Peter's birth, you will have four more girls. You will be surrounded by women at home—just you and the younger Peter, nicknamed "Val." Val will grow up to be a medical doctor, and his two sons, Peter and David, will follow in his footsteps as M.D's.

David actually contacted my mother last week. He is leading the committee for the family reunion this summer and wants me to write a poem for the program. I told my mother to tell him it was fine, as long as it can be composed after the spring semester ends, when I have a little more mental room for inspiration.

It will be the first time that my children will fly on a plane. My son is so excited, but I worry about the other passengers having to hear, "How much longer until we get there?" every five minutes after the plane takes off.

"I hope the kids do okay," I worry to my mother.

"They'll be fine," she reassures, like she always does.

It will also be the first time that my husband has been to Utah and around so many Mormons at one time. I warn him—there might not be any beer at the reunion!

"I'll be okay," he reassures, like he always does, before sliding a flask into his suitcase.

A poem for the reunion? What should I write? I pull out the family album again and look at your pictures. Do I write about your young love with Nellie? Hope and possibilities that are there, but reality that is yet to happen. Or, do I write afterwards, looking back, the way we see patterns only down the road, the texture of the people your love created, and whose love created me?

Is there is some in-between that needs to be captured in the poem, something that dates and faces cannot keep, beyond smiles, jaw lines and tree branches of genealogy that continue to grow past their trunks? I want to say it is the moment the letters left your hands, when they were not yet received, but on their way to being delivered, the seals still shut tight with your lips. I want to say it is the words you formed in your heads that never came out, the way you looked down at your hands and knew they would one day touch each other. I want to write about the distance, the years both before and after your life together-- the years that bridged the miles across the Atlantic Ocean, and later, separated you by death's invisible map.

It will take us over four hours by plane, even with a direct flight, to reach your home this summer. It will take a week of packing before the trip and probably two weeks of unpacking after the trip to cushion our connection. There will be fights between my children. My husband and I will probably irritate each other more times than we will be able to count. Something will inevitably be lost or forgotten, and I will wonder if it is all worth it. There will be tears, not long after the adrenaline from the first minutes of the flight wears off. My husband will take lots of pictures of the mountains, and I will never get to the book I will pack in my carry on.

We will return, and it will take me at least a year to print out the pictures, and then they will sit in the cabinet with the other pictures that are still waiting to be organized in an album.

Thirty years from now my son will say, "Remember when the plane took off for Utah? You couldn't see because I traded you for the window seat, but the sun was shining so brightly that I had to squint to see the runway. And then we started moving and the ground disappeared as we lifted, and then I could almost hear the air against the wing, I could almost see it, and you told me we were flying."

In preparation,
Kathy

Stockholm
April 15, 1902
De Sista Dagars
Heliges Kontor
Hornsgatan 80, 1 re.

My Dear Nellie:

Am very busy but will take time sufficient to drop you a few lines. I am much disappointed in that I have not heard from you now for about 2 months. What can be wrong? Are you ill or have your letters for the first time gone astray? The 2 previous letters to this one I am awaiting replies to, the first letter being dated something like the 27th or 28th of Jan. and the second dated about the 25th of Feb. Hope you are well and enjoying yourself.

Am wondering if you still are in Fairview or if you are in the south or in Salt Lake. As you see from the letter head I am now in Stockholm. Was called from my previous field of labor to this city. My time for the present is employed with the books. Have also to take part in many meetings we have which sometimes causes me some worry.

I enjoy myself splendidly, however, in Stockholm and my new field suits me all right. Spring is soon here in all its grandeur and we feel relieved again. Hope a letter is soon forthcoming from you.

> I remain yours affectionately
> *P. Sundwall Jr.*

Baltimore, Maryland
March 11, 2011

Dear Peter,

I, too, have not written back to you in a few weeks. What
is the reason? This past week it was the stomach virus. The
entire family was gripped in the sours of Exorcist-like vomit, a
movie you are lucky enough not to have seen. It is one film I
wish I had never viewed, with its images of a possessed girl so
frightening I dreamed of her cracked and evil face for years.

I have been busy, too, with my reading, having just finished
my first rough chapter for my Ph.D. dissertation, "Contradiction
in the Love Letters of H.L. Mencken and Sara Haardt," which
paints quite a different picture of the man known as the
"German Valentino," as he continuously wrote to Haardt while
she was hospitalized for tuberculosis. Now, I am turning my
attention to the letters of F. Scott and Zelda Fitzgerald. This
Baltimore love letters project is such a large beast; I hope
it does not eat me in the end. Some days, I see an exciting
landscape of words, voices, and images carried back and forth
across the page like neighbors—a subway map of tangible
love and place that people will be able to point to and feel
in simultaneous connection; all races, classes, sexes: one big
kiss across the page. Other times, I just see a big rusty kettle
of floating debris—an old shoe, a cracked set of dentures, and
my own unsteady hand stirring the pot without a recipe. This
month, the soup is a murky brown, and I can barely make out
the shadow of a vine working its way up the side of the pot's
iron belly. So far, I have noticed a pattern with my Baltimore
love letter couples: sick wives and alcoholic husbands. Last
night, I asked my husband if he would like to hear some of the
beautiful passages from Zelda Fitzgerald's letters, written while
she was institutionalized at Sheppard Pratt Hospital in Towson.

"Nah," he said. "I'd rather just have a drink."

I locked myself into the bathroom, so the kids wouldn't disturb me, and read Zelda's explanations of life while she was hospitalized. I started to worry, because she didn't seem that crazy. In many ways, she seemed very sane. Maybe it is just the intensity that makes the difference between sanity and insanity. While she locked herself in her room for twenty four hours, I am only locking myself in for one. At least that is what I am telling myself.

I told one of my fellow Ph.D. students that we might want to check into Sheppard Pratt for a well deserved "vacation." She agreed, and we imagined a long weekend in white beds, pills brought to us in little white cups, white sandwiches and vanilla custard delivered on clean white trays. Maybe I could find solace living in just one color, instead of interpreting every little shade and shadow that I see.

> Looking for some room of my own,
> *Kathy*

Fairview, Utah
April 6, 1902

My Dear Peter:

Will or can you forgive me? Why I have not written I cannot tell, more than I have just simply let the time go by and have not realized that it has been so long since I wrote. I do not deserve to be forgiven. It isn't that my love for you has grown cold. Love is silent you know. That is why I have been so silent I suppose. I have gone out a great many times with different young men, have enjoyed myself very much, but have always thought how much more I would enjoy myself if my lover were only with me. But I do not appreciate you dear Peter as I should. Nor do I think I will until you return. How proud I will be then to say that you have performed such a noble mission, and that you are my—may I say it Peter? May I say that you will someday be my "husband"? How grand it will be. I wish I could talk with you just for a short time. But it won't be long until I can talk with you for hours and hours. I do wish I could express my thoughts as I should like to. You will not think I am growing faithless? I love you more and more each day. I have thought so much of you today. After meeting a crowd of us "old maids" went out for a stroll. It is such beautiful weather. We were going down to the old mill, but it was so very wet that we could not go. I wanted to go down to a special spot in the meadows before I go. Hope I can yet. I leave next Wed. for S.L.C. Do not know whether I shall go into Arizona or not, rather think I will not go. I should give a great deal if I could go down to see Mama and the children, but I cannot, so will remain for awhile. Remain until my Peter returns.

Had a very pleasant visit with your Mother, Anna, May, Olif, Scott, and Carl last Friday. You may think I am foolish, but I am going to tell you what your mama said, and how nice it seemed. I was talking with Scott. He was sitting on her lap.

She said—Shall I say it? Yes I will. She said, "This is Aunt Nellie, Scott, talk to her." They were all so nice to me. Enjoyed myself so much.

Lois Jorden is to be here soon, she started some time ago. Think she is in S.L.C. now. I shall be so glad to see her. She isn't married. Says she won't love again. She loved a man whom was not worthy of her love. It seems sad doesn't it?

There was a crowd came down and surprised me last Thur. I was completely surprised. We had a very nice time. It is so nice to have so many friends. When I leave Fairview I will have the hopes of returning.

I do not quite agree with Max upon his views. I do not care for a lover that is too silent. Yet I do not care for the flowery talk that Mr. O'Rell said some lovers use, but I think there is nothing sweeter than to have one that you love, and one that you know loves you tell you of his love occasionally. I like Max's views very much and much prefer a silent lover than the one he describes. I think if Mr. O'Rell should know my lover he would say that he is the right kind to get.

Am glad you are well. Hope you will have good health always. I am well. I do hope the people will not be influenced by the adversary much more. Hope you will not have much trouble in your labors.

Spring is here. It does seem so grand. You will excuse this letter Peter but I am so tired, have walked so much today. I will write just as soon as I get into the City.

> With best love and wishes. I remain yours truly
> *Nellie.*

Baltimore, Maryland
March 15, 2011

Dear Nellie,

I find it hard to write back to you today—the disconnect of my
world and yours so wide, as the captions of the earthquake in
Japan are holding my attention, and it is hard to dive into the
realm of love when the news is warning us all that radiation is,
at this moment, riding across the globe.

The death toll is over 10,000 at the moment, and the world
feels paused, waiting to see what comes next. The forthcoming
nuclear plant radiation leaks that the news keeps predicting
are beyond frightening to me. It is the man-made aspect,
I believe: the danger packaged up, held captive inside
containers like hungry and foaming dogs.

"Nuclear power is an amazing thing," my husband replied
when I said nuclear energy should never have been invented.
He is my opposition today, another force to add to the weight
I feel holding everything down past the point of gravity. I
wonder if I flick one object over, like my television, if it will
start an unstoppable unraveling. I stay tight against myself,
so at least I am vertical, and let the kids stay up extra late
watching Cartoon Network while I go through the motions of
my bedtime routine. The night that used to seem so dark now
has shadows of light, a longer life span than it had just a few
days ago.

How would I be feeling if I didn't have a TV, a computer,
a cell phone with global news updates? Would I know the
beat of my feet was on the same earth as the feet of people
halfway around the world, scrambling in every direction from
the devastation of an earthquake? You probably can't imagine
the immediacy of our global knowledge. Did news, always
delivered after the fact, contain the same intensity in your time?

If you didn't know any different, perhaps it did. Maybe the reaction came in the delivery: mothers dropping to their knees in the kitchen from an unexpected knock at the door, children collecting around their father when a thick envelope arrived in the mail.

"It is your perception," I tell myself. "You just feel things more strongly than most people do." I wait for the water to gush out of the screen and knock me over. Are there really people out there who don't feel the wet splattering on their face, a splinter of wood being propelled through the cotton of their shirt sleeve?

Today, Nellie, I am having a hard time identifying with love. I am wondering if love is really a necessity, the way I sometimes envision it to be. Survival has taken precedence today, and love feels artificial and man-made, like the nuclear reactors.

"This is temporary," I tell myself, my favorite motto since entering adulthood and its never-ending responsibility. "Love will return."

You and Peter surely cannot imagine what is happening to your world right now, a hundred and ten years later. Right now, I just hope these letters, including my own, will see another 110 years and not disappear in an invisible wind that looks like nothing but is everything.

> Watching the devastation,
> *Kathy*

Salt Lake City, Utah
April 28, 1902

My Dear Peter:

I have been here nearly three weeks. I said I would write as
soon as I came. I wanted to get a letter from mama before
I wrote. I am not going to Ariz. this summer. I am delighted
with the city. Am staying with an aunt of mine. We live a way
out on 13th E. Just a short distance from the penitentiary. You
see I have to be pretty good. We are very soon into the city
as the car runs very near the house. I have spent a great deal
of my time since I came, gazing around. I have gotten quite
accustomed to the paved streets. It makes me so weary to walk
about on them. There are so many beautiful things to see here
and it will be all the more beautiful as summer advances. The
fruit trees are all in bloom and many other beautiful flowers.

I left a great many very dear friends at Fairview. Am glad I
have not gone so far away but that I can go down to see them
all, this summer. My dear old Grandma is here from Arizona. Is
going to make a visit to Fairview just as soon as the weather is
warmer. Grandma has a great many friends there. She was the
first white woman in Fairview. All of the old settlers know her
very well. They will all be glad to see her again.

When I left Fairview I did not know whether I would go to
Arizona or not. Some of my friends may think I have gone
there. I called in to say goodbye to your folks and your mother
said, "Don't go away down to Arizona" and asked me to write
to them. I spent some very pleasant days at Fairview this
winter. I have been to one dance here, had a very pleasant
time. I enjoyed hearing some home missionaries talk last night.
They have excellent meetings here in Sugar House Ward. Hope
John does not go to Chicago until fall. We can have some very
pleasant times this summer if he does not. Think I shall write

to John. He asked me to write when he was at home during the holidays, but I have not done so yet. I shall be more settled after this, and will write more prompt.

I am so sorry I have been so negligent about writing. I think of you every moment dear Peter. I shall remain true as the violet is blue. I almost wish it were next spring but it won't be very long now. I do hope you are enjoying good health. I am very well. Had a letter from mama today, they are all well.

Lois is at Springville. I think I had a letter from her at Springville.

May our Father in Heaven cause you to be successful in your labors, and a safe return home.

> From your ever true,
> *Nellie.*

Baltimore, Maryland
May 29, 2011

Dear Nellie,

Forgive me. Many weeks have past since I last wrote to you.
My life has turned upside down with the discovery of a large
tumor in my thigh. I found it in the shower, shaving my legs,
as easily as one finds a new penny, though my reaction was
more like discovering a dead body. The downward spiral
started then and there, and was followed through many
doctors' appointments and blood work, and scans, until I
found myself inhaling into a mask on an operating table and
then waking up three hours later to the doctor patting my leg,
saying "It was benign."

I still ache from the ten stitches and feel like a weak wound,
both my body and mind drained of any former confidence. It
reminds me of how I felt after my c-sections: taking slow steps,
winching at the ache and a body that seemed to be someone
else's.

I guess this is the first time I have faced the real chance
of cancer, of that word we have all learned to fear since
childhood, the word that stings with its thorns if you even say
it. The word is so weighted that it seems contagious, as if it
could sneeze on you and you would be next.

"If it is cancer," the doctor said, "we will do a different
procedure, going down more into the muscle, and then we
will radiate the area, but you won't need chemotherapy."

As soon as he said it, I thought about my last entry to you,
and about the radiation in the air this year. I thought it ironic
and uncanny that I might have to get to know her on my own
personal level.

Radiation

March 2011

The news strip flashes its warning
across the bottom of the screen:
Radiation, at this moment,
is riding the wind into Tokyo.
I can almost picture it,
sweet tongues of death,
catching waves of air,
invisible in its clever disguise
of nothing—
a whisper in the ear,
the rustle of a small leaf.
Unlike hurricanes or tropical storms,
radiation does not have a gender,
though I imagine it to be female,
delicately powerful in its silent travels,
destroying everything
without ever making a fuss.

May 2011

If it is cancerous, the doctor tells me,
we will need to use radiation.
I wait, on hold,
to see if I will be placed in the line
for the necessary poison,
the irony that sometimes
you need to kill to live.
Will she breathe into my body,
leaving just enough damage to start over?
Or is she without fingerprints,
a traveling salesman passing

through an already abandoned town?
I wait, and she remains
an unnamed woman.
The end of spring hovers,
humid and breezeless,
against my skin.

In recovery,
Katherine, your great-granddaughter

De Sista Dagars Heliges Kontor
Hornsgatan 80, 1 tr.
Stockholm
May 24, 1902

Dear Nellie:

Will take advantage of this opportunity and write you a short letter and acknowledge receipt of your letters, the last one being dated Salt Lake the 28th and the previous one written just a few days before your leaving Fairview. Am glad to learn that you have good health. I hope your health will continue so. You expressed in your last you hoped you would be more settled after this and write more promptly. I hope you will do it, Nellie. I tell you I do appreciate getting letters often from my sweetheart and have I not a right to look for such letters often? I hope it will not occur again that I must wait so long to hear from you. At these previous occasions when I have had to wait, I had concluded that you were ill or circumstances were so that you really could not write. If these painful delays in your writing me occur again, I shall be tempted not to attribute it to sickness but to wonder if my sweetheart's sacred love is as pronounced and strong as it has been heretofore. You have remarked that it was so hard for you to write and to express your thoughts. Why should it be so Nellie? I find it to be the greatest pleasure to write my Nellie and feel that I should like to write not only every month but twice per month if I thought that you in return could and would write me. I appreciate your letters so much. You must not think that I judge them according to grammar or language or anything of that kind. It is by the spirit and the love you breathe through your letters that I estimate their worth and value of the girl I love. Let your letters be plain and expressive of your love. They have been so, let them continue so. Would, though, like it if in connection with this you would add some items of news regarding yours and my friends you meet etc. Shall we write a little oftener?

I am so pleased Nellie that you have the good will of my folks. How nice it is for myself and you to have their full support and sympathy as it appears we shall have. I was surprised to learn of your having gained my mother's friendship to the extent as was shown by the remarks she made at the occasion of your visiting them. I hope her goodwill will continue and even increase which no doubt it will. Mother writes me occasionally and I appreciate her letters so much for they evince a spirit that is so characteristic of every true mother. However, she never has remarked about you. My sister Anna though has made occasional mention of you and tells how they all like you and appreciate you the more they get acquainted with you.

Rec'd a letter from John the other day. He aims to get to Chicago by August. He aims now to take a M.D. course at the Chicago University. Yes Nellie write him so that he can call on you when he comes to Salt Lake. We have just concluded our conference and had a splendid time, about 35 Elders were present.

Elder William Nilson made another visit to Stockholm and was with us during Conf. He will probably be released during the summer. I was called to labor in Stockholm where I think I shall much enjoy myself. The work of the Lord is progressing here although, maybe, slowly. The other night 2 young ladies were baptized also a lady in the previous week. There have been 54 baptisms in the Conf. during the past winter.

You say the weather is lovely at home. It is so here. You cannot imagine how beautiful Stockholm is beginning to look. It will not be long now until her lawns and parks will be completely green. About next mo. the city will be a most beautiful city, when dame Nature is through with her finishing touches, and not another city can eclipse this one for variety in scenery.

Well, Nellie, I shall bring my letter to a close for this time hoping I shall soon hear from you again. Take good care of yourself. My sincere love to you,

Yours,
Peter

P.S. How are your folks getting along? My best regards to Vina and Mother. What is their address?

Permit me Nell to extend to you a hobson salute. Goodbye.

Baltimore, Maryland
May 31, 2011

Dear Peter,

It is Memorial Day weekend, the long and relaxing weekend
I look forward to every year, full of food and family, without
the pressure of added presents and fuss, travel or large
commitments. In fact, I enjoy it so much that I, like most of the
country, often forget that it is in honor of our Veterans. Our
picnics do not resemble their experiences: burgers instead of
bullet wounds, fresh melon in place of memories.

All of the wars that have occurred since you wrote this letter
to Nellie, a century of killing and enemy swapping like
tired spouses, are still waiting to happen. Your letters are
helpless wings against it, sheets of paper flapping back and
forth through the mail. Yet, I know this is the language, the
communication that has kept even the most depressed soldier
moving forward. As you say, "the love you breathe through
your letters," fills the space of the unfilled, making emptiness
suddenly alive with presence. I think it is your words, too, as
well as Nellie's words, that help to fill the void in my current
life. Your letters make me want to confirm to my children that
they, too, are here both in lineage and progression.

For a moment, just a second, I am with you, in May of 1902.
For just a blink, the computer, the television, the central heat
and air conditioning disappear. My children quickly fad, the
photos release from the photo albums, rewind becomes fast
forward. My husband flirts with me from across the theatre,
and then I am alone with my parents in their bed on a Sunday
morning. Without any siblings yet, I am the proud first child,
then just me and your words, hearing your "Good-bye" as
an actual whisper, and Nellie's sigh on the other end, as she
finishes her first reading of your letter, swallows, and pauses

for a second, before reading it again, almost like it is the first time.

> In honor,
> *one of your great-granddaughters*

S. S. Rumerberg
June 29, 1902

My Dear Nellie:

It is now about AM 5. Am aboard the steam ship Rumerberg, as you will see from the above heading. Am sailing along the coast of Sweden through the Bethany Sea, on my way to Stockholm. I have been away for a couple of weeks visiting my own and cousins in Jamtland, my father's birthplace; also have been visiting the Elders in a couple of branches. I have enjoyed myself very much and I now feel prepared to settle down to earnest work when I get back. Mid summer night (June 24) I had the pleasure of presenting my testimony to about 150 people in a pretty little grove in the country village where my father spent his boyhood days. We have no nights to speak of now, especially in that part of the country where I have been visiting. With exception of a little short period at about midnight it is light the whole 24 hours through.

It is very pleasant sailing now, the boat glides along so smoothly. A very gentle breeze is blowing only. We are sailing close to the coast. The coast is rocky and back of the rocks the majestic woods loom up. For these woods is Sweden celebrated, and the lumber into which these woods are being converted bring a lot of money into this country from many other countries. Looking at the other side of the boat we see, now and then, pretty little islands. These islands usually are covered with woods, but the one we just now are passing happens to be barren with a lighthouse located on its highest point.

If only the influence of some magic wand would transport you here for a little while at least, so that you yourself could gaze upon nature, and see it as it really is. Down in the lower deck you would find a company of men and women representing a variety of ages who have said farewell to their loved ones and friends and are now on their way to the new world. I think you would enjoy such a visit for a little while.

How I would enjoy a conversation with my sweetheart, a real personal conversation of the most confidential kind, one in which we could express our ideas, feelings, thoughts, and sentiments in such a way as one cannot do through the slow and laborious method of writing. It is perhaps of no avail to wish that you were here, and I cannot, I suppose, do otherwise than a pretty song suggests, the words of which I even once in a while, find myself humming, some of the words are "Little Darling dream of me, while the stars are softly gleaming, While I'm far away from thee keep me still within thy dreaming" and "though I'm far away from thee still I'm always near thee" etc.

How satisfying to know that no great length of time remains to hold us separated. How sweet it will be when we can again enjoy each others association. What does my sweetheart say?

It is now quite a while since I received a letter from you. It is so refreshing to get your letters, they bring so much consolence and love. I wish I could get them often. I hope though, that there is a letter awaiting me when I get to Stockholm, in which I hope to learn that you and your folks are well and that you are enjoying yourself in S.L. You probably have met John who, I hope, had time to take you out some.

Well, Nellie, I shall close for this time. Forward my best wishes to your mother and Vina. I should like to know their address. How are they prospering?

Now, Nellie, accept my sincere love and at least ½ doz. Salutes of the Hobson style to make up for the time that has passed since last we exchanged salutes.

Yours affectionately,
P. Sundwall

P.S. N.B. An Elder Stohl of Brigham City departed about a month ago from here, having been released to return home. If he has not called upon you he will probably do so at anytime now. He will leave with you a couple of little pictures. Please accept same as a little expression of my love to you. The little gift (if it isn't too presumptious to call it so) is so little, so trivial that it perhaps would not be out of place to beg of my sweet heart her pardon for sending same. Please overlook it this time. I hope in the future to be in a position to better show my esteem and appreciation of her whom I love most dearly.

My association with Elder Stohl was not so long, but in that time I learned to like him and appreciate him as an energetic and conscientious worker in the Lord's vineyard.

Yours,
P.S.

Your letter of April the 28th is the last I have received.

Baltimore, Maryland
June 2, 2011

Dear Peter,

I begin my reply to you at PM 5 today, not my normal morning writing time, nor my normal productive time, knowing I only have a few minutes before I must stop to take your great-great-grandson to Tae Kwon Do. Right now, you are on a boat, the water moving in rhythmic stretches under your feet. Nellie and I stand on hard ground, reading your letter, its words singing along with the waves of your smooth sentences. The weather has been beautiful today, a warm day with a breeze just light enough to notice. I want to enjoy it before the Maryland humidity permanently kicks in and opening the front door becomes equivalent to entering a sauna. Soon, both kids will be home for the summer and it will be hard to do anything, other than keeping them from killing each other and destroying the house.

My mother has reminded me that the clock is ticking, and I need to start working on the poem for the family reunion in July. I haven't decided what to write about yet. The audience will be composed of your descendants and their families, gathered from all over the country for one weekend in Fairview, Utah. Should I write about you and Nellie during your time, or looking back from mine? Should I capture you during the years of these letters, or when you are older, after your children are grown and are grandparents, themselves? What kind of poem would you want, written in your honor, by one of your descendants? What kind of poem would I want written in my honor, from people yet to be born?

I think I will try to show you in your natural light, through the only lens I possess: my own. I will try to describe you the way I would want one of my own descendents to describe me:

without flair or frills, in the rising sun, the current streaming under the boat, the teacups slightly tilting on the dining room tables, the pen rising, then falling, and then

writing,
your great-granddaughter

Sugar, Utah
June 28, 1902

My Dear Peter:

I am going to write to you today let come what will. If you got every letter I have written in my mind to you, you will or would get one letter every day. Every day there is so much to do. My aunt is a dressmaker, has sewing girls here from morning until night and there is the hum of work all week long. We are so tired when Sunday comes that we know how to appreciate the day of rest. The weather is very warm, one does not feel much like work. We are to stop soon for the summer. I shall be glad.

I have not been very well since I got your dear letter, but am feeling better now.

Peter do not attribute my neglect to my love growing less strong, for I do love you, every day more and more. I can realize how I am blessed in having such a good, noble, and true lover. Since I have come here I have learned more of the wicked ways of the world, and am almost glad I have always been a simple country girl.

My cousin Lois Jorden is here, will remain this summer. She is staying at Bro. L.W. Wilsons. We had a very pleasant time last Wednesday evening, Lois and Sister Wilson came out, Lois and I had a nice time talking, then we gathered strawberries and had berries and cream. Wish you could enjoy some of the nice fruits we are enjoying now. What kinds of fruit do you get in Sweden? You will be at home next year to enjoy the nice fruits will you not? I am going out to Saltair today with Lois and Bro. and Sis. Wilson. It will be my first trip out there. I am so glad Lois is going to remain here this summer. She was going to Canada to be married, but she got word of her brother's death, Hugh- you remember him? He was drowned in a flood. These sad things occur, but it is the Lord's will, and we can only say, "Thy will be done." You see Lois could not be married this spring, so she decided to wait until this fall to return home. I do hope she won't marry the man she intends to now. He is a man of the world and is not a Latter Day Saint. It seems such a shame that she should love one whom is not worthy of her love. When she came down here it was with the resolution to give him up. They had some misunderstanding, but they have since made up. I wrote this letter or what I have written early this morning before breakfast, had to stop to get breakfast and by the time I had the work done it was so stormy I could not go out to the lake. I was a little disappointed but am glad after all because I have time to finish my letter to you and write some more letters that I owe. I had a letter from Mama and it is so very hot down there. She said not to be surprised if they were in Utah soon. O! I shall be so glad if they come back. They were all well. Their address is Tempe Arizona, Maricopa Co.

The Fourth of July will soon be here. I will not celebrate much this year but I hope I won't spend such a dull day as I did last year. I think of the nice time we had two years ago. I have thoughts of the future when I with him whom I love will have pleasant times.

I have met some very nice people since coming here. Do not go out very much, into the city for a ride, and to see Lois. It is very pleasant to ride home on the car in the evening. It is about five miles into town. Am going to take a trolley this summer and see the city. I was at Fort Douglas on Decoration Day. Had a very pleasant time for a solemn occasion.

Thank you Peter for those cards. They are very beautiful. Especially the scene from Stockholm. I should very much like to see the city of Stockholm.

Yes dear Peter I will write oftener. I give you my promise that from now on I will write twice a month at least, and answer your dear letters promptly. I will write if it is possible. Don't think my love is not as strong as before. It is, and always will be. I love you with all my heart. I will write after the Fourth. Hope you are well. Am so glad you are successful in your labors. I accept the Hobson Salute, and send some in return X X X X X X. With my love, from your

Nell.

Baltimore, Maryland
June 12, 2011

Dear Nellie,

Sunday morning, 11 A.M., and I wait for my daughter, Ellie,
to finish gymnastics class. The weather has been scorching
for the past week, over a hundred degrees each day, on top
of the humidity factor. The Utah heat was more breathable, I
remember from my two childhood visits, hot but under control,
unlike our Maryland summers-- weeks of feverish sweat that
leave us wet rags by mid-August. Utah's mountains announced
another land, one without overgrown weeds that crept into our
pretend castle behind my parents' forsythia, without hidden
corners, winding hills, or plant life too rich to be anything but
human, leaves with faces and lips smiling at me from every
backyard bush.

Utah, I recall, was more like a dry open mouth, at least
the area where we stayed close to Salt Lake City, with your
daughter Ann. She was in her late 80's by then, still single,
childless, and bossy. Almost completely blind, her hands told
her the way around her apartment, and she reprimanded my
brother and me for moving things around and disrupting the
tactile map of her home.

I remember there was a water shortage that summer in Utah,
and the plots of grass had turned brown like worn carpets. The
houses seemed to move horizontally across their dry squares,
as opposed to haphazardly, the way they did on my street at
home. Ducks wandered across the bank of the pond in the
middle of your daughter's apartment complex, completely at
ease with their towering human neighbors.

In fact, all life and land seemed calm and less uncertain in
Utah. Perhaps, this was because so much was visible. There
were no hidden possibilities of thorns or fallen branches

that I always felt in Maryland, where we never knew what was around the next bend. In Utah, we could see what was coming and plan accordingly. At home, every corner was a new adventure. In Utah, our rented car moved forward and backwards, and the sky never changed from a dreamy whitish blue. Even when we drove for an hour it was like we had never gained or lost place. The mountains didn't move an inch, strong giants grinding their toes into the earth.

Maryland was partially defined by its tight borders, Pennsylvania, Virginia, and Washington, D.C., dysfunctional lovers that never strayed too far away, all dependent on the irregularities of the map: the dripping gun of the handle of Maryland's Eastern Shore, the heavy hat of Pennsylvania hovering like an aging roof.

Utah wasn't like that for me. I didn't think of it as a state in the same sense of my own state, more like another country. Utah had its own gardens that grew scents that calmed ducks. Utah preferred growing rocks over wild vegetation. The Utah I saw one foggy July morning in 1983 was a massive tongue of earth, rolling out from within its molar mountains with symmetrical precision, the other side of the page I had formally understood as "state". Maryland was my own page, blurry in its layers and lines, and I was unsure as to how to organize these two very different places into the book I knew was labeled "our country".

We rented a gold station wagon with vinyl seats, so greasy my brother, sister and I slid back and forth across the backseat, our legs dark with oil and grime by the time we reached Bryce Canyon, a few hours south of Salt Lake City. The red drips of the canyon reminded me of the sand castle men we made at the beach in Ocean City, only they climbed up into the blue sky and dribbled themselves across the miles until all I could see were melting bodies. The castle men smiled back at me, their individual grins almost unrecognizable in their mass multiplication.

It is true that one cannot fully appreciate natural wonders until they are viewed in person. No picture could fully capture what I was seeing that day. However, I also remember knowing, even then, that I couldn't really process the scene. By the time the impact of the sight was fully formed, I was already back in the greasy backseat, fighting and sliding into my brother over the coveted spot behind our mom, as opposed to the view of Dad's balding head and tan left arm, a half-smoked Camel hanging out the window, its smoke blending into the air before we could catch its disappearing trail.

My geography,
Katherine

De Sista Dagars Heliges Kontor
Hornsgatan 80, 1 tr.
Stockholm
August 13, 1902

Dear Nellie:

Will drop you a few lines to let you know that I am well and enjoying my labors here in Stockholm. I hope you are well and enjoying Salt Lake City. I thank you for your letter of June 28th which came to hand after a long time of waiting. I was of course, pleased to learn that you are enjoying S.L.C. and sorry to learn that your health had not been so well of late. I hope though that now you are well from your illness. Have been disappointed in that I have not heard from you for a month although you kindly promised to write me once in every two weeks at least. I hope you are not ill so that on that account you are hindered from writing me. When I think of the other young men getting letters I ask myself why is it I cannot get a letter from the one I love at least once in two weeks. Elder Morrison, a young man from Richfield who has been to the hospital for a couple of weeks, tells me of the "scorching" he gave his girl for having waited 2 weeks in writing to him. He called her attention to John's Gosp. 14:15. Now I don't mean to "scorch" my Nellie or even scold her, nor hurt her feelings in the least, but how I should appreciate it if Nellie would write at least once in two weeks. I should enjoy, for my part, writing her once in two weeks and why should you not enjoy writing me regular. Why do you Nell allow such long periods of time to slip in between your letters you send me. If I have a girl in whom I bestow my love and who reciprocates my affection for her I would like for her to show her esteem for me, or I may just as well say love, by frequently written letters. What is better evidence that one's sweetheart loves him than to get frequent letters from her in which she unhesitatingly tells him of her adoration for him? What is better evidence to a girl that her love loves her than to get frequent letters from him in which he vows his faith and love to her? That is what I want to do. Let us be more punctual in our letter writing. If you are busy so that you cannot write as lengthy a letter as you would like to write, write briefly. Now Nellie I hope you will forgive me for suggesting this and hope my sweetheart will take no offense at what I have said in this regard. Who knows but that in a few months I shall be home again to enjoy the good company of my Sweetheart again. I notice that one of the Elders who came over in our company is released to return home. So you see it is getting close. Stockholm is delightful and I could spend the winter here to good advantage in the presence of lines in which my interest runs. Am acquainted with some people whose time is employed in creating things beautiful to see, and who give me good encouragement. I have formed the acquaintanceship of a sculptor who is now working on a big design for a water fountain which is indeed beautiful and inspiring. Also another individual who paints the beautiful things in nature.

Elder Swen W. Nilson left yesterday from Copenhagen en route to Zion, so you see he will soon be home again.

Weather here is awful—raining and cold it is nearly all the time. Thanks for stick of sen sen. I appreciate a little chewing of that kind occasionally. It is good for a change and a change is as good as a rest they say. Now, I also thank you for those things represented for the X's, but much better will it not be when conditions are such that one can steal one or two more of those things that the X stands for, from his girl, real ones you know. Well, good bye, accept a L from

Yours affectionately, *Peter Sundwall Jr.*

Baltimore, Maryland
June 17, 2011

Dear Peter,

What My Mother Told Me

I was named after her mother,
a girl who was also a good student,
kept a clean room,
and wore a low bun even after
her dark hair went silver.

I had great aunts and uncles
with voices she could hum,
but never completely imitate.
I tasted copper when she described
the deserts out west,
though I never really saw them.

She said,
That's your grandparents in that picture—
only when they were young.
A man and a woman:
two bodies holding children
like still props.

I took note,
stored the information.
A history of someone?
A girl yet to be filled in
on the last blank line
of the family tree.

I listened,
like a good student.

I was quiet,
like a good student.

I understood the presentation
was the part of the story
I would remember.

Yes, she told me,
You have your grandmother's eyes.
Hmmm. . . she answered,
I don't remember.

Sugar, Utah
August 28, 1902

My Dear Peter:

The reason I have not written is because I have not had very good health for some time. Am feeling some better now. Every day I think I will sure write, but I do not feel like writing or anything else, so I put it off until the next day. Next day comes and goes. I am so very ashamed. I have written to no one but mama, and not very often to her. Have not written in acknowledgement of those beautiful pictures. They are just grand. I was so delighted to get them I haven't words to express my thanks and appreciation for them Peter. Thank you very much. They are simply lovely, and the easel is just as sweet as it can be. I enjoyed the short visit with Elder Sthol the morning he brought them out. Wasn't it kind of him? What beautiful girls they must have in Sweden. Do they all look as sweet as the one in the picture? Sweden is such a beautiful country. Think I should like to live there. If it could only be as my lover said. If I were only transported to talk with you. But it won't be long as you say until we will enjoy each other's company. Then how glad, how glad I will be. When I think of that glad time I wonder if it is really true, wonder if I am not dreaming. I am so happy. Even if you stay until spring it won't be much longer. I may go to Fairview to spend the winter as mama is to return from Arizona next month. Do not know whether Vina is coming or not. Do hope she comes. If she stays there she may marry and remain there always. Mr. Pritchett has been in Utah for some time.

Lois is still here. Do not see her often as she does not come out often and I have not been able to go into see her. Have seen Mr. Neilson once since I came to the city. He called on Lois some few times. Said he had a friend on a mission but did not hear from him often.

I have gone out very little this summer. To the lake once, Lagoon once and Calder's Park once and that is all. Am going to Fort Douglas next Sunday if all is well. Think I will feel better if I get out some. We have had quite cool weather this month. Have had a great deal of wind but not much rain. Seems as though there will be a big storm soon.

Thank you Peter for the beautiful cards. Scene from nature is just grand. What a beautiful spot it must be. People must enjoy life there very much. I can imagine that is you and I under the trees. That statue is grand. I should like very much to see it. Thank you for the sketching. I take delight in looking over the beautiful sketches I have. I smile and think how differently it would be if we were standing at the gate now. That dear old gate. I shall always love that spot where I spent the most happy moments of my life.

I should like to be at Fairview when Bro. Nilson returns. How glad he must be to know that he has filled a mission and is on his way home. Yet his homecoming will be sad in measure.

Indeed I will not take offense at what you have said. I only love you the more for it, if that is possible. I shall try to write often after this, and then when we won't have to write anymore how happy we will be. I thank you again for those beautiful pictures, cards, etc.

Excuse this poor paper and letter. I could not go to town to get better and this is all the kind they had at the store here. I am a little tired now. Hope I will do better next time. Remember I will always love you Peter.

From your ever true. *Nell.*

Baltimore, Maryland
June 23, 2011

Dear Nellie,

I, too, have been trying to write, your last letters pulling at my mind, the guilt of knowing they are right next to my computer, waiting, and still I cannot get to them the way I would like to. Sometimes, it is my health, or my kids' health. Other times, it is teaching or my Ph.D. work, but lots of times it is just me. Artistic guilt is constant.

What about you, Nellie? You never mention a creative need, only the struggle for communication, in keeping up with Peter's pace, with knowing the weight of becoming his other half. Was your struggle with Peter's needs instead, feeling you had to be more, for him instead of you? Did you have something else, a talent that never fully reared its head, caught between the duties of your day? Maybe you were like my mother and motherhood would be your calling. With six children, I can only hope that you found some joy in them. Still, I cannot help but wonder if there was another need you kept to yourself, a shy glimmer of possibility behind your kitchen apron, something else buried in the trunk where you also hid Peter's letters.

Were there days when you looked that smoldering in the face, wondering what might have been? Or, did you keep it smoldering, your life too full with duties to expose even a corner of its presence. Did it tug on you at night? Did it whisper, *Look at me. Look at me. Look at me?*

> Looking at me,
> *Kathy, your great-granddaughter*

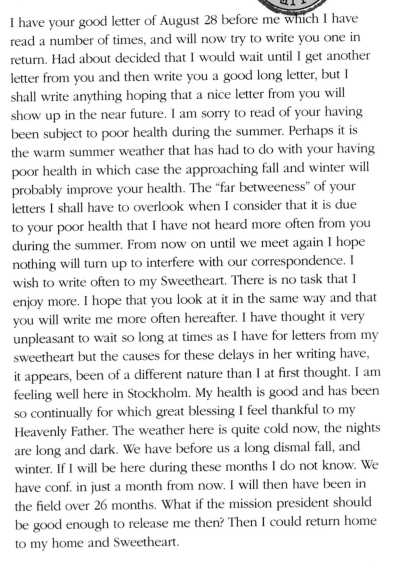

Stockholm den Oct., 1902

My Dear Nellie:

I have your good letter of August 28 before me which I have
read a number of times, and will now try to write you one in
return. Had about decided that I would wait until I get another
letter from you and then write you a good long letter, but I
shall write anything hoping that a nice letter from you will
show up in the near future. I am sorry to read of your having
been subject to poor health during the summer. Perhaps it is
the warm summer weather that has had to do with your having
poor health in which case the approaching fall and winter will
probably improve your health. The "far betweeness" of your
letters I shall have to overlook when I consider that it is due
to your poor health that I have not heard more often from you
during the summer. From now on until we meet again I hope
nothing will turn up to interfere with our correspondence. I
wish to write often to my Sweetheart. There is no task that I
enjoy more. I hope that you look at it in the same way and that
you will write me more often hereafter. I have thought it very
unpleasant to wait so long at times as I have for letters from my
sweetheart but the causes for these delays in her writing have,
it appears, been of a different nature than I at first thought. I am
feeling well here in Stockholm. My health is good and has been
so continually for which great blessing I feel thankful to my
Heavenly Father. The weather here is quite cold now, the nights
are long and dark. We have before us a long dismal fall, and
winter. If I will be here during these months I do not know. We
have conf. in just a month from now. I will then have been in
the field over 26 months. What if the mission president should
be good enough to release me then? Then I could return home
to my home and Sweetheart.

I hope Nellie you are making the best of it i.e. having a good
time and enjoying yourself at the same time—giving attention

to taking interest in matters pertaining to religion that you and I so fortunately are raised and educated in. How nice it will be when I am home and can enjoy my Nellie's good company and we need not keep the matter of our engagement a thing between ourselves only.

I have often thought that I should like very much to get a late photograph of you. I should enjoy it very much. I would only want the print itself and unmounted. I would get it nicely mounted here. I should like a side profile view this time, something like your first picture that you gave me over two years ago. Of course, the picture should only be a "bust" picture as the last one you sent me. The print, you see, you could send along in a letter, and would prefer it to be no smaller than a postal card. Would like the picture to be of "matt" finish. Now, Nellie, I am asking of you quite a favor, but I hope in some way to make up for this favor that I ask of you now. My impression is that a print or two or three would not cost much. If there is any difference much in the cost of the cabinets and a small picture i.e. visit card size, then get the smaller. The smaller size pictures are also nice and also popular here. I was in a reading room yesterday and looked over some of the English and American magazines. In a copy of the "Smart Set" I saw a beautiful poem. Of course I enjoyed it—a love poem it was. Were it not that our summer has faded away I should have copied the poem and sent it to you for in it summer and love are so beautifully painted words. Well, Nellie I shall close for this time wishing you all the blessings of the Lord. With as many X as you will permit me to give you I am

      Sincerely yours,
      Peter

Baltimore, Maryland
June 24, 2011

Dear Peter,

You mention *The Smart Set*, the magazine that H.L. Mencken, a Baltimore reporter, will soon edit. It is interesting timing, since I just finished revising my dissertation chapter about H.L. Mencken and Sara Haardt's love letters this past semester. It makes me realize how small the world of writing actually is. In that understanding, I am also getting more cynical, wondering why I am surprised at eerie similarities when the same patterns repeat every generation.

Sometimes, I even doubt if there is really more than one person on this planet, or if there are just variations of faces and names from the same cut-out, split up across states, countries, and continents. The connection is comforting, to know no one is alone, to know history will continue to repeat. Love will still nod its head in the same way for every generation, always acting like it is the first time it has surfaced, when it is really the millionth, a heavy blindfold used over and over again. But, it is also frightening to realize the duplication, to know history will continue to repeat.

I would like to think that my work will also be passed down after I am gone, that a young great-granddaughter of mine, perhaps unhappy with the scared girl she sees staring back at her in the mirror, will one day pick up a poem of mine and feel a connection, and know she is not alone. But, there is also the possibility that my words will burn up in a computer fire or crumble into yellow flakes of aging paper. I have to be okay with that, and accept that writing is, in the end, for the moment.

For just this moment, *I am.*

Sugar, Utah
Oct. 12, 1902

My Dear Peter:

I have had a very pleasant time since I wrote you last. A day
or two after I wrote you I went out to Fairview to see Mama
and the children. They had just arrived from Arizona. It was so
pleasant to see them again. It had been nearly a year since I
saw them. Then I enjoyed seeing all my friends again. Was at
two dances while there. The wedding dance of Warren Brady's
and Anna Tuckers and one given by the Young Ladies. Had
most pleasant times, when I left I thought to be gone two or
three days but while at Fairview I got word that an aunt of
mine at Springville was very ill and they wanted me to come
down there the day John left for Chicago. I should have liked
to have spent a day or two in the city while John was there,
but I could not.

I have been back some over a week but have been kept busy.
I attended conference last Sunday. At the South gate of the
Temple grounds I met ever so many people that I knew in
Arizona. Among them was a young man I used to go with. Do
you remember me speaking about a missionary that was in the
South the summer you left? It was he I met. He called on me
and I went with him to a concert at the Tabernacle. Heard Miss
Gates sing. I enjoyed it very much. I enjoyed hearing about my
old friends in Arizona also. This Elder is to remain in Utah this
winter as a Y.M.M.I.A. missionary.

There was such a crowd at conference that a great many
people could not get inside either the Tabernacle or Assembly
Hall. There were thousands of people that attended the open
air meeting last Sunday afternoon. The weather was perfect
during the conference. The rain held off until yesterday. Am
sorry you have such rainy weather. Take care of yourself. One

is so apt to get a cold with this cold stormy weather. It is quite cold here now.

Thank you for the card. It is very nice. I should like very much to see the statue. Do you know who the sculptor of the statue is? I was just looking over the pretty cards you have sent to me. I have a great many and they are all very pretty.

The journals are just fine Peter. I enjoy them more and more. They have a puzzle school in them that is very interesting although I can't guess many of them. They are all illustrations representing the names of people, towns, rivers, games, etc.

I must tell you about Vina. She became engaged to a young man there and was so happy, but the next day after they became engaged the young man, Ike Steel by name, met his death by having the earth cave in on him while cleaning out a well. Wasn't it sad? It is as Vina said, she was happy for such a short time. Happy in her new hope I mean. It happened just a week before Mama left, but Vina preferred staying in Arizona. She is clerking in a nice store there at Mesa City now. She says she will never marry now, but she is young and I think this won't blight her life. Poor dear Vina I wish she had come with mama. I do not half realize what it is. I always thought of her as my little sister. It seems almost impossible to think of her as a grown up girl. She may come in the spring, I hope she will.

I called at your home while at Fairview, had a very pleasant time. It is getting late and I will be quite busy next week so will close and write more soon. I shall be so glad to get a letter from you.

> With love and best wishes to you. Goodnight and a X
> *Your Nell*

Baltimore, Maryland
June 27, 2011

Dear Nellie,

This morning I woke up early, at 4:30 a.m., anxious to get back
to my morning routine of writing after spending the weekend
at a friend's house, a single woman without children who I
have stayed in touch with since we were in Sunday school.
It was nice to get away. We ate, talked, ate, talked, ate, then
talked some more.

It was a much needed break from the creative and academic
load that I have been carrying, the house and children that
I can only partially manage on a good day. I came home
feeling refreshed, like I haven't in a long time. Sometimes, I am
envious of other women who are single or without children.
I don't want to be them permanently, but I wouldn't mind a
short-term body invasion, to keep perspective in place.

You seem to grasp the temporality of suffering, viewed in your
acceptance of the tragedy of your sister's poor fiance, killed in
the well a day after their engagement, as well as your patience
while waiting for Peter. You don't seem anxious about the
natural movement of time, as opposed to the way Peter and I
seem to be wired.

I spent a lot of time talking to my friend, also an inactive
Mormon, this past weekend about religion and its innate
nature of keeping troubles hidden from oneself, one's family,
and the rest of the church. It has been over twenty years since
I have been to church and I still remember the multitude of
happy faces each Sunday that seemed to paint the church in
one big mouth crescent across the pews. Even as a young
child, I wasn't able to put on a happy face. Mine stayed stoic
and guarded, my eyes squinting in suspicion. I felt sorry for a
lot of the kids and adults who couldn't stop smiling. I thought

it a difficult road, especially if their minds wanted to pinch the corners of their mouths with sadness the way mine did. Too many smiles became one big frown for me, and I went out in search of others who also couldn't help from frowning. I found people who admitted life sucked a lot of the time and weren't afraid to curse in front of finer company.

Cheese,
Kathy

Stockholm
Nov. 14, 1902

To My Dear Nellie:

How are you now? O.K. I hope. I thank you sincerely for your letter of Oct. 12. Was pleased to learn of your little visit to Fairview and that you paid a little visit to our folks and that you enjoyed your visit there. I have reason to believe that Mother entertains but the best opinion of you. She is however very conservative in her letters regarding you, which of course I also am when writing home. Received just a couple of days ago a good letter from Mother where in she expressed herself so pleased over the prospects of my being home by Xmas. I sincerely hope I shall be released so that I can get home by that time. How nice if I can.

Pres. Skoneky down in Copenhagen has said he would see what he could do in way of letting us off next mo. I have not heard anything yet since he made this promise but I hope to get word one of these days to effect that I may go next month.

We have had an excellent conference. Two of the meetings and a successful course were held in Folkelshus, a popular hall down in the center of the city. Our meetings were well attended also concert. Something like 120 kr. were taken in at the concert. The "Mormon" choir here is making a record. We just held another meeting a couple of evenings ago at the hall down in the city where we had held the previous meetings during the conf. The hall was again filled and we had a fine meeting. The choir was highly complimented after the meeting by strangers who could scarcely believe it was a "Mormon" choir.

That winter is near is evidenced by the short days and long winter nights. We usually light our lamps at about 4 o'clock at which time the street lamps are also light.

Stockholm looks beautiful these dark nights. If one goes down to the quay he sees thousands of lights glimmering in all directions. From ferry boats, steam ships, buildings, street lamps etc. and I tell you the scene is charming.

It was indeed sad about Vina—that she should lose the one she intended to wed and whom she loved. I hope as you do that this event will not blight her for life. It was a little impressing to me to learn that Vina had so soon matured and developed into a big girl. I will no doubt be surprised when I actually see her again. She will probably be quite different from what she was when last I saw her. Is her address simply Mesa Arizona? I shall try to write her a letter.

Well, Nellie I hope you are enjoying life which no doubt you are among your friends and relatives. I hope I shall soon see you again and that we shall have open to us a career of happiness. . .

> With very best wishes to my love from
> Yours affectionately,
> *P. Sundwall*

Can you read this? I doubt it.

Excuse my using such paper.

Write me soon. –X–

Baltimore, Maryland
July 12, 2010

Dear Peter,

We have just returned from our annual summer vacation to
the Poconos with my sister and her family, a week in an old-
fashioned family resort in Pennsylvania, a former escape for
the city dwellers of Philadelphia and New York in your time.
Black and white photographs still hang on the walls in the
lobby- women in pearls and heels hanging out by the pool,
Big Bands shiny with new brass in the Nightclub. Today, it is
called an "old-fashioned" family resort to stress its nostalgic
appeal, not its lack of upgrades. The playground still contains
a rusty merry-go-round and a concussion-causing metal see-
saw. There is no soft rubber groundwork under the swings,
only the screech of old links and the pinch of a child's finger
every hour. My children love it.

"This playground wouldn't be approved today," one father
laughed after picking his crying toddler off of the rough
concrete sidewalk next to the slide. "This was built back when
getting hurt was part of your childhood."

The kids come home sunburned, bloated from s'mores, full of
scrapes and bruises. It is their favorite week of the year. They
can run off through the acreage on their own, and we don't
flinch the way we do at home when we know they have exited
our yard, where predators and certain death are waiting for
them as soon as they are out of our sight. The other parents
on the resort "street" are always home, on their cabin porches
or front lawns, unlike the rest of our year, where human life
outside of the house is scarce. Everyone keeps an eye on each
others' kids at the resort. That is a big part of the vacation
for the parents; the part not mentioned in the pamphlet, the
community of families and the freedom that comes not only

with trust, but with presence. That is what I see missing in today's parenting world. I see shells of houses, of new cars, of jobs and resumes, money passing from account to account, and computers and phones that travel with us like pacifiers. It is the return to "us" that everyone takes away from this vacation.

My mother invited us over for dinner when we returned from our trip, and two missionaries were there: young, energetic boys who gobbled up her meatloaf in seconds. My father tried to stump them with his latest riddles and showed off his recent retirement gifts, a cherry wood plague and watch, to celebrate his years working for the government. The missionaries shook their heads in approval, but they seemed much more excited about the meatloaf than his 30 year trophies. Then, my father opened up his dressing cabinet and told the missionaries to take as many ties as they wanted-- he was through with them! You would have thought someone just opened up a free candy store. The missionaries looked like they were in heaven, sorting through the hundreds of ties that my dad had been keeping since 1970.

"This one is old school," the blond Elder said, his California accent slowing down his words with its peaceful pauses.

"Man, this one is cool," the younger Elder said, his hands cradling a paisley tie from the 80's.

They each finally settled on a handful of wagging tongues, the bottom diamonds of the ties following them home like tails to their bare apartment. I wondered if they immediately hung them in their closet, or if they left them out to view for awhile-- the way we all do with something old, noticing its romantic appeal, the history that feels so much more important than the current movement of air.

> Which are the good 'ol times?
> *Kathy*

Sugar, Utah
Oct. 31, 1902

My Dear Peter:

Your last dear letter came some time ago, but my time has been taken up so since I came back that I haven't had time to write to mama hardly. I had a letter from Vina the same day I received yours, have not ans. it as yet. Dear girl she is very lonely down there.

I haven't gone anywhere since conference. I am saving my good times to enjoy in the future. I can never tell how glad I will be when I get word that you are to start for America. Peter I sometimes think I am dreaming. Is it really true that I have a good, noble, lover and that he is soon coming back to me? Yes, but I am not worthy of him. I wish I were. I will try to be, but I am afraid I will never be worthy.

Have you heard from John since he went east? Hope he is successful in his work.

Am so glad you have good health, my health is very much better now. We have been having most beautiful weather, until today it is cloudy and has rained some tonight.

My cousins Geo and Kate are sitting up until twelve. I will sit up also. It is after ten o'clock now and we talk awhile of ghosts and Jack-O-Lanterns. I will spend the time pleasantly, but I am afraid my letter will not be connected very well. If you come home for Xmas, I will wait until you come to give you a picture but if you do not come until spring I will try to get one just as you say and send to you. The one I sent is so very poor. I hope to get a better one next time.

I am ashamed of this letter but the folks are talking and laughing so I cannot write. I will send it just to let you know I am well and still love you Peter. Take the best care of yourself and come home as soon as you can. I will try to write a sensible letter soon. Hope you have a good time.

> With love and best wishes I am
> Yours only
> *Nell.*

Baltimore, Maryland
July 13, 2011

Dear Nellie,

This is your last letter, hidden by Peter above the kitchen
rafters in his parents' home sometime after 1902. It has been
two years since I began my correspondence to you, and I also
grow weary waiting for an end, closure for the project I began
well before I started my Ph.D. program, before my tumor,
before I learned more than I imagined I ever would about you,
Peter, my children, and myself.

I will end my mission the week before I return, too, to your
physical home and begin a new life without your, or my,
letters. Will Fairview look different than I picture? Will the land
mirror my memories of Utah, ingrained from another time,
a younger girl who went by my name? Will I fit in and feel
a connection with the people known as "my family"? These
questions are the same ones that are asked on any return—by
any soldier, missionary, scholar, or student.

It will not be long now, Nellie. Hang in there.

I see you pause, taking a break from your writing, while you
look across the room, distracted by your cousins and the
festive Halloween night. I almost miss the candle flickering,
the lack of age on your young elbow, the wood clip that holds
your dark hair off of your face, just so.

> Counting down,
> *Katherine Cottle*

Stockholm
Dec. 12, 1902

My Dear Nellie:

How are you? O.K. I hope. I am feeling O.K. Am very busy
today to pack up prior to my leaving tonight. Excuse me for
not being able to write you a decent letter or for not sending
you some token of my unwavering love and esteem for you.
I have been so very busy these last four days, or I should
have written you before. Tonight we hold a concert in a big
hall down in the city. We hope to have a full house. Have 400
tickets printed which we hope to sell. I shall go directly from
the concert to the station to begin my journey homeward. I
expect to go via Copenhagen, Hamburg, Holland, and London
and hope to see many interesting things. I will drop you a
view card from these different points. Hope you rec'd the card
I sent you a few days ago. Last night after making my farewell
talk the saints presented me with a beautiful photograph
album as a memory from Stockholm. What do you think of
that? I remain with love to you

    Peter

Best wishes to Sister Brady and Vina when you write them.

Baltimore, Maryland
July 15, 2011

Dear Peter,

Today, you pack your bags, almost finished with your mission. You do not mention sadness or regret, pride or excitement-- just the facts and the logistics of your return.

Throughout the majority of your letters, I felt as though I related to you better than I did to Nellie. You immediately expressed a love for the arts, and exposed the distractions that you could never completely ignore-- both for your girlfriend and the world around you. I could see my own hand hovering above yours, writing in the dark hours of the morning or the night, always searching for something, one rushed step ahead of itself.

I did not initially relate to Nellie. She seemed two-dimensional compared to you, bogged down with physical work and chores, too exhausted from taking care of other people to explore her own needs. Initially, her letters back to you felt like another set of chores for her, and you were yet another person needing her attention. She didn't seem to need the constant and continual reassurance that you needed. She wrote to you because she loved you, and you wanted her to write, and that was what fueled her responses more than the twists of similes across the page.

As my husband and son have taught me, I can no more make them love language than I can make them stop opposing me. Nor, do I think I would want them to be just like me. They hate to write, yet I know they love me through their daily actions and need for confirmation of my presence. They will never mail me poetic letters of gratitude, nor will they ever compose poems that will measure up to all of the days of our history.

Now, as I read your reply to Nellie's last entry, I find myself warmed by her unconditional stance. Regardless of whether or not you write, regardless of whether or not you baptize, regardless of time or age, she accepts you in a way that you will never be able to accept her or yourself. She holds the hands of the clock even in their bothersome ticks while you push to move them forward, always ahead of their time. She mails her letters, not out of anticipation of what she may receive back, but in what she wants to give. It is not about her, Peter. It never was.

Aren't the letters really about you, Peter, the way mine are really about me, our way of returning to ourselves, our own padding for self-doubt? It is always quicker to come home: the light becomes dimmer, the path shifts downhill. The cities you leave are moving backwards, away from your next stop, letting you go instead of calling you into their arms. A new missionary appears and you are old news, and old news is never as interesting.

      Coming to a close,
      Katherine Cottle, your great-granddaughter

Dominion Line

S.S. "Commonwealth"

Christmas Eve. Dec. 24, 1902

Dear Nellie:

It is now Christmas eve about 7 o'clock pm. We are just
about in mid-ocean sailing on a first class ship by name of
"Commonwealth." At the present we are setting down in
the 2nd class passenger salon. Among the passengers we
find representatives from a number of nations. Among our
emigrants enroute to Utah we find English, Swedes, Danes,
and Hollanders. There are also French and Jewish passengers.
It is interesting to see the little children of the different
nationalities romp about and play together. One little, pretty
French girl, just a few minutes ago, was sitting on one of the
steamer trunks, with her arm around the waist of her smaller
English playmate. Of course neither one could speak to the
other but they were nevertheless friends and intimate ones at
that. We have just amused ourselves by singing songs- English,
Swedish, and Danish ones. We will probably arrange for a
concert of some kind tomorrow.

I am trying to imagine how you at home are enjoying and
spending Christmas. Too bad I cannot be with you to share in
the happy time you will be having. I hope you will have an
enjoyable time both tomorrow and on New Years.

I dropped you a view card at London which I hope you have
rec'd. I had an excellent time in London although I was not
permitted to stay as long as I desired. Saw such magnificent
buildings as Westminister Abbey,--House of Parliament—
Lambeth Palace—London Tower etc. etc. We also spent an
evening in the "Alhambra" Theatre where we saw a number

of the fine artists perform. We left Liverpool the 20th and expect to reach Boston next Monday morning. I will probably go down to New York, thence to Niagra Falls and then to Chicago.

Nellie what do you say if I should stop off at Chicago for 2 or 3 mo.? It isn't sure that I will. It depends a good deal on what father says. I am looking for a letter from him when I reach Chicago. I tell you this so you need not be surprised if I do not come directly home. I should certainly like to come home to you whom I must regard as a true and faithful sweetheart who in 28 mo. of waiting has shown her fidelity and the genuineness of her love which she pledged before I left her. Can I ever show myself worthy of her who has so completely shown her devotion and love? Nellie, I hope so. I shall try so. If I postpone my coming home for 2 or 3 mo. it will be with an object in view by which I hope we mutually will be benefitted.

You know that when I left home it was my intention to do a little studying in art in connection with my missionary labors. While I have been in Stockholm I have had the privilege of meeting an artist or two, especially a Mr. Tollberg, a teacher in the Royal Academy of Art, who showed me much kindness. Through his influence I was admitted to the "Tekniska Skolan" without having to pay the yearly tuition of 50.00 kr. Mr. Tollberg is probably the best engraver and etcher in Sweden. I also had the privilege of calling on Mr. Tollberg at his home to which he kindly invited me. However, I did not accomplish so much in school as I had hoped to. My work at the office was of such a nature that it could not be neglected and consequently I could not attend school regularly and finally had to quit preferring to fulfill my mission rather than quit my missionary labors to go to school. To attend to my missionary labors and go at the same time to school I could not do.

When I reach Chicago I shall write you further regarding my

plans if I decide to stop. The 2 or 3 mo. I spend there will soon speed away and then I shall be home to enjoy your association. I hope Nellie that when we meet again and can be together that our joy and happiness will be so complete that we will feel fully compensated for the long time that we have been separated. I also pray and hope that our Heavenly Father will so ordain it that our future will be one of continual bliss.

I am sorry Nellie that I have no little token to send you. Surely, your love merits something nice in the way of a present, but I hope you will, this time, overlook my failure or neglect in this regard. The pretty chain you sent me is doing me good service. I value it very much. I have quite a nice little charm attached to it.

Well, Nellie, I shall close my letter for this time wishing you a Happy New Year. I hope the new year will have many rich blessings in store for you—and me too. I hope the New Year will soon bring us together and open up for us a happy future, a life of mutual joy and happiness.

> Affectionately,
> P. Sundwall

Dec. 29—

We are now in the harbor just outside of Boston. Probably inside of a couple of hours we will be ashore "our sweet land of America."

Baltimore, Maryland
July 16, 2011

Dear Peter,

It is the day before my 38th birthday, and I write to you as you travel home to the States by ship, your return closer with each capping wave. You admit your desire to stay in Chicago and study art, to continue that part of your life that you could not ignore, to the degree of enrolling in an art school in Stockholm for a portion of your mission.

Your dilemma rests in which need to return to when you reach the States: your girlfriend, your art, a career, or the possibility of juggling all of them if you can delay your final return.

From reading the family history book, I learn that your father will discourage your art and you will end up coming straight home to Utah, moving money in his bank instead of your hand across a canvas. I want to tell you to stay in Chicago, to study now, because you will not get the chance later-- not with six children, a wife, a consuming career, and all that comes with Mormon life. Nellie will continue to be there, time for your art will not. Like a siren, your art calls to you as you move closer to home. Do you hear her whispering in your ear, in that raspy voice that promises so much?

*

I take extra money that we don't have out of the ATM before bringing my son to Artscape, a large summer Arts festival in Baltimore. We take the light rail down, so he can take more graffiti pictures. It is a wonderful afternoon, the city alive with people and air, the sun hidden enough that we can feel it without burning. We look at all kinds of art, eat funnel cakes, and he makes a beaded wind chime in front of the Maryland Institute College of Art. He puts his arm around me as we stroll among the vendors, and I realize it is a date. I enjoy it, because I know it will only be a couple of years before I am replaced, and his camera will want to take pictures of a slender, young female over his aging, tired mother. His camera clicks away the entire day, and we ride back to the county exhausted. His art stays on the memory stick in the camera for months, but I promise him it will not be erased.

With all good intentions,
a mother

Chicago
Jan. 5, 1903

My Dear Nellie:

Your letter was on hand when I reached Chicago on
New Year's Day. I have enjoyed myself very much here
in my brother's company. Since writing you on the "S.S.
Commonwealth" I have been sight seeing in Boston,
Cambridge (the home of Harvard University), Buffalo, The
Niagara Falls, and a number of places in this city. Did you get
the letters I mailed you from Boston and souvenir card from
Buffalo? On the card I think I forgot to state "Sugar 1904"
and consequently it may not reach you. Yesterday we heard
the celebrated Lyman Abbot and Dowie (Elijah the Restorer)
preach which was very good. They have a good choir here
and some bright and active young people in the church.

Nellie, your last letter has given me much uneasiness. I cannot
understand what can be wrong. I certainly must think strangely
of your letter. You say you wish you have not gone to the city,
and also that I will cease to love you. What can this mean
Nellie? Such expressions fill my mind with strange forebodings.
What is wrong now that her in whom I had such implicit faith,
should not just previous to my homecoming give me cause
to doubt? You say you have something to tell me (apparently
something special) and then you add that I will cease to love
you. Can it be possible? I hope not. Too bad if anything has
occurred that will shake my faith in you. I have had every
confidence in you and thought you to be the best and sweetest
girl it had my fortune to meet and who pledged to me her love
and faith. During our long separation you have been faithful
and maintained your good reputation, won the esteem of my
folks, and since leaving Stockholm I have meditated much on
how when I reach home my joy would be made complete
in that I would be permitted to associate with my true and

noble sweetheart. I sincerely hope Nellie that I shall not be disappointed in these expectations. I hope that when I get home I shall find Nellie to be the true, sweet, pure, and noble girl that she was when I left her. And yet you tell me I will find you quite different. Until I hear from you I shall not feel at rest and I hope that something you have to tell me is nothing of so much consequence after all or that will give me course to no longer love you.

How soon I shall be home I cannot say. Maybe in a few days. Maybe not. The folks are very anxious for me to come. While it would be grand to see them and you it would also be of great benefit for me to remain a couple of months. I am looking for a letter from them tomorrow which may have some to do in deciding whether or not I shall go home at once.

Write at once Nellie and tell me all. In case I am gone before your letter reaches Chicago, it will be forwarded back, and if I am here (as there is a strong likelihood of my being) I shall then be consoled to know what it is you have to tell me.

Regards from John and love from your Peter

Baltimore, Maryland
July 19, 2011

Dear Peter,

The last letter Nellie sent you is missing from the collection, perhaps destroyed in fear, more likely destroyed in anger, hidden away somewhere separate from the rest of Nellie's sedate words; the black sheep pulled away from the rest of the herd. Even a glimpse of doubt pulls the rug out from under you, Peter, and I know your mind has already multiplied into the thousands: doubt X fear = misery. The girl in the picture labeled Nell, the one you held up as perfection throughout your mission, has suddenly become human. Regardless of the actual details of her digressions, she has shifted in your mind. The stool has wobbled and fallen.

Did she kiss another man? Get drunk? Whatever the sin, she has crumbled away from you, just days before your return. Was it on purpose, so that she didn't have to live up to the unattainable sketch you created of her in your mind?

Did she need for you to know that the real Nellie was not always beautiful, not always strong, and not always able to handle your inflexible perception?

You will get over this, Peter. You will still love Nellie, in spite of whatever she did and whatever she will do in the future. And she will love you in return, in spite of yourself.

> In spite of myself,
> *A woman.*

The University of Chicago
Jan. 15, 1903

My Dear Nellie,

Your letter came to hand O.K. I was certainly glad to hear
from you. You see, your previous letter made me uneasy.
The sensational remark or two that you made in your letter
regarding that I would cease to love you etc. were not
agreeable things to hear. I couldn't quite reconcile myself to
the thought of losing my little sweetheart. To think that all
would be up between me and her whom I truly loved was
I assure you painful. You were so to the point with your
statements that I really thought that something serious had
occurred. I'm glad though that that is not the case.

I will probably see you soon and hope you will explain all to
me. I hope it will be nothing that will lessen my esteem for
you in the least regard, but to the contrary I want to love my
Nellie more and more as a true lover should do who has a
true sweetheart. Scarcity or the "far-betweeness" of your letters
also gave me a little dissatisfaction and I used to wonder why
I could not get letters regularly from you. Circumstances which
you have not clearly explained or that I have not been able to
fully grasp or understand may have been responsible for this.

Well, I won't say anymore this time about these things. I hope
to see you soon and talk with you. How nice Nellie it will be,
providing I have your full and complete and undivided love
and affection. I hope my Nellie hasn't remained true to her
vow made 28 mo. ago just because she made the vow and
because she feels she had ought to be good to her promises.
I want my Nellie to feel that I am the only one for her, and
the only one whom she can sincerely devote herself to. My 28
mo. of experience out in the world among a variety of people
and under various circumstances has not altered my estimation

and love for Nellie one iota. Now I hope the case is the same with you. You have had quite awhile to reflect on the merits or demerits of him to whom you gave your promise,--as to whether you really loved him or not, I hope and believe Nell that your decision is the same as mine.

How nice to see you again. I hope to find you the same girl you were when I left—Changed to some extent, of course, i.e. more matured and with some womanly qualities more manifest or brought out.

Say Nellie order some of that delightful moonshine and weather we had when I used to call at your romantic home on the corner. How exciting it was, wasn't it? Well, Nellie, if you can't arrange to get any of that weather, we'll try to do the best we can until "summer comes again" when I hope opportunities will be given us to bask in or enjoy some of the wonderfully delightful nights experienced in 1900.

What do you say Nellie? Now, Nellie, in the last letter or two you have been very scarce about those X's. What does that mean? Are you reserving them until I get home? If so you'll have to pay them back in good measure and with interest too. What do you say to this?

Now, Nellie, I haven't told you a thing about what I'm doing here in the "windy city." Have spent two weeks here with John, now, but do not know if I shall or can stay longer. Would like to stay another 4 weeks, then I could go to Zion feeling O.K. My teacher says 6 weeks will finish me up and prepare me for active work in the R.R. Service. So you see I should like to stay that length of time or 4 weeks at least to get the benefit of a training that will certainly be of much value to me. I have been paying my way and have now before me a note from Western Union Telegraph Co. asking me to call up to their office tomorrow. Undoubtedly I have a position awaiting me if I should want it in the Western Telegraph Union's service.

Should I want to accept it and I certainly would do it if I were to stay as I desire to. All the folks at home are urging me to come home at once. John and I have written them to try to convince them of the benefit and advantage of my staying the 4 or 6 weeks and taking the training of "finishing up" in a trade that will probably be my vocation for the next few years. The folks it seems are very restless and it appears will not be at ease until I get home. I shall probably leave first part of next week. The prospects are so good for a month of "affective and valuable experience" that I do not so much like to leave here now, but I suppose I shall have to do it anyway.

With love and a X
I am Peter

Baltimore, Maryland
July 20, 2011

Dear Peter,

I leave you waiting this morning, the day before we are to
leave for the family reunion in Fairview, Utah, for the right
decision, to pick the path that will take you down the rest of
your life. Your indecision shines through your words—your
worry about your relationship with Nellie, your career plans,
the last wobbly leg of your mission.

I feel the same uncertainty—about my family, my writing, and
my recent decision to return to academia as both a student
and a teacher. It doesn't end. If I could, I would tell you that
everything will work out fine. Nellie will be there for you.
You will learn to see her as a woman in the flesh as opposed
to letters, which will be more complicated than you ever
imagined, but also more real. You will be successful in your
career and church, and any problems you and Nellie have
will take a back seat when your children arrive. They will
distract you from your constant worries, as children deplete the
extra time that might be used for excessive self-examination.
You will be married for 57 years, raising your family in your
parents' house in Fairview. That corner house will become the
life-long home for you, you and Nellie, and then your own
children. You will forget the time that you wished to return to
it, and you will eventually only understand it as the body of
your family, the heart beat created by the people living under
its roof.

Before I finish packing for the trip, I show the family history
book and your letters to my children, pointing to pictures
of you and Nellie, and then flip through a hundred pages of
names and pictures of your descendants.

"These are the people we are celebrating this weekend in

Utah," I tell them. They cannot understand how so many pages can come from just two people.

"They look funny," my son says, about both of you. "Old time people."

"She is pretty there," my daughter remarks, pointing to Nellie's younger picture, then gestures to her older one, "but not there."

You are pictures in a book to them, stories and frames of another time. I saw that same distance when I was a child, and my mother pointed to your photographs, explaining who was related to whom. The pictures were black and white foreign lands, without flaws, and I imagined them in slow motion, words and actions able to be rewound and spliced.

"These are your great-great-grandparents," I tell the kids.

"He was an artist, like you," I tell my son.

"She was a mother, like you might be," I tell my daughter.

My son's mind is already past the book I am holding, looking into the kitchen, eyeing up the brownies on the stove.

"When's dinner?" he asks.

I open to one of your letters and show my daughter. "These are their love letters," hoping she might be impressed. She starts to grab them, and I notice chocolate on two of her fingers.

"Don't touch them!" I bark. "They are valuable."

"When's dinner?" my son repeats, and I close the letters, snapping the book shut.

"Never-mind. Maybe you two will appreciate this one day when you are older!"

I place the books in the dining room, on top of the china cabinet, away from dirty fingers and grabby hands, and return to my life-- burning dinner, breaking up fights, cleaning up messes.

You and Nellie are safe there for today, for now. Inside the book, your pictures continue to stare in serious contemplation. I will keep you up there, hidden, out of reach, until my children are older. Until my children are older, I will keep you up there, hidden, just out of reach.

I Remain Yours,
I am Katherine Elizabeth Cottle

Frames.

Read at the Sundwall Family Fairview Reunion, Sanpete
County, Utah

July 22, 2011
I. 1905

Only one baby, in perfect white,
not an ounce of spill or exhaustion--
A tight triangle of lace and gaze,
two new parents as sure as
any possible future.

The carved wooden chair peeks out
within the formal background,
blending into Nellie's dark bun,
shadowing Peter's fair face
like a warm fire.

It is quiet, with a silence of bare smiles,
hands folded neatly in your laps.
It is the year your family has just begun.

II. Summer 1931

In a blink, 6 children are balanced to your right,
almost enough to tip the scale:
3 standing, 3 sitting,
an even game of pick up sticks
against the open Utah sky.

They are strong and young,
faces echoing your own,
without the years of holding still,
mending skinned knees and broken hearts,
of watching them grow,
both away and towards you,
as children learn to do.

III. June 22, 1959

There are almost too many bodies
to squeeze into this warm summer day.
Barely enough room to hold the white cake
on a table between you,
waiting to be lit in celebration
of your 55th wedding anniversary.
It is hard to know who are the children,
and who are the spouses,
heads and faces looking
every which way but forward.
One boy bites his lip under a cowboy hat.
One girl places her hand on Nellie's shoulder.
It is the inevitable side effect of volume,
when your own grow into others' own,
when family branches away from its trunk.

IV. July 22, 2011

Today, your descendants gather--
some remember you, some are too young.
Some can still hear your voices,
and some can only imagine.

The frames, at this moment,
extend past the four sides of a square,
into the lives you started and those which continue,
scattered across our shrinking world.

The frames become the people
who are here right now,
standing where you once stood,
listening where you once lived.

Today, for a few special hours,
the pictures come together.
A new album appears, then overflows:
framed and frameless, all of it, from you.

About The Author.

Katherine Cottle is the author of a memoir, *Halfway: A Journal through Pregnancy* (2010), and a poetry collection, *My Father's Speech* (2008), both published by Apprentice House. Her recent critical work appears in *Critical Insights: Zora Neale Hurston* and *Muses India: Essays on English-Language Writers from Mahomet to Rushdie*. She teaches at Goucher College and is a doctoral candidate in English at Morgan State University.

Apprentice House is the country's only campus-based, student-staffed book publishing company. Directed by professors and industry professionals, it is a nonprofit activity of the Communication Department at Loyola University Maryland.

Using state-of-the-art technology and an experiential learning model of education, Apprentice House publishes books in untraditional ways. This dual responsibility as publishers and educators creates an unprecedented collaborative environment among faculty and students, while teaching tomorrow's editors, designers, and marketers.

Outside of class, progress on book projects is carried forth by the AH Book Publishing Club, a co-curricular campus organization supported by Loyola University Maryland's Office of Student Activities.

Eclectic and provocative, Apprentice House titles intend to entertain as well as spark dialogue on a variety of topics. Financial contributions to sustain the press's work are welcomed. Contributions are tax deductible to the fullest extent allowed by the IRS.

To learn more about Apprentice House books or to obtain submission guidelines, please visit www.apprenticehouse.com.

Apprentice House
Communication Department
Loyola University Maryland
4501 N. Charles Street
Baltimore, MD 21210
Ph: 410-617-5265 • Fax: 410-617-2198
info@apprenticehouse.com • www.apprenticehouse.com